Perfecting Your
PURPOSE

Also by David D. Ireland, PhD

Activating the Gifts of the Holy Spirit

Failure Is Written in Pencil

What Color Is Your God?

Why Drown When You Can Walk on Water?

Perfecting Your
PURPOSE

40 Days to a More Meaningful Life

David D. Ireland, PhD

WARNER
Faith®

New York   Boston   Nashville

Unless otherwise noted, Scriptures are taken from the HOLY BIBLE: NEW INTERNATIONAL VERSION®. Copyright © 1973, 1978, 1984 by International Bible Society. Used by permission of Zondervan Publishing House. All rights reserved.

Scriptures noted The Message are taken from *The Message: The New Testament in Contemporary English.* Copyright © 1993 by Eugene H. Peterson.

Scriptures noted TLB are taken from *The Living Bible,* copyright © 1971. Used by permission of Tyndale House Publishers, Inc., Wheaton, Illinios 60189. All rights reserved.

Scriptures noted NRSV are taken from the NEW REVISED STANDARD VERSION of the Bible. Copyright © 1989 by the Division of Christian Education of the National Council of The Churches of Christ in the U.S.A. All rights reserved.

Scriptures noted NLT are from the *Holy Bible,* New Living Translation, copyright © 1996. Used by permission of Tyndale House Publishers, Inc., Wheaton, Illinois 60189. All rights reserved.

Scriptures noted KJV are taken from the King James Version of the Bible.

Warner Faith.
Time Warner Book Group
1271 Avenue of the Americas, New York, NY 10020

Visit our website at www.twbookmark.com
The Warner Faith name and logo are registered trademarks of the Time Warner Book Group.

Printed in the United States of America

First Warner Books printing: April 2005
10 9 8 7 6 5 4 3 2 1

Library of Congress Cataloging-in-Publication Data
Ireland, David
    Perfecting your purpose : 40 days to a more meaningful life / David D. Ireland.
        p. cm.
    Includes bibliographical references.
    ISBN 0-446-57824-X
    1. Christian life—Biblical teaching. 2. Christian life—Meditations. I. Title.

BS680.C47I74 2005
248.4—dc22   2004019854

This book is dedicated to all the people who
have struggled to discover their life's purpose and
are also struggling to perfect it. I had you in mind when
I wrote this book to help you answer the question:
How do I perfect the purpose for which God has created me?
May you discover your purpose and find the
conviction to perfect it.

CONTENTS

Step #4: Have the Right Stuff

Step #5: Live By a Code

Step #6: Bury the Past

Step #7: Win the War Against Discouragement

Step #8: Overcome Fear

Step #9: Learn to Connect on a Deeper Level

Step #10: Shout from the Housetop

The Search for a More Meaningful Life

The cry of the human heart is to find meaningfulness in life. You can spend your whole life searching for value, meaning, or even purpose, but to no avail if God is not heading your search party. *Perfecting Your Purpose* is about following God's lead so that He can point you to your purpose and help you perfect it. As you do so, a deeper meaningfulness will arise out of your life.

Over a 40-day journey you will find solid answers to the question: *How do I perfect the purpose for which God has created me?* Forty days is not an arbitrary number; it is the period God used throughout the Bible to transform a nation or a person when someone approached Him with a major problem that required His wisdom as the Divine Mechanic to fix it. Ten specific occurrences are cited in the Bible. Whenever a person engaged in a 40-day habit-changing period, the result was always mind-boggling: either a nation or a person was transformed. Therefore, I call this 40-day period a *Transforming Interval.* My heart's desire for you as you read this book over the next 40 days is that God will use it as a Transforming Interval in your life.

Billy Graham's fiancée, Emily Regina Cavanaugh, broke his heart by telling him that she was more in love with another suitor, Charles Massey. Rather than wallowing in sorrow, the young Billy Graham decided to turn to God for comfort. During that time, he also came to accept his purpose to preach. Dr. Graham writes, "I now had a purpose, an objective, a call. That was when the growing up began, and the discipline to study."[1]

Similarly, when I discovered that God's purpose for my life was for me to become a preacher, I eagerly devoured every book I could find on the ministry. Although I continued working as an environmental engineer, my mind was preoccupied with thoughts about my newfound life's purpose. Discovering what God intended when He created me was incredible. I found out what God had in mind when He thought of creating David Ireland. There was a definite intention about my life's purpose. I was not an accident or an afterthought. In God's foreknowledge, He designed my life, my purpose, and mapped out ways for me to discover that intention. And since He's not one to play favorites, He has done the same for you.

The Book's Aim

This book pursues three goals. The first is to help you confirm your life's purpose through a series of self-discovery exercises. Self-discovery is about becoming more self-aware and determining who you are and who you are *not*. It also shows what you're gifted to do and what you're not gifted to do. It is about arriving at your own "aha" moment as a delightful response to the internal question: *What did God create me to be?*

Since it is my conviction that no one can achieve his or her destiny independent of God's involvement, drawing closer to God will be one of the ways that self-discovery occurs. Reading this book will assist you in building a stronger relationship with the Lord.

Second, this book aims to help you perfect your purpose. I want to help you hone the skills to further mature you in your life's purpose. I plan to help you take this fledgling idea of what you were put on earth to do and—like a consummate gardener—grow it, purge it, shape it, and see it blossom into full maturity. Merely discovering your purpose is not enough. Often, there are a myriad of reasons, including life's distractions, why you don't end up with a perfected purpose.

Have you ever asked a child to bring something to you that you may have forgotten in another room of the house? I can remember when my children were small. I would say, "Danielle, can you bring Daddy's eyeglasses from the upstairs bedroom?" Her response would be innocent and eager: "Sure, Daddy!" However, the scenic journey from the living room to the bedroom was full of fun, adventure, and plenty of stops along the way. No less than thirty minutes after my request, and after she had played with the hallway light switch, teased her little sister, combed the hair of a doll, and done God knows what else, Danielle would snuggle next to me with one of her books and urge me to read her a story. There would be no eyeglasses in sight or in mind. I would have to hold back my frustration in recognition that she was distracted by all the household sights that met her curious little eyes. I would repeat the request or walk upstairs in defeat to get the glasses.

Keeping your purpose in view and actively pursuing it require avoiding the rabbit trails that life's distractions can bring. Thus, knowing how to avoid distractions will be advantageous in perfecting your purpose.

Third, this book presents the benefits of practicing a 40-day habit. Although you will learn valuable principles over the short span of 40 days, the greater blessing will be in adopting them as lifetime habits. I remember a friend in college who refused to study regularly throughout the semester. He attended every party and even created his own parties when there was a lull. It all came crashing down on him during finals week. He decided to consume excessive amounts of caffeine to stay awake and cram for his exams all at once. To my amazement, he stayed awake for several days straight, studying like a madman. On the day of his biggest exam, however, he fell asleep—right in the middle of the test. When he was awakened, he immediately passed out and had to be rushed to the emergency room. The moral of this story is: don't look for quick answers to long-term success. Instead, create a lasting habit that's based on daily practice.

In other words, if you're looking for a magic pill or formula, put this book down. Grab the TV remote, and surf for an infomercial that can help you achieve your goals in no time flat. But if you're looking for real answers that translate into lasting change, this is your book. Read on! Let's begin the 40-day journey in perfecting your purpose.

How to Read this Book

This book is designed to be read in 40 days in a study group or by yourself. There are 40 chapters, each written in a devotional format to be read thirty minutes per day. If you are a morning person, before scurrying around the house getting dressed, preparing breakfast, and attending to your family's needs, commit to starting your day by reading a chapter each morning. If you're a night owl and you have your quiet, reflective time in the evening, this book will be an excellent way to end your day. In either case, read one chapter a day and complete the exercise at the end of each chapter, which reinforces that day's lesson. You may also choose to use a journal to capture all of the feelings, emotions, and changes that the Holy Spirit will evoke in your life over the next 40 days. Although you will be tempted to jump ahead and read more than one chapter a day, try to restrain yourself. Through the exploration and application of timeless principles gleaned from biblical characters who participated in these 40-day journeys, you will develop life skills that will assist you in perfecting your purpose.

If you choose to rally some of your friends, coworkers, or members of your congregation to form a study group, the 40-day study will be enriching and exciting, especially as you eyewitness others experiencing a Transforming Interval with God. One approach is to select a group leader who will coordinate an ideal time for the group to meet—whether weekly or biweekly—and discuss the chapters. The leader will also facilitate a group approach to completing the exercises for a particular day's lesson. You will learn quite a bit through the group discussion while having lots of fun with creative ways to complete the exercises.

Americans love guarantees, especially those that have a credible guarantor standing behind the product. God guarantees that you will develop a lifetime habit that promises a companion reward if you are willing to commit to 40 days of reading the text and following through with the exercises.

Don't end up like the dad who purchased a swing set for his son after months of hearing the youngster whine. This father, like many others before him, did not see the need to read the instructions. "It's a waste of time. I can just wing it!" he reasoned. After hours of frustration, he left the swing set unassembled, and Johnny's spirit was crushed. Reading this book—and applying its principles—is the equivalent of reading the assembly instructions to discovering and perfecting your life's purpose.

Before you begin the 40-day journey, I would like you to choose a friend who is willing to hold you accountable to complete the journey. Let your friend know how serious you are about perfecting your life's purpose and that their partnership will help motivate you to keep your 40-day commitment. Afterward, complete the following form and make your commitment to the process of self-discovery official. My signature indicates that I've already prayed for God to use this book to help you perfect your purpose.

My Commitment

Through God's grace and strength, I commit the next 40 days to discovering how I may have a more meaningful life as I seek to perfect my life's purpose.

_____

Your Name

_____

Your Partner's Name

David D. Ireland

David D. Ireland, PhD

The LORD will fulfill his purpose for me;
your love, O LORD, endures forever—
do not abandon the works of your hands.

(Psalm 138:8)

Step #1

Search for Purpose

*"I know the plans I have for you," declares the L*ORD*, "plans to prosper you and not to harm you, plans to give you hope and a future."*

Jeremiah 29:11

DAY 1

Understand the Power of 40 Days

Perfecting Your Purpose offers a solution to a problem that you may have been complaining about and you've finally decided to do something about it. Great! You have taken the first step, a powerful step, toward a solution to the problematic question: *How do I perfect the purpose for which God has created me?*

Throughout the Bible people were weighed down by that same question. To answer it, they chose to enter into a 40-day period to seek God in a unique way.

Sociologists look for patterns in human activities to make predictions about society, culture, and human behavior. Likewise, theologians look for patterns in God's behavior or His Word—the Holy Bible—to predict human outcomes when people adhere to those divine patterns. Without such prescriptive advice life would become more unpredictable, yielding greater uncertainties, and leading to increased depression, instability, and the lack of fulfillment in people's lives. Thankfully, these patterns exist, and we can explore them.

In looking for a biblical pattern regarding one's purpose, I found ten biblical references to a period of 40 days. In each instance incredible benefits befell the men and women who practiced a 40-day habit of pursuing God in order to discover and perfect their purpose.

40 Days: The Transforming Interval

In the Scriptures, the number 40 symbolizes a fresh start, deliverance, freedom, salvation, a firm foundation, completion, and healing. On each occasion when the biblical character practiced the required habit for 40 days, the result was a personal or national transformation. For instance, the Ten Commandments—God's moral code for humanity—were handed to Moses following a 40-day period of fasting. And Joseph—an exciting Old Testament character—gave orders for his deceased father, Jacob, to be embalmed over a span of 40 days. Embalming symbolized laying aside the pain of the past. Before launching His public ministry, Jesus went into the desert for 40 days. During that time He fasted and prayed, thus crystallizing in His heart the eternal mission of bringing salvation to humanity.

Since this 40-day period is so results-oriented, I call it the Transforming Interval, and I hold this Transforming Interval high as a pattern for modern-day people to follow. The assurance of a transformed life through practicing a 40-day habit is not another human effort that promises unrealistic results. Practicing a habit for 40 days is a classic theological observation that can guarantee a result—the perfecting of your purpose. And as you advance in your purpose, you are pursuing your God-given dream, turning it into a reality.

Using the Next 40 Days to Transform Your Life

The way in which you use the next 40 days is extremely important. At stake during this Transforming Interval of 40 days are your life-altering decisions—decisions about your marriage, or perhaps whom you marry; decisions about your children and issues that will shape the kind of people they will eventually become; decisions about your business or career. These issues are critical to your life and require God's wisdom. In perfecting your purpose, you obtain God's wisdom by following the pattern established in Scripture—the 40-day Transforming Interval.

In the book of James we read that a double-minded person is "unstable" in all his ways (1:8). Despite your intellect, your wealth, your talent, or your area of gifting, being double-minded about right decisions in the major areas of your life leads to instability in *every* area of your life. Right decisions come from being focused, purpose-driven, and in tune with God's wisdom. That's why James tells us that if any of us lack wisdom—in living, business, money management, parenting, any significant area—let him ask God, "who gives generously to all without finding fault" (1:5). There's no fault in conceding that God has the precise answers regarding the critical areas of your life. Rather, I commend you for your willingness to set aside the next 40 days to gain clarity about where your life is headed.

Setting aside 40 days is like taking a journey in which you are focused on a destination. Two years ago, my wife and I took a cruise from Washington State to Alaska. Everything we needed was provided on that ship—food, entertainment, fitness, night life, you name it, it was there. The staff provided impeccable service. Marlinda and I didn't have to lift a finger. All we had to do was focus on our destination, and it was an unforgettable experience. I want you to focus on the destination of perfecting your purpose during this 40-day journey. It, too, will be an unforgettable experience. This journey will direct you to the destination that God intended you to reach from the foundation of the world.

Consider the life span of Americans—men are expected to live to age 74.1, and women are anticipated to have 79.5 years of life. The decision to take the next 40 days and work toward perfecting your life's purpose will be a small investment compared to your expected span of 27,047 days (for men) or 29,018 days (for women). God's 40-day pattern has proven effective over thousands of years in the Scriptures. If you are serious about perfecting your purpose, dedicate the next 40 days to taking strategic action that can propel you into one of the most exciting seasons of your life.

40 Days to a More Meaningful Life

One of the men I most admire in the Bible, although he was quite unusual, is the prophet Ezekiel. Whenever I read the book named after him, I am amazed by his incredible prophetic antics that show a dogged allegiance to God's instructions. He was not a sophisticate like the statesman Daniel or an intellectual debater like the apostle Paul, but I take my hat off to Ezekiel as a man of action. In the fourth chapter of Ezekiel, we find the prophet responding to the weakened, sin-ridden state of his nation, Israel. God called for

Ezekiel to communicate a word picture of the dilapidated moral and spiritual state of the country and its people by lying on his left side for 390 days and on his right side for 40 days (Ezek. 4:4-8). Try explaining the prophet's assignment to someone who is unspiritual, and not only will he think Ezekiel was crazy, but he will consider calling the insane asylum to have you picked up should you talk about mimicking the prophet's behavior. Despite Ezekiel's eccentricity, you will find four specific lessons from this man's 40-day Transforming Interval with God that you can easily apply to your situation.

In exploring Ezekiel's 40-day Transforming Interval, you will learn how to (1) gain an understanding of the power of 40 days; (2) establish a deep conviction to fulfill your purpose; (3) solidify an unforgettable experience with God; and (4) discover the joy of knowing that your purpose is not hidden in some out-of-the-way place, but was under your nose all along. By the way, congratulations! You've already begun your journey toward a more meaningful life. You're in your first day, and you're learning the power of 40 days.

Spiritual Answers to Physical Problems

Most people think that every natural or physical problem calls for a natural or a physical solution. Not so! Many physical problems can be solved by applying a spiritual solution. Consequently, turning to this book, which is biblically and spiritually centered, for a solution to your natural problem of achieving a greater meaningfulness to your life was a wise action. Ezekiel knew well the correlation between the natural and the spiritual, and so he answered God's call to serve the natural needs of his nation by performing a spiritual act. This is what God said to him:

> *Then lie on your left side and put the sin of the house of Israel upon yourself. You are to bear their sin for the number of days you lie on your side. I have assigned you the same number of days as the years of their sin. So for 390 days you will bear the sin of the house of Israel.*
>
> *After you have finished this, lie down again, this time on your*

*right side, and bear the sin of the house of Judah. I have assigned you
40 days, a day for each year.*

(Ezek. 4:4–6)

Ezekiel's act of lying on his left side for 390 days, to demonstrate
a need for the Israelite people to return to God, and then on his
right side for 40 days in further demonstration of the same need,
shows that he understood how God's spiritual solution could solve
a natural problem. The number 40 throughout Scripture means a
time of completion. Thus, closing out this prophetic demonstration
by lying on his right side for 40 days, Ezekiel was announcing that
the Lord wanted the spiritual waywardness of the Hebrew people
to end. They were no longer to live aimlessly by abandoning their
call as the people of God. They were no longer to live apart from
the pursuit of their purpose. They were no longer to live without
the benefit of meaningful lives.

Ezekiel heeded God's word, and the 40-day Transforming Interval occurred. The people of Israel saw their weakened state, but
chose to continue in it. What about you? After the 40-day journey,
will you continue to live the way you used to? The 40-day journey
toward perfecting your purpose is designed to help you develop the
habits that can produce a lifelong change. Three main benefits produced by this change are (1) a life of purpose overcomes aimlessness; (2) a life of purpose focuses your energy; and (3) a life of
purpose keeps you observant.

1. A Life of Purpose Overcomes Aimlessness

The first benefit is that aimless living ends when you know *why*
you've been created and what you've been created to do. A person
caught in a cycle of purposelessness tends to jump from one career
path to another or perhaps from one relationship to another in
search of meaning. This unpredictable pattern may be slow or fast
paced. If the movements are slow, an aimless person will participate
in some exciting activity, albeit for the wrong reasons. Conversely,
the deception associated with a fast-paced, busy lifestyle is that it
creates an illusion that progress is occurring when all along a person may simply be going around in circles.

I was surprised in the middle of my counseling session with a precious couple when the wife blurted out her annoyance with her husband's lack of focus with his life and construction projects at their home. According to her descriptive words amidst her sobs, her husband had started numerous projects, but completed none of them. In his defense, he said that all of his projects were great ideas that would drastically improve the quality and appearance of the house, even increasing the property value. There was such a great difference of opinion, I did what I had never done before in a counseling session. I said, "Let's go for a ride to see this house."

Once we arrived, I was speechless. The husband had started at least ten different projects over the years. There was a big hole in the backyard where a swimming pool was to be located. A half-completed pantry in the kitchen, an opening in the walls of the master bedroom for a shower that had no shower, a circular drive-way that had only one opening, and a number of other construction jobs "in progress" showed me that the wife was right. Her husband was full of wonderful ideas, but he lacked the follow-through to finish them so he jumped from idea to idea, leaving frustration in the home and in her heart. He was deceived. His busyness in starting projects had blinded him from the need to complete them.

2. A Life of Purpose Focuses Your Energy

The second benefit is that your energies will become focused like a laser beam when you're living a life driven by purpose. A scattered life speaks of purposelessness. But a focused life conveys that your aim is sure and your life has continuity.

If you are always trying your hand at fifteen different things simultaneously hoping that something sticks, your energy level is probably depleted, and it's likely that you've had very little success. The benefit of working in harmony with your life's purpose is similar to installing an energy conservation device in your home. You will achieve a great output of energy with minimal loss in efficiency.

Recently, the local gas company sent workers to my neighborhood to check the energy efficiency of all the homes it serviced. At

my house the workers wrapped the hot water tank and the five feet
of exposed ductwork in the boiler room with a fire retardant ma-
terial to contain the energy within the unit. As a result, my monthly
bill dropped by a few dollars, and the gas company reduced the energy requirements stemming from the Ireland household. Admit-
tedly, this reduction was small, but when the energy savings from all
the homes in my neighborhood were added up, the company
gained a significant savings. Similarly, when you redirect your energies toward your purpose you will gain greater efficiency in every
area of your life. The more you distance yourself from aimless living,
the closer you come to living a life directed toward your purpose.

3. A Life of Purpose Keeps You Observant

The third benefit of living according to your life's purpose is that
it keeps you observant. You can miss your life's purpose by thinking that it's too obscure. Your purpose may be near, but you overlook it because you're not paying attention to the opportunities
obscured by your emotions, both good and bad. Your network of
friends can be doorways that lead you closer to your destiny or walls
that hinder you from reaching it. Even your trials and disappoint-
ments can lead to untold opportunities if you are observant.

In the Atlanta Yellow Pages under the listing of restaurants, there
is an entry for the Church of God Grill. The peculiar name arouses
much curiosity, and Charles Paul Conn, author of the book *Making
It Happen*, tells the story about when he dialed the number:

> *A man answered with a cheery, "Hello, Church of God Grill!" I
> asked how his restaurant had been given such an unusual name, and
> he told me: "Well, we had a little mission down here, and we started
> selling chicken dinners after church on Sunday to help pay the bills.
> Well, people liked the chicken, and we did such a good business, that
> eventually we cut back on the church services. After a while we just
> closed down the church altogether and kept on serving the chicken
> dinners. We kept the name we started with, and that's Church of God
> Grill."[1]*

Imagine if the proprietor had raised his nose in the air and pre-
sumptuously said, "God called me to be the director of a mission.

And I am going to do it even if it kills me." Guess what? It would have killed him! The reality is that right under his nose, he was able to discern that the missions venture was floundering (no pun intended) while the chicken business was taking off.

You and I will benefit from being observant over the next 39 days.

DAY 1 Points to Reflect Upon

Taking the next 40 days to journey with God to a destination of perfecting your purpose is essential to your critical life decisions. Discovering my purpose earns me the benefit of

1. ending aimless living.

2. focusing my energies like a laser beam.

3. helping me become more observant about my life so that I gain the best opportunities.

DAY 2

Establish Conviction:
The Fuel of Purpose

People with conviction are hard to forget. Something about their commitment not to back down, not to back out, or not to allow themselves to get backed into a corner is remarkable. Their goals are too important to be disrupted by mere obstacles. Ezekiel was that kind of prophet. When challenged by God to lie on his left side for 390 days and on his right side for 40 days as a prophetic act—which symbolized sinful Israel's need to return to God—the man of God took action without hesitation (Ezek. 4:1–8). Ezekiel shared God's conviction that a moral change was needed so that the people of God could return to their original purpose. This conviction made the difficult physical challenge easy.

True Conviction from God

Ezekiel's conviction so consumed him that he had the passion he needed to carry out the prophetic act of lying on his sides. The key to discovering your purpose is to locate the source of conviction. True conviction that is gripping, persuasive, and moving originates from God. The prophet heard God's heart toward Israel, and conviction was born in his heart that triggered his purpose to call Israel to repentance and right relationship with God.

1. Conviction Brings Clarity

Too many people meander about, hoping that something exciting and rewarding happens to them. They are unaware that adopt-

ing a conviction to a cause or a purpose would trigger the excitement they seek. Conviction brings clarity to direction and plans because it draws a line in the sand. Conviction cries: "No more
meandering. No more messing around. No more waiting for something to take place." Conviction says: "Today is the beginning of
change." When Ezekiel positioned himself on the floor, it was clear
that he wanted what God wanted for his nation. It was clear that he
did not want Israel to stay in hopelessness and despair. He drew a
line in the sand with his act of conviction.

When Paul was riding to Damascus, his heart burned with the conviction that he needed to incarcerate Christians because he despised
their faith. He thought it was cultish and an offense to the "true"
worship of God (Acts 9:1–9). His actions, although misguided, were
in response to his conviction. However, as Paul neared the city, Jesus
threw him to the ground, and he looked up, saw a vision, and heard
these unforgettable words from the Son of God: "Saul, Saul, why do
you persecute me?" Paul abandoned his former theological views,
which had no place for the divinity of Christ, and instantly became a
wholehearted, fully devoted follower of Jesus. This radical shift, though
sudden, was also supported by Paul's deep conviction that Jesus was
indeed Lord and that he ought to obey His words without question.
Perplexed by the transforming encounter with Jesus and the question
about why he was persecuting Jesus, Paul asked,

> *"Who are you, Lord?"*
>
> *"I am Jesus, whom you are persecuting," the Lord replied. "Now
> get up and stand on your feet. I have appeared to you to appoint you
> as a servant and as a witness of what you have seen of me and what
> I will show you. I will rescue you from your own people and from the
> Gentiles. I am sending you to them to open their eyes and turn them
> from darkness to light, and from the power of Satan to God, so that
> they may receive forgiveness of sins and a place among those who are
> sanctified by faith in me."*
>
> (Acts 26:15–18)

That encounter with God gave Paul a conviction that led to a
purpose, and he spent the rest of his life fulfilling it. Years later, Paul
was still laboring to perfect that purpose when he wrote, "When I

preach the gospel, I cannot boast, for I am compelled to preach. Woe to me if I do not preach the gospel" (1 Cor. 9:16)! In other words, Paul had a true conviction that gave him clarity about his purpose. He made no bones about it; he did not vacillate. He was called to be a preacher, and he wore his conviction as a badge of honor.

What has God burned in your heart as a conviction that you want to spend your life championing? If you are not sure, don't despair. Over the next few days I will help you discover your purpose. Thereafter, your conviction about that purpose will deepen as you strive to bring it to perfection.

2. Conviction Brings a Warrior Spirit

Warriors have no difficulty fighting for what is theirs. They will fight you tooth and nail to secure their possessions, their property, or even the promises they feel rightfully belong to them. Have you ever seen a lion resting? He looks so docile and meek that the uninitiated can be fooled into thinking that the lion is simply a big house cat. Make that mistake and it will likely cost you your life. When I travel to the East African nation of Kenya for missions work, I frequent on my downtime one of their national game parks to witness the wildlife in their natural habitat. There is a gated area at the entrance to the park. You pay your fee, you're told to stay in your vehicle, and you're pretty much on your own from there.

Every time I go through the park, my Kenyan drivers relay stories about the foolish stunts of tourists who get caught up in the adventure and forget where they are. The often tragic stories hit the local papers, and the Kenyans shake their heads in dismay because they never would have considered such foolishness. The foreigners got out of their cars because they saw lions at rest, looking meek and gentle. In a few moments their lives were snatched from them or they were irreparably harmed because they did not discern a "warrior" at rest. Lions devour things; that's what they do. If you mistake that because you see them asleep, that will be your last mistake.

Without conviction you are simply a tamed house cat, but with conviction you will be a warrior. Whether at rest or in action, you will be known as a warrior. Conviction gives you a cause to live for, a battle to fight. Without a conviction, life seems dull and meaningless. Without a deep conviction that your purpose is valuable, priceless, and indispensable, the purpose fritters away. But when you adopt a conviction that God has given you a purpose to live for, that conviction will summon a warrior spirit within you that will guard the treasure inherent in your purpose. Conviction removes passivity. Conviction eliminates mediocrity. Conviction forces you to make up your mind about the direction you're going in and about the direction you're *not* going in. Conviction summons the warrior at rest within you to arise and enter the battle for the perfecting of your purpose.

When Ezekiel lay on his right side for 40 days, he was engaging in a prophetic act for the welfare and purpose of his nation. He was not going to let it disintegrate into a mediocre, sinful nation made up of people who had lost their way. He was going to do his part as a prophet—a spokesperson for God—to see his nation return to God and to its purpose. The prophet's conviction turned him into a fighting machine.

A Life of Purpose Shows Cooperation with God

You show your genuine cooperation with God by ordering your life according to purpose. Living according to God's purpose shows that you are in harmony with His will, His plan, and His overall strategy for the human race. Your life takes on greater significance because it feeds into a greater purpose—God's ultimate objective for the world.

The apostle Paul instructs us that "in him [Christ] we were also chosen, having been predestined according to the plan of him who works out everything in conformity with the purpose of his will, in order that we, who were the first to hope in Christ, might be for the praise of his glory" (Eph. 1:11–12). This passage helps us to see that when we bring our lives under God's leadership, we participate in His master plan. Being in Christ means that you have accepted Christ as your Savior, and the outcome of that decision is that you surrender completely to His entire plan for your life as you grow in relationship with Him.

You don't want to miss out on the joy of knowing that you are a partner with God in His overall plan for humanity. Your participation in the will of God brings you into the greatest company of all time—the family of God.

When Martin Luther, the sixteenth-century German monk, refused to go along with the party line of the Roman Catholic Church regarding what qualifies someone for salvation, he demonstrated a true conviction to the Scriptures claiming that the just shall live by faith. Although she was a nun, Mother Teresa felt her calling was to live among the poor rather than in the convent. Her conviction came after she heard a voice that said, "Go to the poor. Leave the convent. Live with the poorest of the poor."[1] The voice was none other than the Lord. She obeyed, and her impact on the poorest of the poor in Calcutta, India, is a testimony the world over.

These two people demonstrated a sincere conviction to their purpose by their willingness to lay down their lives. They were not going to be stopped by fear because their conviction brought them courage. People who are gripped by fear seldom show conviction to move toward their purpose. They are intimidated by the anticipated statements of family members, colleagues, or friends. Courage is like the vaccine for the virus of fear. It will protect your spiritual immune system from the ravages of fear so that you can walk in your God-given purpose.

As you seek to discover and perfect your life's purpose, may you do so with courage and a deep sense of conviction that God's will and your purpose are one and the same.

DAY 2 Points to Reflect Upon

Ezekiel was a man of deep conviction, which fueled the actions that defined his purpose. Similarly, your convictions should catapult you toward perfecting your purpose.

1. What issues do you constantly find yourself championing? List them and highlight the ones about which you have the greatest conviction. Commit to championing them!

2. Conviction summons the warrior spirit within you to do battle against the things that try to kill your purpose.

3. A life of purpose shows cooperation with God.

God is giving me a time of rest, growing in Him, allowing Him to shower me with his love. This will be a time of memories with family, study in the word, writing, fun with new friends. These last weeks of leading in singles has been a blessing but this season is over and on to the new....

Solidify an Unforgettable Experience

The self-discovery aspect of uncovering your purpose is unlike other forms of information gathering. It usually results in an unforgettable experience. While I am a staunch believer in academic pursuits, the process of undertaking an arbitrary course of study and even graduating doesn't pack nearly the emotional punch of studying with a life purpose in hand.

When Ezekiel lay on his right side for 40 days, he was not only symbolically bearing Judah's sins but also conveying to God's people their need to walk out their purpose without being encumbered by wayward living (Ezek. 4:6). Either they had forgotten or never discovered their purpose as individuals or as a nation. The prophet's unusual actions, though he did them in obedience to God, became an unforgettable experience that sealed his life purpose as a prophet to the nation of Israel.

Throughout the Bible unforgettable experiences frequently launched someone into his purpose, and I am captivated by Moses' unforgettable experience at the burning bush.

Ingredients in Discovering Your Purpose

Moses' experience reflects three powerful ingredients in discovering your purpose. As God is preparing you to have an unforgettable experience that catapults you toward your life's purpose, here's what you should notice about yourself: (1) feeling ordinary frustrates you;

(2) the thought that something big is missing from your life gnaws at you; and (3) the idea of your big dream dawns on you.

1. Feeling Ordinary Frustrates You

The account of the burning bush is presented in Exodus 2–3. Moses had escaped to Midian—a neighboring land east of Egypt—after killing an Egyptian soldier. Although Moses was considered a prince in Egypt, having been raised by Pharaoh's daughter, he was of Jewish origin, and his commitment to his people provoked him to kill the Egyptian soldier who was punishing an Israelite slave. After spending 40 years in the wilderness and having married and fathered two sons, Moses was tending the flock of his father-in-law, Jethro.

The job of tending to the needs of Jethro's flock had become routine and commonplace to Moses. He had succumbed to the notion of feeling ordinary, especially in light of his former position as a prince in the most revered nation in the known world. He had surrendered to the role of a shepherd, and, the flock was not even his own.

Perhaps his frustrations led Moses to incorporate sightseeing into his shepherding duties as he took the flock to "the far side of the desert" (Exod. 3:1). In journeying toward Horeb—the mountain of God—Moses became intrigued by a burning bush that was not consumed by the fire (Exod. 3:2–4). Burning bushes are not unusual sights for shepherds living in deserts and arid climates. Self-combustion is commonplace in scorched lands. God simply wanted to get Moses' attention, deal with his frustrations, and give him a marching order—a life purpose.

God spoke to Moses from within the burning bush: Moses was to deliver the children of Israel from more than four hundred years of Egyptian bondage and relocate them to a land flowing with milk and honey. After Moses heard that, his frustrations about feeling ordinary became even more pronounced. He said to God: "Who am I, that I should go to Pharaoh and bring the Israelites out of Egypt?" (Exod. 3:11). God's response was: "I will be with you" (Exod. 3:12).

A state of frustration exists when you are dissatisfied with unresolved issues or unfulfilled needs. Not knowing your purpose is quite frustrating. You can benefit from frustration by recognizing that these feelings are a precursor to discovering your purpose. Have you ever seen the movie *The Karate Kid*? The star character, Daniel LaRusso, learns the martial art of karate to avoid being bullied by neighborhood kids. After taking lessons from a wise karate expert, Daniel discovers that he is quite good at the art. In fact, he becomes good enough to win a championship against members of a rival school who were also the neighborhood bullies. Daniel's drive to learn self-defense came from his feelings of frustration. Again, we see how frustration can be positively positioned to propel you toward discovering your life's purpose.

2. Something Big Is Missing

When I was a boy, I loved to play pranks, especially on my siblings. (The truth is that I still love to play pranks.) I was the third of four children in my family, and I was the child most prone to creating unnecessary conflicts. One evening I decided to hide my sister Paula's mattress. I took the blanket off her twin bed, removed the mattress, and remade the bed by spreading the blanket over the box spring. I placed her mattress in my room, on top of my bed and underneath my blanket. The moment she walked into her bedroom she noticed that her mattress was missing. I knew that would happen, but my intention was to see the effect of her search. You should have seen my father's face when Paula approached him with the question:"Dad, have you seen my mattress?" His look was so shocking that I couldn't help myself. I burst out laughing and was soon rolling on the floor. Of course, she quickly realized that I was the perpetrator of the zany stunt.

In the same way, when purpose is missing from your life, you will recognize that something big or meaningful is missing. Often you discover that meaningful activity or objective when you ask yourself the question: What am I willing to die for? Or phrased another way: Why am I here?

God's assignment to Moses gave him something to risk his life for. It answered the question of why he was placed on the earth. When you discover your life's purpose, it will so consume you that you will eagerly strive to become a champion for your cause, which very well may be your divine assignment. God called Moses to go back to Egypt and lead the one million plus Israelites into the Promised Land. The task was definitely bigger than Moses; he did not have the needed resources, manpower, or relationships among his Hebrew constituency. All he had was a word from God and a companion promise: "I [God] will be with you" (Exod. 3:12).

The assignment was the something big that Moses was missing. When their lives are filled with busyness, demands of others, deadlines, and who knows what other expectations, many people don't recognize the void that purposelessness creates. It becomes pronounced only when it grows to a large size.

Are you noticing the big thing missing from your life? In seeking out that something big, look for satisfaction. What will satisfy your thirsty heart? Whether you long to make a small or large contribution to the world around you, you find satisfaction in obedience to your calling and assignment. You may not have had a dramatic supernatural experience like Moses did with the burning bush. But if you sense that something big is missing from your life, you are on your way to discovering your purpose. Purpose satisfies the soul. Therefore, when you feel satisfied about the direction and activities of your life, you are on the right road to fulfilling your purpose.

3. The Idea of the Big Dream Dawns on You

Moses fled Egypt at age 40 because his secret was out—he had killed an Egyptian soldier. The soldier was beating a Hebrew slave: one of Moses' own people. The day after he killed the soldier, Moses separated two Hebrews from fighting. His question to the man in the wrong—"Why are you hitting your fellow Hebrew?" (Exod. 2:13)—revealed his big dream to one day see his people freed from the devastating ravages of slavery. But it was not until age 80 that Moses began to walk out that big dream.

For 40 years Moses' big dream lay dormant. Can you imagine how he must have felt—not knowing whether his big dream of seeing the Hebrews live in freedom would ever happen? It probably worked in him an array of emotions stemming from anger, disappointment, and hopelessness to perhaps abandonment of his big dream.

The moment God raised the idea of his returning to Egypt to orchestrate the deliverance of the Hebrews, Moses' big dream resurfaced. Armed with a charge from the Lord, he knew that his big dream was sanctioned. It was God's idea; it was God's big dream too. What is your big dream? It may seem outlandish or far-fetched, but if you had God's mind on the matter, wouldn't it seem more plausible? Absolutely! What you need is a word from God about your big dream.

Your big dream is a pathway to your purpose. Be honest. What is your big dream? Are you doing anything to accomplish it? If not, you must. It will give you satisfaction because it is a significant entry point to your life's purpose.

If you determine that your present big dream is unrealistic and that it is not an assignment from God, you should abandon it immediately. Don't waste your emotional energy trying to walk out that dream. If your big dream does not coalesce with God's will, then it is a nightmare. Don't negotiate ways to keep it brewing. It will be only a distraction from God's purpose for your life, and it will be a constant source of frustration.

Allow me the privilege of helping you to release the wrong big dream. It is a prayer to almighty God, Creator of earthly and eternal purposes. Get in a quiet place for a moment and pray this prayer:

Heavenly Father, You alone know what is best for me.
You love me and will always love me, even when I stray from Your will for my life.
Now I return to You for guidance and direction.
I want Your will for every area of my life. Please wash the strong emotions from my heart and mind that have come from this big dream.
Help me to let it go right now.
And replace it with Your big dream for my life.
I ask You this in Jesus' name. Amen.

While in this posture of prayer, take a moment to reflect on the unusual incidents in your life at this moment. Can any of them be like a burning bush experience? Recently, I counseled a young man who had relocated to the East Coast for a new job. After a few years, the job did not work out, and his frustration mounted as he tried to make sense of God's will about where he should live. I shared with him that the job might have been his burning bush experience to relocate his family to the greater New York area. With that perspective, he relaxed and found peace of mind.

Don't ignore any sighting of burning bushes. Follow Moses' steps: (1) he stared at the burning bush; (2) he went closer to inspect the burning bush; and (3) he received a revelation about the meaning of the burning bush. These three steps can be replicated in your burning bush experience. The end result will be the discovery of an assignment from God involving your life's purpose.

DAY 3 Points to Reflect Upon

My journey toward my purpose happens as

1. I change my perspective behind the frustrations of feeling ordinary.

2. I notice that something big is missing from my life.

3. I accept the idea that my big dream is achievable.

love God most. Hate the sins that cause heart death sickness take you sins to from God away

DAY 4

Discover the Search Engine for Purpose

Google is one of the most powerful search engines on the World Wide Web. If you surf to the Web site www.google.com and type in a word, this search engine looks through almost five billion Web pages of information in moments to locate all of the sites that reference your subject.

Similarly, if you went to God's search engine to gather a greater understanding about His purpose for your life, I would encourage you to perform two different searches back to back. First, you would type in the word *love*, and second, you would key in the word *hate*. These two powerful human emotions embody the keys to unlocking your purpose. Ezekiel discovered this principle because his *hate* for the moral bankruptcy of his people along with his undying *love* for the Lord moved him to lie on his left and right sides as a prophetic sign (Ezek. 4:4–8).

Ask yourself these two vital questions: What do I love most? And what do I hate most? I am referring to your love or hate of items, processes, vocations, and the like, not people. Jesus made it quite clear that if we intend to follow His leadership and submit to His behavioral requirements, we have only one option of behavior toward people—to love them. In Matthew 5, Jesus set forth the social law of love:

> *You have heard that it was said, "Love your neighbor and hate your enemy." But I tell you: Love your enemies and pray for those who persecute you, that you may be sons of your Father in heaven. He*

| 23

causes his sun to rise on the evil and the good, and sends rain on the righteous and the unrighteous. If you love those who love you, what reward will you get? Are not even the tax collectors doing that? And if you greet only your brothers, what are you doing more than others? Do not even pagans do that? Be perfect, therefore, as your heavenly Father is perfect.

(vv. 43–48)

What Do You Love Most?

Jesus made the requirement of loving others, regardless of their race, creed, ethnicity, or socioeconomic status, a requirement to being one of His disciples. In fact, not only are we called to love those who do good toward us, but verse 44 instructs us to love our enemies—those who hate us. In much of the New Testament the English word for love translates from the Greek word *agape*, which means the God kind of love. This type of love is awakened by a sense of value in an object; a love that puts self aside in an effort to help and bless others. The unselfish nature of the God kind of love is based on the way that God interfaces with us. It also reflects the way we should love people throughout the global community. There is no wiggle room for a misunderstanding of our need to apply the God kind of love in every type of relationship—be it adversarial or friendly. We are required to love people, not to hate them.

My usage of the love/hate dynamic in locating your life's purpose stems from Isaiah 61:8, which reads, "For I, the LORD, *love* justice; I *hate* robbery and iniquity. In my faithfulness I will reward them [God's people] and make an everlasting covenant with them [God's people]" (italics mine). This verse points back to my two original questions: What do you love most? And what do you hate most? By answering these questions, you will find your purpose.

Isaiah prophesied that God loves justice. God's behavior, plans, and actions often center on performing acts of justice toward His creation. My point is this: whatever you love most, you will spend your time doing. Therefore, your purpose is often hidden in what you love to do.

Have you given any thought to what you love to do? I love explaining things to people, and this love has manifested itself as a teaching gift. I enjoy debating about controversial or philosophical subjects that demand logical thinking and sharp communication skills. Hence, part of my life's purpose is to empower people who need a ready defense against intellectual bullies and false teachers bent on misleading people.

People who have pursued their life's purpose because they discovered what they loved to do are numerous in the Bible and throughout postbiblical history. Take David, for instance. He loved entertaining the presence of God through personal worship. As a shepherd boy, he sang and played his instruments before the Lord. As he grew into adulthood, he continued pursuing this passion. As a result, 2 Samuel 23:1 said of him: "These are the last words of David: 'The oracle of David son of Jesse, the oracle of the man exalted by the Most High, the man anointed by the God of Jacob, Israel's singer of songs.'" Among all of his great accomplishments—killing the fearsome Goliath, a nine-foot-tall giant of a man; becoming king of the nation of Israel; using his keen military mind to save his people—David was known as "Israel's singer of songs." The King James Version of the Bible translates these words as the "sweet psalmist of Israel."

David's love of worship positioned him to pursue his God-given purpose of writing hundreds of songs, dozens of which made it into the book of Psalms. These psalms have aided millions of people in finding peace, comfort, and emotional help throughout history—although their primary purpose is to guide people toward a more meaningful relationship with God. For example, David authored the most famous psalm—the Twenty-third Psalm—commonly referred to as the Shepherd's Psalm. The Message, a modern translation by Eugene Peterson, offers a refreshing perspective on this timeless psalm. Take a moment to enjoy it:

> GOD, *my shepherd!*
> *I don't need a thing.*
> *You have bedded me down in lush meadows,*
> *you find me quiet pools to drink from.*

True to your word,
you let me catch my breath
and send me in the right direction.

Even when the way goes through Death Valley,
I'm not afraid
when you walk at my side.
Your trusty shepherd's crook
makes me feel secure.

You serve me a six-course dinner
right in front of my enemies.
You revive my drooping head;
my cup brims with blessing.

Your beauty and love chase after me
every day of my life.
I'm back home in the house of GOD
for the rest of my life.

(Ps. 23:1–6)

What do you love most? Don't overlook the significance of your answer because it may contain the direction that you have been waiting for. Use this question as a self-discovery tool to guide you to your purpose.

What Do You Hate Most?

It often seems much easier to see the value of love than the value of hate. I suspect the reason is that people seek love and run from hate. In fact, in its most general form the word *love* occurs 310 times in the King James Version of the Bible. The word *hate*, on the other hand, appears 87 times. Despite its fewer times mentioned in the Scriptures, hate offers a service that you should not underestimate or ignore. Human beings, particularly Christians, just hate to think that there could be any value in hating something. Nevertheless, hate has its benefits.

Ask yourself: What do I hate most? Then zero in on hate from two perspectives. First, think of the things that trouble you—the things that you avoid. For example, I just hate wasting time, so I keep my distance from and minimize my involvement with people who like to waste time. This aspect of hate is not an indicator of purpose. Second, think of the things that you hate so much you're always thinking of ways to fix or solve the problems that they present. This second perspective is the one I want you to consider here.

I hate chaos and confusion in people's lives. Seeing projects or organizational systems of any size in disarray irritates me. But over the years I noticed that I was constantly being drawn into situations involving these areas. After a time of introspection and after receiving positive feedback following many of my restructuring tasks, I discovered that I have a gift of administration and organization. The very antithesis of the things I hate—chaos and disorder—is the area where one of my strongest gifts lies.

How would we achieve order if there were no chaos to straighten out? What place would there be for administration if there were no misaligned or improperly structured organizational systems and projects to fix? Lurking behind the emotion of hatred is an internal magnet that draws such problems to us.

You need to reconsider this issue so that you use the hatred appropriately—not to despise the area of your gifting or purpose, but to propel you toward it. I used to become angry when I saw disorder, especially within organizations, but once I changed my attitude, I was able to see my purpose being fulfilled as I solved the problems within the organizations. Now I gain a great degree of personal satisfaction from this area of my life.

Let's go back to God's words in Isaiah 61:8: God hates robbery and brutality. In light of this statement, God's need to establish moral laws to safeguard society against robbery and brutality is understandable. What God hates, He establishes a means to correct. God also puts a similar hatred in the hearts of people who will champion His interests.

Moses hated the Egyptians' brutality against the Hebrews. He found his purpose as he began correcting the very thing he despised. He did not fight with God's instruction to return to Egypt and deliver his people from bondage.

How about you? What do you hate most? If you search intently, you may discover that there is a gift lying beneath the surface of the things you hate most—the very things that may lead you to your purpose.

DAY 4 Points to Reflect Upon

Discovering my purpose can occur if I input the words of *love* and *hate* into God's search engine.

1. What do I love most? Take a moment and write down the top five things that you truly love doing. No matter how elementary or silly your answer may be, write it down.

2. What do I hate most? Jot down five of the top things that you hate doing, but always find yourself being called upon to do.

3. In reviewing the list of things that you love to do and hate to do, which ones recharge your emotions? Cross out the ones that drain you since they won't benefit you in discovering your purpose. Discuss with a friend the gifts that he or she has observed in you when you are engaged in tasks related to these items. This analysis may help you see that your life's purpose is in the things that you love most or hate most.

love

1. Serve – cook, bake,
2. Humor – tell stories – write
3. Read – learn, grow in God
4. Music – ministers to me.

hate.

1. choas –
2. Being unorganized
3. not following through

Step #2

Know Where You Are Going

I long to accomplish a great and noble task; but it is my chief duty and joy to accomplish humble tasks as though they were great and noble. The world is moved along, not only by the mighty shoves of its heroes, but also by the aggregate of the tiny pushes of each honest worker.

Helen Keller

DAY 5

Explore Where You Would Like to Go

In the first four days of *Perfecting Your Purpose* you learned a few principles that should have helped you discover your God-given purpose. Now that you have an idea about your life's assignment, the next question I want to help you answer is: What are the secrets that will help me perfect my purpose? Simply put: What do I do now? My answer is: explore where you would like to go, or better yet, explore where *God* would like you to go.

Over the next four days (Days 5–8), my objective is to help you (1) explore where you would like to go; (2) evaluate the level of difficulty in getting there; (3) keep your ideas quiet, at least for now; and (4) get a sample of the results you want to attain. Each day one of these four gems will be unearthed as I endeavor to help you answer the question: What do I do now? These four ideas originated from the wisdom behind Moses' instruction to the twelve spies he dispatched to explore the Promised Land over a 40-day period.

Moses learned that hard decisions—ones that affected his life-long direction and the lives of people he influenced—could be made at the end of 40 days of exploration. After he led the children of Israel out of Egypt and into the wilderness, Moses' purpose was just beginning to unfold. The next phase of his assignment was to lead the people from the wilderness into the Promised Land (Exod. 3:17). Moses' overall quest was all about fulfilling God's desire for *his* life. It was not about how he could twist God's arm so that God would bless his self-centered plans. Moses desired to find God's purpose for his life and perfect that plan.

In the wilderness, God nudged Moses to proceed with the second phase of his assignment—leading the people into the Promised Land—by saying, "Send some men to explore the land of Canaan, which I am giving to the Israelites. From each ancestral tribe send one of its leaders" (Num. 13:1–2). The expedition of these twelve spies took exactly 40 days (Num. 13:25).

The overarching goal was to scout out the land, gather information, and return with a good report that would encourage the fledgling band of ex-slaves in the wilderness about possessing the Promised Land. Although only two of the twelve spies embraced a positive perspective toward attaining the big dream (Num. 13:31–32; 14:6–9), the four guiding principles we saw at the beginning of this chapter are the exact guidelines Moses prescribed to his explorers. These principles will also work you if you are a modern-day explorer seeking to discover and perfect your life's purpose.

Explore where you would like to go. This maxim could be rephrased: Where would God like you to go? When you approach your quest from the latter perspective, it keeps you focused on this reality: your purpose is perfected as you seek God's agenda for your life. We can become consumed with our dreams—those that have absolutely nothing to do with God or the improvement of humanity. In the eyes of society, it appears that we are merely ambitious or driven. But the internal, pivotal question remains unanswered: Did my life on the earth fulfill its purpose? To avoid the internal frustration created by living without God's direction in your life, you must explore where *God* would like you to go.

Moses needed to regroup after he escaped the clutches of the powerful Pharaoh and the mighty Egyptian army. While the Israelites were encamped in the desert of Paran, a divine manifestation occurred (Deut. 33:2; Hab. 3:3). Moses received the heavenly revelation to send twelve spies to search out the Promised Land (Num. 13:16). The wilderness site of Paran was later incorporated into a blessing that Moses spoke over the children of Israel just before his death: "The LORD came from Sinai and dawned over them from Seir; he shone forth from Mount Paran" (Deut. 33:2). Moses referred to God's instruction to send the twelve spies into the Promised Land as a type of shining forth or revelation of the *next step* toward perfecting his purpose.

Tackling Tough Questions

Similarly, in your quest to perfect your purpose, you need to be absolutely sure of your next step. Perfecting your purpose is similar to taking a journey where God's plan becomes your road map. Moses was on a journey to the Promised Land, and he checked with God periodically to verify that he was on the right track. Checking in with God is about quieting your life to hear God's heart regarding your course. Contemplative reflection and thoughts center on questions such as: Am I in the right place? How do I really feel about what I'm about to do? Do I feel good about myself based on my life's direction? These questions help you remain connected to your purpose. They also help you disconnect from wrong ambitions, wrong directions, or double-mindedness concerning your life's purpose.

Dr. Billy Graham gives the personal description of his struggle as he sought to understand how to perfect his life's purpose:

> *In August of 1949, I was so filled with doubts about everything that when I stood to preach and made a statement, I would say to myself: I wonder if that is the truth. I wonder if I can really say that sincerely. My ministry had gone. I then took the Bible up into the high Sierra Nevada mountains in California. I opened it and got on my knees. I pled, "Father, I cannot understand many things in this Book. I cannot come intellectually all the way, but I accept it by faith to be authoritative, the inspired Word of the living God!"*[1]

During this time of soul-searching and self-discovery, Dr. Graham found inner peace and resolved his approach to his faith. Within the next twenty-four months he soared to national prominence.

You can secure the confidence to walk out your purpose through quiet times with God. Turn a portion of your morning into a reflective period of solitude and prayer. While reclining in your bedroom or another private space in your home, ask God this question: "Lord, is my life in the center of Your purpose?" Immediately get still and listen for the Lord's quiet response to your heart. Consider the thoughts that flash in your mind. Survey a Bible verse or past sermon theme that comes to mind. Any one of these re-

I have a peace when I'm with my children grandchildren (handwritten)

sponses could be God's way of saying to you: "You're on the right track; press on." Or He may be saying: "Make an adjustment because you've veered off course." Even God's silence can be an indication of His affirmation of your life's direction. Yet there are times when God's silence leaves you with an uneasy feeling, which indicates that you're off course. Conversely, your sense of inner peace is one way that God assures you that you're in sync with His will. Isaiah tells us, "You [God] will keep in perfect peace him whose mind is steadfast, because he trusts in you" (26:3). God's peace, which He plants in the hearts of His children ensures that they are anchored in an ongoing relationship of trust.

In the article "All the Right Moves" in *Fast Company* (May 1999), chess master and sought-after mentor Bruce Pandolfini is quoted as saying, "My lessons consist of a lot of silence. I listen to other teachers, and they're always talking . . . I let my students think. If I do ask a question ('why are you making that move?') and I don't get the right answer, I'll rephrase the question—and wait. I never give the answer. Most of us really don't appreciate the power of silence. Some of the most effective communication—between student and teacher, between master players—takes place during silent periods."[2]

We, too, can learn from God in His moments of silence as we allow the sweetness of the Holy Spirit to calm our hearts and affirm our directions through His peace.

In the quiet desert place, Moses heard from God about *next step* issues. Next step plans must originate from God. Be assured, the thought of advancing you toward your life's purpose is already in God's heart. Your struggle with discovering your life's purpose should be behind you at this point. Now, the objective is to get God's thoughts about the course you ought to take to perfect your purpose. What good is it to know your purpose if you have no plan to flesh it out? A plan outlines an intentional approach to perfecting your purpose. God could have easily given Moses a comprehensive overview of the Promised Land without the use of a twelve-man scouting expedition. But He chose to tell Moses to search out the land. God's job is to give you a purpose for living and help you discover that purpose. It is *your* responsibility to search out the purpose.

Search Out Your Purpose

I believe the divine intent behind giving us the responsibility for searching out the next steps lies in our need to understand our purpose through the five senses. God wanted Moses to have information gained from touching, seeing, smelling, hearing, and tasting. Gaining a glimpse of your destiny through spiritual knowledge is one thing, but natural knowledge is also required to formulate a complete strategy.

Moses' commands to the twelve spies were to

> *"go up through the Negev and on into the hill country. See what the land is like and whether the people who live there are strong or weak, few or many. What kind of land do they live in? Is it good or bad? What kind of towns do they live in? Are they unwalled or fortified? How is the soil? Is it fertile or poor? Are there trees on it or not? Do your best to bring back some of the fruit of the land." (It was the season for the first ripe grapes.)*

> (Num. 13:17–20)

Moses desired to understand and evaluate the agricultural quality of the land, the inhabitants' preparedness for battle, and the soundness of their cities against a military campaign. The spies were also to bring back a little taste of the fruit. Moses outlined a thorough investigation of the Promised Land before he formulated a plan to advance his purpose—God's assignment.

Exploring where you would like to go is about formulating a research strategy. As Moses sought information and fruit to satisfy the need of his five senses, likewise you should explore your intellectual and emotional curiosities regarding your next step. Keep in mind that the painstaking work of investigation often involves trial and error. You won't know what things are like unless you search them out. Some things are readily known or easily determined through minor research, while other items require more effort and call for persistence and patience. Regardless of the difficulty, 40 days is a good period to gather this information. As Moses did, choose capable people to aid you in the process. Don't try to gather all of the data by yourself. It will be too time consuming and difficult. Choose people who are not afraid of difficult challenges, and invite them to gather data to support various aspects of your purpose. In many cases, the information that you are seeking already exists. It may simply be one telephone call away or the input of a few key words in the search category of an Internet search engine like Google. And presto, the information will pop up on your computer screen.

Establish a search for the next steps toward perfecting your purpose with a significant degree of commitment and persistence. Moses recognized the urgency for occupying the Promised Land. The moment he heard God's suggestion to send spies to explore the land, he selected the spies and dispatched them. If you are really passionate about perfecting your purpose, demonstrate this passion by immediately exploring what the next steps toward your purpose entail.

DAY 5 Points to Reflect Upon

In exploring where you would like to go, consider these tips:

1. Spend a few moments contemplating these tough questions: How do I really feel about moving forward in this season of my purpose? Do I feel good about myself based on my life's direction? *yes!*

2. Pursue further knowledge of where you would like to go by conducting several word searches in a search engine like Google regarding your purpose.

3. Read the parable of the persistent widow in Luke 18:1-8. As you read, ask yourself this question: Am I as determined as the widow in searching out and fulfilling my purpose?

3/06 - My purpose is allowing God's love to flow through me to my family, to write, be with solid friends, no more chasing dreams, just God!

DAY 6

Have a Mountaintop Experience

Have you ever had a mountaintop experience? I'm talking about standing on top of a huge mountain that overlooks a city. What an experience! If you climb high enough, you can see for miles around.

When I was on a recent speaking engagement to the East African nation of Kenya, my host took me to see the view from the mountainous area of the Great Rift Valley. The Rift Valley, located in the southern portion of Kenya, ranges in elevation from an estimated 1,300 feet below sea level (the Dead Sea) to approximately 6,000 feet above sea level. The main section of the valley continues from the Red Sea southwest across Ethiopia and south across Kenya, Tanzania, and Malawi to the lower Zambezi River valley in Mozambique. It extends approximately 3,000 miles (4,830 km) from northern Syria to central Mozambique.

If I had a powerful telescope from where I was standing in Kenya, I would be able to see not just the cities below, but such a broad expanse of land that I could also see whole countries. The interesting thing about mountaintop experiences is that everyone can appreciate them, but few people boast about the climb. Our focus today is evaluating the level of difficulty in response to the question: What do I do now? As you recall, Moses gave twelve spies an assignment to explore the Promised Land. One of their tasks was to "see what the land is like and whether the people who live there are strong or weak, few or many. What kind of land do they live in? Is it good or bad? What kind of towns do they live in? Are they unwalled or fortified?" (Num. 13:18–19). These questions aimed at gathering information that would help Moses strategize how to lead the Israelite army and capture the land God promised them. In other words, Moses had to evaluate the level of difficulty involved in climbing the mountain of his purpose.

How High Can You Climb?

Upon their return from the explorative study conducted over 40 days, ten of the twelve spies gave a bad report. Although two spies, Joshua and Caleb, vehemently opposed the fear-based opinions of their counterparts, their lone voices did not sway the crowd. The debilitating report of the ten spies was intended to prevent the Israelites from embracing God's purpose for their lives. They said,

> *"We can't attack those people; they are stronger than we are." And they [the ten spies] spread among the Israelites a bad report about the land they had explored. They said, "The land we explored devours those living in it. All the people we saw there are of great size. We saw the Nephilim there (the descendants of Anak [huge people] come from the Nephilim). We seemed like grasshoppers in our own eyes, and we looked the same to them."*

(Num. 13:31–33)

The ten spies regarded the task of defeating the inhabitants as insurmountable. In essence, they drew a conclusion before getting started. They did not want to climb too high to fulfill their purpose.

When I think about the ten spies, I am reminded of the African impala when it's trapped. These animals can jump to a height of more than ten feet and cover a distance of greater than thirty feet. Yet these magnificent creatures can be kept in an enclosure in any zoo with a three-foot wall because they will not jump if they cannot see where their feet will fall. Similarly, the ten spies made no room for faith, for God's power, or for the synergistic ability of people who were passionate to fulfill God's purpose for their lives. The spies looked at the size of their opponents and made three conclusive remarks that thwarted their future plans toward perfecting their purpose.

First, they concluded that the inhabitants were "of great size." In other words, they were too large to conquer. Second, they looked at themselves in light of the physical stature of their adversaries and passed another paralyzing verdict: "We seemed like grasshoppers in our own eyes." This statement conveyed that they altered their view of themselves based solely on how they felt. They felt dwarfed in contrast to their opponents. Third, the ten spies said about themselves, "We looked the same [as grasshoppers] to them." The spies assumed that the native inhabitants saw them the way they saw themselves.

If you want to talk yourself out of your purpose, hang around people like these ten spies and you'll be too petrified to consider climbing the mountain that leads to perfecting your purpose. The spies succeeded in talking themselves out of advancing in their purpose before they had begun the ascent. They had fallen into a common trap. They focused on the difficult task of climbing the mountain rather than the joy of standing on the mountaintop. I am not suggesting that you should discount the climb ahead of you. Daring to pretend that the climb won't be tough or worse, that it does not exist, would be foolish and delusional. You must acknowledge the rigor of the climb to the mountaintop toward perfecting your purpose. Yet the ones who make it to the top—those who perfect their God-given purpose—are the ones who recognize that an evaluation of the difficulty of the climb is not an adequate reason to abandon the journey. This is especially true since you've not even begun the ascent.

Dr. Martin Luther King Jr. delivered perhaps the most famous speech of the twentieth century—"I've Been to the Mountaintop." He declared,

> *Well, I don't know what will happen now. We've got some difficult days ahead. But it doesn't matter with me now. Because I've been to the mountaintop. And I don't mind. Like anybody, I would like to live a long life. Longevity has its place. But I'm not concerned about that now. I just want to do God's will. And He's allowed me to go up to the mountain. And I've looked over. And I've seen the promised land. I may not get there with you. But I want you to know tonight, that we, as a people, will get to the promised land. And I'm*

happy, tonight. I'm not worried about anything. I'm not fearing any man. Mine eyes have seen the glory of the coming of the Lord.[1]

Dr. King honestly and candidly admitted to the world that achieving racial harmony and equality is a difficult goal. Nonetheless, he was at peace because he had been to the mountaintop, and God had allowed him to see the proverbial Promised Land—humanity's embrace of justice and reconciliation among the races. Unlike the ten spies, Dr. King distinguished the difficulty of the climb to the mountaintop from the appearance of its invincibility and intended to make the climb nonetheless.

Get Ready to Climb the Mountain

If you focus on the value and worthiness of your goal, coupling that with God's divine initiative fueling your purpose, the level of difficulty facing you will not feel so overwhelming. Passion will thrive against difficulty any day.

As the story goes, one evening while a man was driving down a country road, he lost control of his car and wound up in a ditch. He walked to the closest farmhouse and asked for help pulling the car out. The farmer said, "Sure. Let me hitch up Dusty and you'll be out in no time." A few minutes later the farmer appeared with Dusty—an old, swaybacked, almost blind mule. After Dusty was hitched to the car, the old farmer cracked the whip and said, "Pull, Buck, pull." Nothing happened. The farmer cracked the whip again and said, "Pull, Clyde, pull." Nothing happened. He cracked the whip again and said, "Pull, Dusty, pull." Dusty began to pull until finally the car was out of the ditch. The man thanked the farmer and then said, "I'm really curious. If your mule's name is Dusty, why did you say 'Pull, Buck,' and 'Pull, Clyde'?" The farmer said, "Well, you know Dusty's old and he doesn't see too good, and he doesn't have much confidence. If he thought he had to do all the work himself, he'd never even try." Similarly, you must remember that you are not alone. God is in there pulling with you, helping you reach the mountaintop.

Joshua and Caleb, the two spies who had a positive report, counseled the Israelites, "Only do not rebel against the LORD. And do not be afraid of the people of the land, because we will swallow them up. Their protection is gone, but the LORD is with us. Do not be afraid of them" (Num. 14:9). Like Dusty, the Israelites needed encouragement that there would be help on their side. But Joshua and Caleb talked to no avail. The picture painted by the ten spies had already dried on the canvas of the people's hearts. They were not able to see beyond the level of difficulty to advance in God's promises and seize the land.

What about you? Are you up for the climb? To perfect your purpose, you must be willing to climb a mountain that may be full of challenges, obstacles, and potential hindrances. In evaluating the level of difficulty, you will face the question: Is God calling me to do this? If your answer is yes, climbing the mountain will be an adventure in faith rather than a death trap. I'm learning to truely trust in God not self

After 40 days exploring the Promised Land, Joshua and Caleb were not going to let a few giants and ten fearful men stop them from perfecting their purpose. The conviction that they wanted to impart to the Israelite assembly was: "The land we passed through and explored is exceedingly good. If the LORD is pleased with us, he will lead us into that land, a land flowing with milk and honey, and will give it to us" (Num. 14:8). Caleb and Joshua were trying to get the people to prepare for the climb by putting first things first. They reminded the Israelites that the will of God was for them to seize and occupy the Promised Land. If they labored to please God, perfecting their purpose would be a cinch because God always blesses those who please Him.

> *One day an expert in time management spoke to a group of business students. He said, "Okay, time for a quiz." Then he pulled out a one-gallon, wide mouth Mason jar and set it on a table. He produced about a dozen fist-sized rocks and carefully placed them, one at a time, into the jar. When the jar was filled to the top and no more rocks would fit inside, he asked, "Is this jar full?" Everyone in the class said, "Yes." Then he said, "Really?"*
>
> *He reached under the table and pulled out a bucket of gravel. Then he dumped some gravel in and shook the jar causing pieces of gravel*

to work themselves down into the space between the big rocks. Then he asked the group once more, "Is the jar full?" By this time the class was on to him. "Probably not," one of them answered. "Good!" he replied. He reached under the table and brought out a bucket of sand. He started dumping the sand in the jar and it went into all of the spaces left between the rocks and the gravel. Once more he asked the question, "Is this jar full?" "No!" the class shouted. Once again he said, "Good." Then he grabbed a pitcher of water and began to pour it in until the jar was filled to the brim.

Then he looked at the class and asked, "What is the point of this illustration?" One eager beaver raised his hand and said, "The point is, no matter how full your schedule, if you try really hard you can always fit some more things in it!" "No," the speaker replied, "that's not the point. The truth this illustration teaches us is: If you don't put the big rocks in first, you'll never get them in at all." We need to be sure the "big rocks," the most important things, are priorities in our lives.[2]

If the Israelites evaluated the level of difficulty associated with pursuing their purpose in light of putting the big rocks in the jar first, climbing the mountain would be a rewarding adventure. Doing God's will and striving to please Him were the two "big rocks" that Caleb and Joshua tried to put into the jar—the hearts of the assembly—but fear caused the people to resist.

Wilma Rudolph was the twentieth of twenty-two children. She was born prematurely, and doctors didn't expect her to survive her infancy. She did, but at the age of four, she contracted double pneumonia and scarlet fever, which left her with a paralyzed left leg. At the age of nine, she removed the metal leg brace she had depended on for five years and began walking without it. By thirteen, she had developed a rhythmic walk, which doctors said was a miracle. That same year, she decided she wanted to compete in races. She entered her first race and came in last. For the next three years, she came in dead last in every race she entered. But she kept running until the day came that she won a race. Eventually, the little girl who was not supposed to live and then who was not supposed to be able to walk would win three Olympic gold medals in track events.[3]

Don't fall into the trap of looking at the level of difficulty before you. Look at the pleasure of standing on the mountaintop—accomplishing your life's purpose.

DAY 6 Points to Reflect Upon

Climbing the mountain that leads to perfecting my purpose happens when

1. I look at the mountaintop and not the level of difficulty involved in the climb.

2. I refuse to allow negative, fearful people to sway me from starting the climb toward perfecting my purpose.

3. I put the big rocks into the jar before the smaller ones. The first rock is committing to doing the will of God, and the second rock is striving to please God in every area of my life.

Keep Your Ideas Quiet for Now

How much stock should you put in the opinion of others when it comes to perfecting your purpose? I usually answer the question by saying it depends on who's giving the opinion and how much that opinion harmonizes with God's.

Sometimes the most brilliant people don't have a clue when it comes to understanding God's purposes for someone else's life. That is why I always say, "Never let anyone else dream for you because he'll always dream too small!" Keeping your ideas quiet during the exploratory phase of the journey toward perfecting your purpose is an ingenious practice that Moses employed during the 40-day mission of the twelve spies. The spies had to maintain the secrecy of their mission. If the inhabitants of the Promised Land got wind of the fact that a covert mission was under way to investigate how *their* homes and lands could be taken away by the Hebrew refugees from Egypt, they certainly would have marshaled a powerful attack against them.

The Early Stages of the Journey

The twelve spies returned safely to Moses and their group without being noticed by the inhabitants (Num. 13:26). Although ten of the twelve spies had a fear-based perspective that halted the mission of perfecting their destiny, at least they got this portion of their command correct. They kept their mouths shut while they gathered pertinent data about the ascent to their purpose. Knowing how to keep quiet in the early stages of your purpose is critical because that's when you are most uncertain if, in fact, you're headed in the right direction with your life. Three principles that helped the spies keep focused and quiet during the exploration were (1) they were under God's orders; (2) they were public servants; and (3) their future depended upon how they handled the mission. I'd like to help you understand how to apply these principles in your life as you perfect your purpose.

1. You're Under God's Orders

When you're sure that your life's purpose originated in God's heart, and you are en route to perfecting your purpose, you are under God's orders. The twelve spies knew that Moses sent them to explore the Promised Land because he was under God's orders. In fact, God said to Moses: "Send some men to explore the land of Canaan, which I am giving to the Israelites" (Num. 13:1). Since Moses was under God's orders, they, too, became subject to His command. As the spies trudged through the hills, valleys, and rocky and flat areas in Canaan, they moved ahead because *they were under God's orders.* If you can envision yourself as a soldier who is under the direct command of God when you are investigating various dimensions of your purpose, your encouragement and enthusiasm about your mission will grow. Think about it—the God of the universe gives you His personal order. God Himself is interested in your future. Your purpose reflects His orders!

The spies could not open their mouths prematurely or unwisely, or they would have failed God. No one starts off with the notion: I don't care if I fail God. As a pastor of a congregation of multiple thousands, I have never met anyone within or without the church who wanted to fail God. The converse is usually the case; everyone wants to please God. If it is too difficult or too inconvenient to please God, however, some people refuse the mission at the onset. Such was not the case with the twelve spies. All of them wanted to cooperate with the clandestine mission. They knew that they had to keep their mouths shut, at least during the exploratory phase. Life and death were at stake if the emissaries could not keep their secret.

2. You're a Public Servant

The twelve spies, representing the Israelite community, were public servants entrusted with the life purpose of the entire group. Acting on their own—even if it felt convenient—would jeopardize the perfecting of that purpose. Likewise, you become a public servant to your family, friends, and even the greater society by perfecting your God-given purpose.

As a public servant, you are charged with a certain responsibility, and you are given the appropriate authority to carry out the mission. You must fulfill the order with a certain measure of decorum in your conduct, speech, and morals. Additionally, the perfecting of your purpose should make the world a better place for everyone. This level of responsibility should help you control what you say and to whom. In other words, seeing yourself as a public servant helps you to keep your ideas quiet for now.

If you risk sharing your dreams prematurely, your purpose may die from the poison of criticism. Criticism kills dreams and thwarts your life's purpose. Hearing toxic comments about your plans being too grand or too lofty puts a stranglehold on your purpose. Unconsciously, your life's purpose dies in your soul without having a chance for you to work on it.

Many years ago, Victor Kiam, the Remington shaver entrepreneur, ignored a chance to obtain exclusive rights to an unknown product because colleagues criticized it. The product was Velcro. Kiam's perspective today is that "it's just another blip in the road." He said, "Besides, if I hadn't learned from that lapse of judgment by not having confidence in myself, I never would have bought Remington."[1]

Then there's the story of the woman who was bent on improving her marriage by trying very hard to please her ultracritical husband. He always seemed the most cantankerous at breakfast. If the eggs were scrambled, he wanted them poached; if they were poached, he wanted them scrambled. One morning, with what she thought was a stroke of genius, the wife poached one egg and scrambled the other and placed the plate before him. Anxiously, she awaited what had to be his unqualified approval. He peered down at the plate and snorted, "Can't you do anything right, woman? You've scrambled the wrong one!"[2]

3. Your Future Is in Jeopardy

In the middle of a conversation have you ever thought, *Pardon me while I take my foot out of my mouth?* You recognized that what you said was not correct or was just plain dumb. All of us have been there, and we know that sometimes what we say can jeopardize our future.

A little bird was flying south for the winter. He got so cold that he froze up and fell to the ground in a large field. While he was lying there, a cow came by and dropped manure on him. As he lay there in the manure, the bird began to realize how warm he was. The manure was actually thawing him out! He lay there warm and happy, but soon he began to complain about the odor. A passing cat heard the little bird complaining. Following the sound, the cat discovered the bird under the pile of manure and promptly dug him out—and then ate him. The moral of this story is threefold. First, not everyone who drops manure on you is your enemy. Second, not everyone who digs you out of a pile of manure is your friend. Third, when you're in the manure, keep your mouth shut—don't complain! The third point is our focus: don't say anything while you're checking things out.

The twelve spies were clear on this point. If they told anyone of their mission, the inhabitants of Canaan probably would kill them. On top of that, the group's purpose would have been jeopardized. The spies understood that their silence protected their purpose. Premature scrutiny can jeopardize your purpose. In the infancy of any major plan, particularly a life direction, you must fully embrace your dream, but recognize that others' early scrutiny may cause you to inadvertently abort that dream. Your silence protects you from detailed scrutiny—and possibly envy and ill will—as you attempt to perfect your purpose.

During the first two years following my commitment to whole-heartedly serve Jesus Christ, I began having aspirations to become a pastor. The idea seemed extremely odd to me because I had just completed my master's degree in civil engineering and landed a great job in the field. No matter how I rationalized the idea, however, the desire would not go away. I kept wrestling with the thought that I should prepare myself for a life and career as a pastor. Sometimes the idea seemed far-fetched, while at other times the notion seemed appealing and exciting. One day I surrendered to the idea that I was going to become a pastor. After the question of my life's direction was solved, I told my plan to an older Christian man whom I deeply admired for his Bible knowledge and his fatherly demeanor. To my surprise, he shot down the idea, saying that there were already too many ministers and pastors and that the last thing we needed was one more. Each attack made me more insecure about what I thought was God's plan for my life.

Despite my friend's comments, the thought of becoming a pastor would not leave me. At first, I tried to push the desire away, rationalizing that he was right and that I must be wrong. *C'mon*, I thought. *I'm an engineer. Why would God cause me to throw away five and a half years of educational training and make me a minister?* But the desire would not leave me. After I recovered from that emotional blow, I enrolled in seminary and also took every ministerial training class offered by my local church. As they say, the rest is history.

In hindsight, I realize that I should not have shared my purpose so prematurely. My zeal to share my excitement with others jeopardized the purpose for which my life was destined. At the onset of my journey, I did not have the strength of conviction to allow for intelligent questions, strong objections, or intense scrutiny. I needed time to gather data, grow in internal assurance, and work out the emotional and psychological issues surrounding my understanding of God's purpose for my life.

When God speaks to the heart of His creation, nothing can thwart the power inherent in His word. God spoke to my heart, even though I was spiritually immature to His ways. The writer of Hebrews puts it this way: "The word of God is living and active. Sharper than any double-edged sword, it penetrates even to dividing soul and spirit, joints and marrow; it judges the thoughts and attitudes of the heart" (4:12).

Be encouraged! In the early stages on the journey to perfect your purpose, learn to guard what you say. Treasure the benefit that silence brings to your purpose. During this phase of purpose, let the inward excitement help you grow spiritually. Thank God for giving you a unique purpose that is specific to your personality. Right now, the idea is your little secret between you and God. Discuss the idea with God during private times of prayer and worship. Later, at the right time, you will be able to share your newfound purpose with others.

DAY 7 Points to Reflect Upon

Keeping your ideas quiet at the onset of the journey to perfect your purpose can be a challenge. Here are a few exercises to remove the temptation of sharing your ideas prematurely:

1. Write one page in your journal concerning your newfound excitement about your purpose. Describe how you feel about the possibility of doing something big, exciting, and a fulfillment of God's plan for your life.

2. In your journal, list three specific reasons why you need to keep quiet for now about your purpose. What emotional traps do you need to avoid? Or what criticisms do you need to circumvent?

3. Since this phase of your purpose requires quietness, how has your relationship with God been improved?

DAY **8**

Sample the Fruit

Before the twelve spies started on the 40-day exploration of the Promised Land, Moses said to them: "Do your best to bring back some of the fruit of the land" (Num. 13:20). There's nothing like testing things before you marshal a full-scale effort to perfect your purpose. Moses wanted to see the fruit, squeeze the fruit, and possibly taste the fruit that came from the Promised Land. He probably figured that the fruit would be a good indicator about the rest of the land. Good fruit would motivate and encourage the Israelites to face the challenge of defeating the Canaanites in order to possess their property as God's Promised Land.

Don't get me wrong. Moses was not planning to change his mind about occupying the Promised Land; he just wanted to sample the fruit from the place that God had foretold was "a land flowing with milk and honey" (Exod. 3:8). A sampling of fruit from the place of your destiny encourages you when the time comes to fight any opposition that stands in the way of your purpose.

Tell Me Like It Is!

It's just like my high school baseball coach used to say to me and my teammates after hearing us brag about how well we thought we could play: "Don't tell me. Show me." Moses wanted to see what God was talking about when He used glowing words like "a land flowing with milk and honey" to describe the Promised Land. So, he told the spies to bring back Canaanite fruit to sample upon their return to the camp. That would settle any questions regarding the richness of the land. Was God telling it straight, or were the terms inflated? A sample of the fruit would be a good representation of the rest of the land.

I remember hearing a story about an interview for an assassin at the CIA, a highly classified position that is hard to fill. After a few applicants went through background checks, training, and testing, the possible choices were narrowed down to two men and one woman, but only one position was available. The new recruit had to be tough, which all three finalists claimed to be.

The day came for the final test to see which person would get the job. The CIA agents administering the test took one man to a large metal door and handed him a gun. "We must know that you will follow your instructions no matter what the circumstances," they explained. "Inside this room, you will find your wife sitting in a chair. Take this gun and kill her." The man got a shocked look on his face and said, "You can't be serious! I could never shoot my own wife!" "Well," said a CIA agent, "you're definitely not the right man for this job then."

They took the second man to the same door and handed him a gun. "We must know that you will follow instructions no matter what the circumstances," they explained. "Inside you will find your wife sitting in a chair. Take this gun and kill her." The second man looked shocked, but nevertheless took the gun and went into the room. All was quiet for about five minutes, and then the door opened. The man came out of the room with tears in his eyes. He said, "I tried to shoot her. I just couldn't pull the trigger and shoot my wife. I guess I'm not the right man for the job." "No," a CIA agent replied, "you don't have what it takes. Take your wife and go home."

They led the female finalist to the same door and handed her the same gun. "We must be sure that you will follow instructions no matter what the circumstances. This is your final test. Inside you will find your husband sitting in a chair. Take this gun and kill him," an agent said. The woman took the gun and opened the door. Before the door even closed all the way, the CIA men heard the gun firing. One shot after another for thirteen shots. Then all hell broke loose in the room. They heard screaming, thrashing, and banging on the walls for several minutes, and then all went quiet. The door opened slowly, and there stood the woman. She wiped the sweat from her brow and said, "You guys didn't tell me the gun was loaded with blanks! I had to beat him to death with the chair!"

Although the CIA agents were testing the woman's capacity to execute drastic orders, she meant business. In the same matter-of-fact way, God meant every word He said to Moses: "The land flows with milk and honey." Nonetheless, Moses wanted to see for himself that the purpose God had called him to perfect would be extremely fruitful and satisfying.

The spies successfully returned with a sampling of the land's fruit, and their testimony to Moses was: "We went into the land to which you sent us, and it does flow with milk and honey! Here is its fruit" (Num. 13:27). The spies "cut off a branch bearing a single cluster of grapes. Two of them carried it on a pole between them, along with some pomegranates and figs" (Num. 13:23). Could you imagine grapes so large that it took two adult men to carry a single cluster? I would love to have seen those bananas, grapes, and pineapples. They must have been humongous!

Sampling Fruit

What would be a sample of the fruit from the land of your purpose? In the early days of exploring God's purpose for my life, I sampled many types of fruit along the way to understanding and embracing my newfound pursuit to become a minister. The more books I purchased and read on the ministry, the more I hungered for knowledge and experience. The more I questioned pastors about the vocation, the more I longed for that same opportunity. The more I spoke to people about God's willingness to help them, the more I longed to do this service all the time, in every place. These intentional activities were fruit-sampling opportunities. I ate; I enjoyed; I longed for more. These experiences encouraged me to keep journeying toward the goal, no matter how daunting the task may have seemed.

In our church, we introduce teens and young adults to people working in the professions that they are contemplating. This quasi-mentoring relationship helps to demystify the professions so that the young people can see, feel, understand, and sort out some questions that could not otherwise be answered. If this opportunity is not in your reach, there are other approaches to sampling the fruit of your purpose. Consider making an appointment with someone who is heavily involved in the field that holds your attention. Seldom will you find someone who is unwilling to discuss his or her occupation and the training requirements with you if you're clearly interested.

In your quest to perfect your purpose, sample fruit along the way. The fruit gives you a glimpse of what you should expect when you're fully engaged in your purpose. If you discover that the fruit is inadequate, you must reconsider whether you're headed toward God's purpose for your life. Doing this is extremely important because if you're not motivated by the fruit you sample at the beginning of your journey, you may take a mediocre approach to perfecting your purpose.

John Garner, former U.S. Secretary of Health, Education, and Welfare, said, "An excellent plumber is infinitely more valuable than an incompetent philosopher. The society which scorns excellence in plumbing because it is a humble activity and tolerates shoddiness in philosophy because it is an exalted activity will have neither good plumbing nor good philosophy; neither its pipes nor its theories will hold water."[1]

Mediocrity is not an option if you view your purpose as God's best plan for your life. You must be vigilant about happily pursuing your purpose with excellence. This need for a positive attitude reminds me of the story of the man who watched two masons working on a building. One worker continually frowned, groaned, and cursed his labors. When asked what he was doing, he replied, "Just piling one stone on top of another all day long until my back is about to break." The other mason whistled as he worked. His movements were swift and sure, and his face was aglow with satisfaction. When asked what he was doing, he replied, "Sir, I'm not just making a stone wall. I'm helping build a cathedral."

Suppose you were the man observing the two masons and you were an apprentice who sought to venture out on your own after extensive training. Would you act like the whistling mason or the one who could not see how his role played a valuable part in the construction of a cathedral? Let's turn the question around. Of the two masons, which one would you like to mentor you in the craft? Which one do you think would give you feedback about his work—a sample of fruit—that would encourage you to pursue masonry? The answer is a no-brainer. If you sampled fruit from the complaining mason, you would throw away your trowel and wheelbarrow and pursue a more rewarding occupation. But if you sampled fruit from the happy mason, you would sign up for a lifetime membership in the professional society of masons. Be careful about whose fruit you sample.

Fruit is a wonderfully motivating factor. Sampling the reward that awaits you will certainly stir you toward achieving great things.

DAY 8 Points to Reflect Upon

Here are a few exercises to help you sample the fruit found in the land of your purpose:

1. Make an appointment to have a fifteen- to thirty-minute interview with someone who is doing what you would like to do. Write your top five questions beforehand so that you maximize your fruit-sampling moment.

2. Make a list of the fruit you have already sampled that is germane to your purpose.

3. Ask God to bring some fruit into your life confirming that the purpose He is perfecting in your life is a land that flows with milk and honey.

Follow the
Right Voice

*How can one pity anyone who is doing the will of our Lord? Is
there anything sweeter on earth than to do the will of Him one
loves? And if it gives one some trouble to carry it out, the sweetness is all the greater.*

Charles de Foucauld
Meditations of a Hermit

DAY 9

Determine Who Is in Charge

One day a lion, proud of his mastery of the animal king-dom, decided to make sure all the other animals knew he was the king of the jungle. He was so confident that he bypassed the smaller animals and went straight to the bear. "Who is the king of the jungle?" the lion asked. The bear replied, "Why, you are, of course." The lion gave a mighty roar of approval.

Then he asked the tiger, "Who is the king of the jungle?" The tiger quickly responded, "Everyone knows that you are, O mighty lion."

Next on the list was the elephant. The lion faced the elephant and addressed his question: "Who is the king of the jungle?" The elephant immediately grabbed the lion with his trunk, whirled him around in the air five or six times, and slammed him into a tree. Then he pounded him onto the ground several times, dunked him under water in a nearby lake, and finally threw him on the shore.

The lion—beaten, bruised, and battered—struggled to his feet. He looked at the elephant through sad and bloody eyes and said, "Look, just because you don't know the answer is no reason for you to get mean about it!"[1]

Answering the question of who is leading as you perfect your life's purpose is unavoidable. Either God is at the helm or you are. Both cannot lead at the same time. The lion saw things differently once the elephant helped him understand life in the jungle. The lion quickly adopted a fresh perspective of leadership and submission to authority. Although it appeared that he was in charge, he quickly realized that looks are deceiving. The elephant wielded the quiet authority and true leadership of the animal kingdom. Similarly, God's style of leadership is unassuming and quiet, but if you attempt to challenge Him, you will quickly learn who really is in charge.

Over the next four days (Days 9–12) we will examine a 40-day episode that captures a Transforming Interval in the life of a man named Noah. Sometimes standing alone is the right decision, even when it feels wrong. Noah became the laughingstock of his community because he decided to build an ark—a foreign vessel to the people of his day—in obedience to God's warning of a forthcoming 40-day flood. The 40 days of constant rain went down in biblical history as God's way of starting fresh. Everything and everyone died except Noah, his family, and the animals spared by the ark's protection.

This 40-day episode demonstrates that anyone can get a fresh start as long as he is willing to go the way of God's salvation. The principles that are held up as lessons to practice over the next four days include (1) accepting God's leadership on a personal level; (2) avoiding advice from people who don't listen to God; (3) valuing the salvation experience as real and transformational; and (4) building your ark—a safe place that shelters you from life's storms.

Accepting God's Leadership

In chapters 6 through 9 in the book of Genesis, God introduces a rainstorm that lasted 40 days and 40 nights because of the continued sinfulness and disobedience of the human race (Gen. 6:11–13). Only Noah and his family submitted themselves to God's prescribed way of life. The society needed to be completely revamped to reflect virtues attained through righteous character, community, and culture.

To attain this noble objective, the Christian community must take an active role in demonstrating and upholding Jesus' commandment to "'love the Lord your God with all your heart and with all your soul and with all your strength and with all your mind'; and, 'Love your neighbor as yourself'" (Luke 10:27). Noah embraced this perspective. However, this idealized view was non-existent in the society in which he lived.

During the days of Noah, God decided to clean house because civilized humanity can be accomplished on a large scale only when individuals embrace it. Noah became the precursor of all those who would accept God's leadership on a personal level. Noah demonstrated that God was the Chief Executive Officer of his life.

How about you? Who is the person in charge of your life, your decisions, or your money? Is God truly your leader? To help you answer this soul-searching question, I will walk you through a spiritual audit that Noah used to demonstrate the authenticity of his faith and complete submission to God's leadership.

The spiritual audit centers on five questions:

1. Am I grieved by the things that grieve God (Gen. 6:6)?

2. Do my family and friends recognize and respect my relationship with Christ (Gen. 6:9)?

3. Do I carry out God's commands (Gen. 6:22; 7:5)?

4. Do I see my purpose as a spiritual calling from God?

5. Am I intentional about my spiritual development (Gen. 8:20–22)?

1. Am I Grieved?

The Bible clearly states, "The LORD was grieved that he had made man on the earth, and his heart was filled with pain" (Gen. 6:6). As a pastor, I can't help feeling the pain of someone's unfulfilled desires when his concerns are poured out in a counseling session. In that transparent moment seldom do I ask him why he feels the way he feels. Often enough the person seeking solace has tried everything to remedy the situation and his last resort is to try to gain comfort from a listening heart. Although God was not in a counseling session with Noah, He needed no one to counsel Him. He was communicating to Noah about His pain and disappointment with the constant disobedience and sinfulness of humankind, and about how humankind had grieved Him. The Scriptures captured no questions, feedback, or comment from Noah. His silence affirmed his understanding of God's heart. Noah was grieved by things that grieved God.

If God is your leader, the things that grieve Him—sinful behavior, acts of injustice, inhumane treatment of other human beings, and even a disregard for His ways—must grieve you. This feeling of sorrow must then move you to act the way God would act and, when God carries out His justice, to side with Him unhesitatingly. Noah built the ark without quibbling about why only eight people—his family—would be saved from destruction.

2. Do My Family and Friends Respect and Recognize My Relationship with Christ?

The way others see you is a good indicator of your submission to God's leadership. You can fool strangers, but you cannot fool family and friends. The Bible tells us that "Noah was a righteous man, blameless among the people of his time" (Gen. 6:9). This verse provides two angles from which God wants us to see Noah. The word *righteous* speaks of an external quality while the word *blameless* is an internal one. The English word *righteous* comes from the Hebrew word *tsaddiyq* (pronounced tsad-dak), which means "just and lawful." This character description of Noah signifies that he was just in a moral and forensic sense. He wanted to be morally correct and righteous in the eyes of the courts. In essence, the way he conducted his business affairs could stand up under legal scrutiny and be deemed righteous. The English word *blameless* comes from the Hebrew word *tamiym* (pronounced taw-meem), which means "complete, full, entirely without blemish." Noah was a man whose integrity was known to family and friends because it emanated from within.

I am reminded of the story of a little boy who held on to his mother's hand while listening to a minister who used great, swelling words to eulogize his deceased father. Rev. Smith proclaimed, "John was a good man: a good husband, who loved his wife. He was a good father, who was always there for his son." At that point, little Johnny tugged on his mother's dress and whispered, "Mommy, we're at the wrong funeral."

If you have a relationship with Christ, your family and friends must acknowledge that you have been transformed by that relationship. And the transformation dictates the way you carry yourself in familial and business relationships.

3. Do I Carry Out God's Commands?

What greater accolade could be credited to Noah than this: "Noah did everything just as God commanded him" (Gen. 6:22)? When Christian Herter was governor of Massachusetts, he was running hard for a second term in office. One day, after a busy morning of chasing votes (and going without eating lunch), he arrived at a church barbecue. It was late afternoon, and Herter was famished. As he moved down the serving line, he held out his plate to the woman serving chicken. She put a piece on his plate and turned to the next person in line. "Excuse me," Governor Herter said, "do you mind if I have another piece of chicken?" "Sorry," the woman told him. "I'm supposed to give one piece of chicken to each person." "But I'm starved," the governor said. "Sorry," the woman said again, "only one to a customer."

Governor Herter was a modest and unassuming man, but he decided that this time he would throw a little weight around. "Do you know who I am?" he said. "I am the governor of this state." "Do you know who I am?" the woman said. "I'm the lady in charge of the chicken. Move along, mister."[2] Noah's obedience to God was demonstrated in that he "did all that the LORD commanded him" (Gen. 7:5), just as this woman did.

Is God the leader in your life? The question is best answered by having the testimony, "I did all that the Lord commanded me to do." There is no such thing as partial obedience. Submission to God's leadership in your life occurs when you carry out all of the Lord's commands in every area of your life.

4. Do I See My Purpose as a Spiritual Calling from God?

When the order came down to Noah, "make yourself an ark" (Gen. 6:14), he pursued that purpose as a spiritual calling from God. Noah had to recognize and help his family to understand that behind the natural process of cutting down the cypress trees, measuring the planks, nailing the pieces of wood together, sealing the wood with pitch—a tarlike substance that waterproofs wood—was a clear acknowledgment: my purpose is a spiritual calling from God. There is no other way to submit to God's leadership in every area of your life, the nonspiritual as well as the spiritual, unless you see the direct connection between your purpose and God's calling.

If you are a carpenter and you recognize carpentry as one of your purposes for being put on earth, you must also see your vocation as God's calling on your life. Don't despise what you do, thinking that only spiritual things, such as preaching, writing books that promote the Christian faith, or penning Grammy Award–winning worship songs, reflect a spiritual calling. If what you do serves people and promotes a good society, and you can honestly say that you like who you are becoming, settle the issue in your heart: your labor reflects God's calling.

During World War II, Winston Churchill, Great Britain's prime minister, wanted to raise the morale of the nation by stirring the people with pungent words of hope. He toured the country visiting troops and factories in the central cities and in out-of-the-way coal mining towns. On one visit to the hardworking coal miners, Churchill urged them to view their significance in the light of the overall national effort for victory against Hitler's regime. He told them, "We will be victorious! We will preserve our freedom. And years from now when our freedom is secure and peace reigns, your children and children's children will come, and they will say to you, 'What did you do to win our freedom in the Great War?' And one will say, 'I marched with the Eighth Army!' Someone else will proudly say, 'I manned a submarine.' And still another will say, 'I guided the ships that moved the troops and supplies.' And still another will say, 'I doctored the wounds!' " Then the great statesman paused. The dirty-faced miners sat in silence and awe, waiting for him to proceed. "They will come to you," he shouted, "and you will say, with equal pride, 'I cut the coal! I cut the coal that fueled the ships that moved the supplies! That's what I did. I cut the coal!' "[3]

The rest is history. Churchill's speech spurred the nation to victory. Your perspective makes all the difference. Make Jesus Lord of the spiritual and natural areas of your life!

5. Am I Intentional About My Spiritual Development?

After the 40-day rainstorm ended, the dying of people and animals ceased, and Noah, his family, and a pair of each animal were saved, Noah emerged from the ark. The first thing he did was to build an altar to the Lord (Gen. 8:20). What a role model! If it were me, I probably would have wandered off exploring what happened to the earth over the course of the Flood. Not Noah. He sought God! You must approach spiritual development with intentionality. No one grows spiritually without mapping out a plan—whether in the mind or in a journal.

In his book *Wild at Heart*, John Eldredge notes that every man needs three things to become passionate for God: (1) an adventure to live for; (2) a battle to fight; and (3) a beauty to rescue.[4] Although Eldredge was writing specifically to men, women also need a clear spiritual road map that points them to an adventure to live for, which is attained through spiritual development. Certainly, you can stumble onto the next rung of the spiritual ladder, but that does not reflect God's complete leadership of your life. When God is in full charge, you are eager to learn of His plan for your spiritual advancement. Through prayer, Bible study, intimate worship, and full surrender, you learn how to draw close to God. Then you can map out a plan for your ongoing spiritual transformation and growth.

This five-point audit should help you answer the question: Am I in charge, or is God the leader of my life? There is no hiding when you're in charge. The converse is equally true: there is no hiding when God is in charge of your life. The world will see it because you cannot hide God's favor and blessings upon a life surrendered to His leadership.

DAY 9 Points to Reflect Upon

Determining if God is in charge of your life means that you have to be able to answer yes to the tough questions of Noah's spiritual audit:

1. Am I grieved by the things that grieve God?

2. Do I see my purpose as a spiritual calling from God?

3. Am I intentional about my spiritual development?

DAY 10

Listen to God

I'm sure that you are familiar with this cliché: cheap advice is expensive. This axiom helps you understand that seeking the advice of the least expensive professional, because it is the frugal thing to do, may be more costly in the long run if the counsel is faulty. This cliché helps you to be mindful about the people you listen to.

Before God issued an alert to Noah about the coming flood, the earth had never experienced a 40-day continuous rain. In the early days of God's creation, a supernatural irrigation system watered the landscape and vegetation. No rain was necessary. God's own underground watering device sustained the plant and animal life.

However, when humanity's sin became so great, God was grieved, and He decided to put an end to His creation, allowing only Noah and the seven others in his family—his wife, their three sons and their wives—to remain. God decided to start all over again in populating the planet with people and animal life. Corruption precipitates destruction and new beginnings. In reflecting on this cycle, you are poised for a fresh start with God if you need it. There are times when you simply have to start over again. Whether it is after a bout with failure, a divorce, the loss of a job, or even the death of a loved one, starting over again is a natural part of life.

Unlike Noah, the other inhabitants of the earth did not experience a fresh start. They did not listen to God or to Noah's warnings, for that matter. As a consequence, they experienced destruction and annihilation while Noah experienced salvation and life. The difference came down to one simple principle: if you listen to God, you will avoid destruction.

Imagine what would have happened if Noah had dismissed God's warning to build an ark by listening to the crowd who probably mocked him mercilessly. Can't you hear their mockery as he was laying out the cypress wood for the construction of the ark? "Noah, what are you doing?" "You're building what, an ark? What's that?" "Noah, you're crazy! I hope you come to your senses!" The early environmentalists probably yelled: "Why don't you stop cutting down all those cypress trees?" The animal rights activists might have tried to stop him by asking: "Where is your permit to catch and load all these animals into this contraption you call an ark?"

Had Noah heeded the faithless chatter of the majority, he would have perished alongside them. People whose lifestyle is fraught with sin are deafened to the voice of God. *Sin* means "to miss the mark." The Greek word for sin comes from archery. When an archer shot his arrow toward a target and missed, the Greeks would say, "He sinned." Also, when a soldier tried to slash his opponent with his sword but missed, the onlookers would say, "He sinned." *Sin* is a directional word. The people in Noah's day were considered "corrupt in God's sight" and "full of violence" (Gen. 6:11). Their lives had veered off course; sin had ruined them. They were not hitting God's target of righteousness or holiness, or even having a God consciousness.

Positioning Yourself to Hear God

I wish that I could thumb my nose at those wayward people, but I recognize that the same thing could happen to me. Each of us is one decision away from a scandal. In a single moment, if your guard is down and you're in a vulnerable place, you can make the wrong decision. And before you know it, you'll be on the evening news hiding your face from the television camera. Noah practiced two things as a lifestyle to keep himself in a position to hear from God. His twin secret is revealed in one verse: "Noah was a righteous man, blameless among the people of his time, and he walked with God" (Gen. 6:9). In succinct language, Noah had two legs to his success in avoiding the advice of the crowd and hearing from God: (1) he walked in integrity; and (2) he walked with God.

1. Walk in Integrity

God's plan to replenish the human race with Noah as the progenitor was founded on the man's integrity. Integrity is the building block of society. Integrity is also the building block of a person's life. To establish a lifestyle of integrity, you must not allow the opinion of the masses to dictate your choices of the heart. How far would Moses have gone if he had taken a poll in Egypt? What would Jesus Christ have preached if He had taken a poll in the land of Israel? What would have happened to the Reformation if Martin Luther had taken a poll? It isn't polls or public opinion of the moment that counts. It is right and wrong, and leadership that begins by possessing a heart of integrity.

The Bible has a great deal to say about this business of guarding the heart. In Scripture the word *heart* refers to your mind, your will, your emotions and spirit—your inner being, the real *you*, everything that is the essence of who you are. And the integrity of your mind or soul determines your actions and well-being.

That is why Solomon said,

> *Above all else, guard your heart,*
> *for it is the wellspring of life.*
> *Put away perversity from your mouth;*
> *keep corrupt talk far from your lips.*
> *Let your eyes look straight ahead,*
> *fix your gaze directly before you.*
> *Make level paths for your feet*
> *and take only ways that are firm.*
> *Do not swerve to the right or the left;*
> *keep your foot from evil.*

(Prov. 4:23–27)

When Solomon called the heart a "wellspring," he used a word that's not in our common vernacular. A wellspring is a *fountainhead,* the source of water that either nourishes or pollutes everything downstream. What flows out of your heart determines the nature of your thinking and behavior. It results in your choices, in what you decide to make your most meaningful activities. It determines what and whom you love. No wonder we are admonished to guard the heart; it is the seat of integrity.

Unlike deceitful corporations that instruct their accountants to "cook the books," believers are to periodically perform "audits" on their hearts to assess their true condition. You cannot hear God clearly if your heart is consumed with the affairs of this life or the voices of the masses of people who walk in spiritual deafness. Like the CPA firm that annually checks the financial records of the church where I serve, we must regularly go through a checklist of items that reveal how we are doing in matters of the heart.

We should audit what I call our spiritual DNA. (You may already know that this stands for *deoxyribonucleic acid*, but I dare you to say that five times fast!) DNA is the genetic "fingerprint" that helps to determine who each of us is. Our criminal justice departments have come to realize that DNA has a superior degree of accuracy in identifying people, and it's been used both to incriminate and to acquit those who have been accused of a crime.

Similarly, your spiritual DNA determines your **d**eeds, your **n**ature, and your **a**ffections. Deeds, including words, are from that "wellspring," the heart. These words can be negative (profanity, verbal abuse), or positive (complimentary language). When I audit my heart, I must also look at the way my deeds reflect my *values*. My activities point to the values I cherish, good or bad.

My heart is influenced by my nature—the temperament that helps to form my priorities. Values speak loudly of who I am. They testify not just to what I'm doing, but to what I'm like inside.

Your heart is prejudiced by your affections—the emotional realm of the things you love. In other words, what gives you pleasure shapes your spiritual DNA. And, in turn, your spiritual DNA reflects your integrity. If your relationship with God does not protect your affections, your heart will slowly gravitate toward the culture of the society around you. Noah walked blamelessly before God, which deafened his ear to the voice of fallen culture while, at the same time, kept him open to hearing the voice of God.

Don't be misled into thinking that you're stuck with whatever spiritual genes you inherited. You inherit general tendencies, but when Solomon said to "guard your heart," he implied that each of us can assess those tendencies and correct our behavior accordingly. If Noah was able to live above the misguided and sinful society of his day by walking blamelessly, so can you. That's why you must guard your heart and your deeds. They point to whether you are "patrolling" or guarding the heart, as Solomon charged you to do.

2. Walk with God

A farmer asked the district superintendent to assign a pastor to his community. "How big a man do you want?" asked the superintendent. "Well," the man replied, "we're not overly particular, but when he's on his knees we'd like to have him reach heaven." Walking with God is all about reaching heaven when you speak. It was said of Noah that "he walked with God" (Gen. 6:9). What a powerful testimony given the widespread rejection of God that was occurring in his day. Walking with God comes simply by making a decision. However, it will require that you reduce the importance of the crowd's opinion in your life.

A soap manufacturer and a pastor were walking together down a street in a large city. The soap manufacturer casually said, "The gospel you preach hasn't done much good, has it? Just observe. There is still a lot of wickedness in the world, and a lot of wicked people, too!" The pastor made no reply until they passed a dirty little child making mud pies in the gutter. Seizing the opportunity, the pastor said, "I see that soap hasn't done much good in the world, for there is much dirt, and many dirty people around." The soap manufacturer replied, "Oh, well, soap is only useful when it is applied." And the pastor said, "Exactly, so it is with the gospel."

DAY 10 Points to Reflect Upon

To audit how well you are listening to God, consider these points:

1. Perform a quick audit of your spiritual DNA. What can be known from your **d**eeds, **n**ature, and **a**ffections?

2. How are you shielding yourself from the world's chatter so you can hear God's voice loud and clear?

3. Read Proverbs 4:20–27 and meditate on the importance of guarding your heart.

DAY **11**

Allow God's Love to Rescue You

The 40-day Flood during Noah's time was designed to cleanse the earth of all corruption, violence, and godless living. God grieved that His creation did not want to honor Him or desire to worship Him. Therefore, He chose to rid the earth of this corruption by eliminating all human beings and animals with the exception of Noah's family and the sampling of animals invited onto the ark. We can easily see that the number 40 represents moral cleansing, or in one word: salvation. Noah acknowledged that the highest purpose for his life was to honor God, and the Lord said to him: "Go into the ark, you and your whole family, because I have found you righteous in this generation" (Gen. 7:1). As God shut the door to the ark, it became clear to Noah that God's love rescued him (Gen. 7:16).

Being rescued by God's love reflects God's desire to have fellowship with His creation. Noah alone among his contemporaries chose to respond to God's love; everyone else sought his own purpose outside God. Saint Augustine voiced his view of humanity's purpose this way: "You [God] have formed us for Yourself, and our hearts are restless till they find rest in You." In response to the question, what is the chief end of man? the Westminster Catechism answered, "The chief end of man is to glorify God and enjoy Him forever."[1]

God's action of extending salvation to Noah was a reflection of two things. First, it was said of Noah that he had "found favor in the eyes of the LORD" (Gen. 6:8); second, he "was a righteous man, blameless among the people of his time, and he walked with God"

(Gen. 6:9). Noah's blameless character caused him to pursue a relationship with God, but God's favor—not Noah's good name—precipitated his salvation. God extended His favor (a free act of kindness) to Noah. This account portrays the salvation experience that Jesus made available to all who recognize their alienation from God and choose to respond to His invitation to have a personal relationship with Him.

Answering God's Call

As a boy, I attended a small Methodist church in my neighborhood. Although the minister had good intentions, he never taught the message of God's saving grace. He gave short sermons each week directed to build character and heighten our concern for fellow human beings. I never heard a single message on how Jesus can transform the human heart when we accept Him as the Savior of our lives. As a result, I evolved into a scientific atheist by the age of thirteen. During this same time, my family stopped attending church.

When I started college at sixteen to major in mechanical engineering, I was a full-fledged scientific atheist. My thoughts were: *There is no God. Earth is the only heaven or hell that one will ever experience if there's such a thing as heaven or hell.* The Christians at Fairleigh Dickinson University in Teaneck, New Jersey, tried their best to share the faith with me. Although they were passionate about their relationship with Jesus Christ and spoke about a personal transformation that occurred in their lives, it made no sense to me. I was blinded by my unwillingness to listen without filtering their assertions through my prejudices. Each time they spoke to me, I thought, *Christianity is for mindless people because it is not reasonable to believe that your life can be transformed by inviting Jesus Christ to forgive you of your sins.*

After a few years of debating with them and observing the consistency of their lives with their faith claims, I sat on the edge of my dormitory bed and prayed, *God, if You're real, come into my heart and change me.* This occurred on July 6, 1982. Miraculously, I was immediately changed. Three things became evident to me in the following days: (1) experiencing salvation truly changed me; (2) my worldview was radically transformed; and (3) I wanted the world to experience what I had just experienced.

1. Salvation Changes You

What I experienced is described graphically in Noah's 40-day ordeal. I became a recipient of God's salvation. His love rescued me from a life of waywardness, unfulfilled purpose, and banishment to an eternal hell. Noah understood as well as any human being could grasp the reality that "the LORD was grieved that he had made man on the earth, and his heart was filled with pain" (Gen. 6:6). And Noah did not want to contribute to God's grief or pain.

Walking in God's salvation is the most powerful way to convey your appreciation of God. If you value God, you must value His greatest gift to humanity: salvation through Jesus Christ. In Noah's day, salvation was typified in the fresh start given to the earth. I, too, received a fresh start when I repented of my sins and invited Jesus to be my Savior and Lord.

The day after I invited Christ to accept my life as an offering, I noticed that I was transformed. The gaping void that was in my life was completely gone. I used to consume Eastern philosophy books, searching for answers to questions such as: Why am I here on this earth? What's life all about? Is there more to life than getting a good education, marrying, and making lots of money? I was empty and disillusioned by my scientific atheism, which offered no answers to such soul-searching, intellectually honest questions. On the day that I gave my life to Jesus my soul found rest in God. I was transformed from the inside out. No more wrestling with such questions or contemplation about life's meaning. As He had done for Noah, God shut the door to my ark of safety—His salvation—and I received a fresh start. My sins had been forgiven, and my life—the real life God had foreordained for me—could start.

2. Salvation Changes Your Worldview

The famous hymn "Amazing Grace" was written in the late 1700s by John Newton, a former slave ship captain who was overwhelmed by the mercy that God had extended to him. However,

Kenneth Osbeck writes, "For the next several years [Newton] continued as a slave ship captain, trying to justify his work by seeking ways to improve conditions as much as possible, even holding public worship services for his hardened crew of thirty each Sunday."[2] Newton eventually discontinued the unrighteous occupation because he could not reconcile his new faith in Christ with a lifestyle that enslaved other men for the selfish, greedy practices of people who did not allow God in their lives. Indeed, our natural tendency as human beings is to rationalize rather than recognize sin. But the personal transformation that occurs at the cross of Jesus Christ convicts us to change when our worldview is out of alignment with God's message of salvation.

A worldview is a set of beliefs that address the most significant issues of life. According to Professor Ronald Nash, every worldview should address five major areas of life: "God, reality, knowledge, morality, and humankind."[3] As a Christian, I formulated my worldview from a biblically based perspective that is anchored by seven foundational questions:

1. Who is God, and what is His view of life?

2. What is the Bible, and what does it indicate about life?

3. Who is Jesus, and what is His view of life?

4. Who is the Holy Spirit, and what is His role in my life?

5. Who is man, and what is expected of him when he lives among others?

6. What is the role of the fellowship of believers in developing a Christian community?

7. What is my responsibility toward the society in which I live?

Your answers to these questions determine your worldview. As Christians, we must take our answers from the Bible. According to the Westminster Catechism, a Christian is a wholly devoted follower of Jesus Christ who also acknowledges that the "Holy Scripture [the Bible], given by inspiration of God, is necessary because the works of creation and providence are not sufficient to give a saving knowledge of God."[4] Therefore, the Bible is integral to constructing a Christian worldview.

After receiving a fresh start through God's salvation, I can no longer choose to believe whatever I want to believe and call myself a follower of Jesus Christ or a person who walks with God. To bring doctrinal coherence to the Christian community and eliminate heresy throughout the ages, the church established creeds—succinct statements of faith—cowritten by notable church fathers as they participated in important councils such as the one at Nicea in A.D. 325. Two creeds accepted within the Christian community are the Nicene Creed and the Apostles' Creed. The Apostles' Creed says:

> *I believe in God, the Father almighty,*
> *creator of heaven and earth.*
> *I believe in Jesus Christ, His only Son, our Lord.*
> *He was conceived by the power of the Holy Spirit*
> *and born of the Virgin Mary.*
> *He suffered under Pontius Pilate,*
> *was crucified, died, and was buried.*
> *He descended to the dead.*
> *On the third day He arose again.*
> *He ascended into heaven,*
> *and is seated at the right hand of the Father.*
> *He shall come again to judge the living and the dead.*
> *I Believe in the Holy Spirit,*
> *the holy universal Church,*
> *the communion of saints,*
> *the forgiveness of sins,*
> *the resurrection of the body,*
> *and the life everlasting. Amen.*

The Apostles' Creed was used historically in the church's liturgy at baptisms. The practice of baptismal candidates reciting the creed prior to immersion dates to the beginning of the third century in Rome. While such creeds provide an overview of the fundamental doctrines of Christianity, in a general sense, they provide a framework in which people who have experienced God's salvation can adopt a worldview that is consistent with their newfound faith. Sharpening your focus on your God-given purpose must also be reflected in your acceptance of God's love for you. Embracing salvation is the way you accept God's love. Establishing a biblical worldview is the way you reflect Christ's salvation to the world around you.

3. Salvation Makes You Excited About God

Have you ever been around someone who just married the love of her life? She cannot contain her excitement; she wants the whole world to know. Somehow she skillfully weaves the exciting news into the dialogue in hopes that you, too, will share her enthusiasm. Becoming a Christian is much the same way. After you invite Christ to forgive you of your sins and accept you into His family, an inner peace coupled with an unspeakable joy grips your heart. This rush of excitement for God seems to overtake you. And you are urged from within to tell someone else about your newfound relationship with Christ. Behind it all is your genuine desire for everyone in the world to share the same experience. I suppose this type of personal transformation and ensuing excitement made Noah go against culture as he built the ark.

Have you ever seen a sidewalk turned inside out because a little acorn fell between the cracks? An acorn cannot move sidewalks. But when you set the acorn free to be what it was created to be, you've got an oak tree on your hands. The law of the oak transcends the law of the concrete. When an acorn is embedded in the ground, the power of its nature is released, which overpowers the strength of concrete. When you accepted Jesus Christ, you received the acorn of the Spirit, who wants to become the oak of your life to move aside the concrete of your problems. As the big pieces of concrete are being moved aside by God's inner workings, your excitement builds to the point that you just can't contain it.

Everyone needs to know what's happened to you; everyone needs to have the same experience. This is how I felt after receiving Christ as Savior.

One of the most noticeable signs of this inner joy was that I would awaken each morning with sore jaws. Unbeknownst to me, as I lay in bed each night contemplating God's goodness in giving me a fresh start with my life through His salvation, I had a big smile on my face. When morning came around, my jaws were aching.

This is a great place for me to ask you, Have you accepted Jesus Christ as your personal Savior? If you're not sure or your answer is no, I want to invite you to take a moment and find a quiet place because I am going to ask you to pray a powerful prayer. It is the prayer of salvation. Your sins are about to be exchanged for Christ's salvation. Are you ready? Then pray this prayer:

Almighty God,
thank You for sending Your Son, Jesus Christ, to die for my sins.
I am a sinner; I have lost my way as I sought to perfect my life's
*   purpose.*
Please forgive me. Come into my heart, Lord Jesus, and wash away my
*   sins.*
Live Your life in me.
I accept You today as my personal Savior and my Lord.
I ask you these things in Jesus' name. Amen.

Congratulations! You are now what the Bible calls "born again." You have now become a Christian in the biblical meaning of the word. Perfecting your purpose is sure to happen. Please read on!

DAY 11 Points to Reflect Upon

Here are a few exercises to help you enjoy the fresh start that comes as you have been rescued by God's love:

1. Write in your journal five things about God's love for which you are thankful.

2. As Noah had to stand against the culture of his day, reflect on the ways you must resist the allure of compromise with this world's culture.

3. Is your worldview totally Christian? How would you answer this question: Who is Jesus, and what is His view of my life?

Come Out of the Rain!

When chaotic things occur—within society, your family, or your inner being—a safe shelter is needed to escape from the temporary or long-term storms. The corrupt lifestyle of other people and the broken culture created by their values made Noah seek a safe shelter. The behavior of human beings became so offensive that "the LORD was grieved that he had made man on the earth, and his heart was filled with pain" (Gen. 6:6).

The Bible's portrayal of God's emotions toward the fallen culture made Him a perfect shelter for Noah or anyone else who desired to seek refuge. In God's words to Noah we find answers for modern-day people seeking shelter from life's storms. The biblical account states:

> *The earth was corrupt in God's sight and was full of violence. God saw how corrupt the earth had become, for all the people on earth had corrupted their ways. So God said to Noah, "I am going to put an end to all people, for the earth is filled with violence because of them. I am surely going to destroy both them and the earth. So make yourself an ark of cypress wood; make rooms in it and coat it with pitch inside and out."*
>
> (Gen. 6:11–14)

Based on the scriptural account, we recognize the impact of the storm on societal and personal levels. A storm is a violent disturbance of affairs—be they civil, societal, cultural, or familial. Storms are disruptive, and those hit by their force must seek out a shelter if they desire to be rescued from the impact. In Noah's day, which is similar in many respects to our day, the storm forced him to seek a safe haven if he was going to achieve any semblance of purpose in his life.

Seeking Shelter from Life's Storms

The root of the societal storm that Noah faced is evident in the words *corrupt* and *full of violence*. It was centered on errant ideology and values that created social unrest. Values include interests, pleasures, preferences, duties, moral obligations, desires, and wants of human beings. On a personal level, storms shape people's values by moving them along a certain life course and direction. Values can produce behavior, which helps to establish social boundaries. That is why Jesus was so adamant that when we have new life stemming from personal salvation, we must shape the culture and values around us by becoming *salt* and *light* (Matt. 5:13–16).

These two metaphors describe Christians who practice their spiritual experience on a societal level. *Salt* speaks of a preservative that anchors the good qualities in society, while *light* symbolically represents goodness and righteousness. Jesus used these terms to describe the lasting, positive change possible in society when individuals set out to influence the lives of others. Implementing this practice would demonstrate the fundamental principles of faith, compassion, equality, justice, and the love Jesus prescribed for humankind.

Noah did three things to escape the storm created by the societal unrest and the violence prevalent among the people: (1) he pursued God; (2) he pursued God's purpose for his life; and (3) he pursued becoming a role model.

1. Pursue God

Although most of us are unable to introduce large-scale cultural change because of the limited sphere of our influence, we have the power to quiet a storm's impact on our lives when we allow the message of God's love to change us individually. We find the safest haven from the storms of life in the shelter of salvation. Once we are changed personally by accepting Him as Savior and Lord of our lives, Jesus offers us this shelter:

> *Do not worry about your life, what you will eat or drink; or about your body, what you will wear. Is not life more important than food, and the body more important than clothes? Look at the birds of the air; they do not sow or reap or store away in barns, and yet your heavenly Father feeds them. Are you not much more valuable than they?*
> (Matt. 6:25–26)

The wisdom of these words indicates that God knows our daily needs. We must: "seek first his kingdom and his righteousness, and all these things [daily needs] will be given to [us] as well" (Matt. 6:33).

Noah's soul found rest and shelter as he sought *first* the kingdom of God and His righteousness. God became Noah's shelter from the rainstorm because "Noah was a righteous man, blameless among the people of his time, and he walked with God" (Gen. 6:9). You cannot get any clearer than verse 9: if you want to escape the impact of the storms of this life, pursue God. This verse does not suggest that you pursue God's blessings; rather, you should pursue God's person. Noah did not walk with God to avoid the storm or its impact. He sought God because he loved God. Pursue God with this same purity of heart, and you'll be sure to escape any storms that may be looming over the horizon of your life.

2. Pursue Your Purpose

The Bible calls us to become agents of change. Effecting positive change in the world is at the core of loving our neighbor as we love ourselves—Jesus' pattern of influencing society. I am keenly aware of the power of prayer and the need to assume and maintain the responsibility of intercession—standing before God in prayer for the needs of the land (see Ezek. 22:30). I understand this portion of the Bible's teaching, and I wholeheartedly practice this principle. The stark reality, however, is that on many levels you cannot change society or even make specific people change.

Keep in mind, God Himself was unwilling *or* unable to make societal change or to make the people of Noah's day—or our day—change. What makes you assume that you have the responsibility or the ability to change people or culture? I am not saying that God was powerless to rectify the problems or the people. Since God does not force His will upon society or individuals, change has to occur through noncoercive methods. God has limited the display of divine power in order for it to work through love and not through force or compulsion. God's respect of humanity's free will reflects an intentional limitation He places on Himself. Human beings have a personal choice to do *or* to believe whatever they choose. Furthermore, humans have the freedom to ignore whatever they choose. Looking at this divine restriction another way, we understand that God has the highest form of power in that He is able to give His creation the freedom and ability to make their own choices and act on them. God chose to put this format in place. Thus, His power was really on display all along by His willingness to make us truly free.

Noah found shelter in perfecting his purpose. Noah's purpose was displayed in a threefold way: (1) he walked with God; (2) he lived a blameless life before the world, which was a by-product of his relationship with God; and (3) he executed all the assignments that God gave him. Noah found shelter from life's storms by serving God.

Noah interpreted God's instruction to build an ark as an assignment—a large part of his life's purpose. As he labored to build the ark, his soul found rest from the storms of life. Noah knew that God was about to solve the problems of corruption and violence by the subsequent flood.

When you're buffeted by the storms of this life, you find a safe haven when you advance in your purpose. Put on your game face, plow full speed ahead toward God's assignment for your life, and you will have a sense of inner peace and fulfillment. Although you should still try to positively shape and influence society, realize that your respite is not in your success in transforming broken people or culture, but in your desire to hear the same words God said of Noah: "Noah did all that the LORD commanded him" (Gen. 7:5).

3. Pursue the Status of a Role Model

One of the highest distinctions you can ever earn is being called a role model. Role models are people who intentionally see the need to represent a certain quality of behavior before the world. Coercion or fear of retaliation should not be the basis for choosing to become a role model. In other words, you should not seek to become a role model by default. The nobler route is to choose to be a positive influence because so few are choosing that position. And the people around you need an example that can point them in the right direction. Choosing to become a role model is also choosing to become a leader. A leader shows others the way because he or she first learned the way.

Noah was described as "blameless among the people of his time" (Gen. 6:9). This is the language of role models. People could not speak negatively concerning his dealings or the way he carried himself. Because Noah lived blamelessly above the broken culture of his day, he was considered a role model. To accomplish such a feat required great conviction, especially when the societal culture was so deplorable. As we look back to the Roman world during the first and second centuries, we see that Rome similarly demonstrated a ruined culture through its cruelty. Its brutality was captured by the entertainment found in placing Christians and wild beasts together in the arenas. Spectators received pleasure from seeing lions, tigers, and other ferocious animals tear human beings limb from limb. The famed author Francis Schaeffer reminds us,

> Let us not forget why the Christians were killed. They were not killed because they worshipped Jesus. Various religions covered the whole Roman world. . . . Nobody cared who worshipped whom so long as the worshipper did not disrupt the unity of the state, centered in the formal worship of Caesar. . . . The reason the Christians were killed was because they were rebels. . . . We may express the nature of their rebellion in two ways, both of which are true. First, we can say they worshipped Jesus as God and they worshipped the infinite-personal God only. The Caesars would not tolerate this worshipping of the one God only. It was counted as treason.[1]

Although the Bible does not reference any threats on Noah's life, it is clear nonetheless that to live above any brutal culture that celebrates violence, especially as a role model, an individual needs deep conviction. Without appearing egotistical or self-congratulating, you gain a wonderful feeling as you see yourself riding above the turbulence caused by societal storms.

DAY 12 Points to Reflect Upon

There are three simple ways you can escape the destructive impact of life's storms:

1. Pursue God. Identify three things that you do to pursue God.

2. Pursue God's purpose for your life. Identify three ways that you are engaged in pursuing God's purpose for your life.

3. Pursue the status of being a role model. What are three things you recognize as proof that you are becoming or have already qualified as a role model?

Step #4

Have the Right Stuff

There are three things that if a man does not know, he cannot live long in this world: what is too much for him, what is too little for him and what is just right for him.

Swahili proverb

DAY 13

Make the Transition

B efore launching His public ministry, Jesus went into the desert for 40 days to fast and pray. During that time, Jesus' eternal mission to bring salvation to humanity was crystallized in His heart. Over the next four days of the journey into perfecting your purpose, we will examine the four specific obstacles that Jesus faced prior to starting His work. This study will allow you to glean principles for building the lifelong habits that ultimately will perfect your purpose. In observing how Jesus overcame these obstacles you will (1) learn to make smooth transitions into your life's purpose; (2) overcome the impulses and appetites of the flesh; (3) conquer the enticement of the world's system; and (4) establish a life dependent on the worship of God.

The model of Jesus' desert experience shows that over the course of 40 days, you can purify your intentions and discover a supernatural power that fuels your lifelong mission. Ask yourself this question: Do I have the right stuff? Another way of framing the question is: Do I have the presence and blessing of God upon my mission? Don't launch anything significant without receiving this divine affirmation.

Making Smooth Transitions

Transitions reflect the death of one phase of life and the birthing of another. The transition of a caterpillar into a multicolored butterfly is an excellent example. This transition occurs in four phases. First, an egg hatches, and second, a caterpillar emerges. After it sheds its skin a few times, it reveals yet a third stage: pupa or chrysalis. In two or three weeks, the pupa makes the transition into a beautiful fly-ing creature—the butterfly. The butterfly displays a dimension of God's handiwork and creative genius. You make this kind of smooth transition when you move into your purpose.

The biblical account regarding Jesus' transition from the carpen-ter's shop to the preacher's pulpit occurred after a 40-day episode of fasting and prayer in the desert. According to the gospel of Matthew, the Transforming Interval happened this way: "Jesus was led by the Spirit into the desert to be tempted by the devil. After fasting forty days and forty nights, he was hungry" (4:1–2). The desert is a place known for its barrenness, heat, dryness, and isola-tion. Jesus needed this retreat to commune with God before transi-tioning into full-time ministry. In verses 1 and 2, we learn two essential ingredients that helped Jesus make a smooth transition into His purpose, namely: (1) He was led by the Holy Spirit; and (2) He went to a place of isolation to commune with God.

1. Being Led by the Holy Spirit

The smoothest transition that you can experience is to allow the Holy Spirit to lead you from where you are to where God wants you to be. Jesus explained that a principal function of the Holy Spirit is to lead us into *all* truth:

> *When he, the Spirit of truth, comes, he will guide you into all truth. He will not speak on his own; he will speak only what he hears, and he will tell you what is yet to come. He will bring glory to me by tak-ing from what is mine and making it known to you. All that belongs to the Father is mine. That is why I said the Spirit will take from what is mine and make it known to you.*

(John 16:13–15)

These three verses point out that God's sons and daughters should expect the Holy Spirit to lead them into truth, tell them the truth, and reveal hidden truth. All of these methods of leading peo-ple will ultimately bring glory to Jesus. This is quite a benefit for us Christians—to be able to have a special Guide to lead us at every turn. The Holy Spirit of God is not just an ordinary personality. He possesses all knowledge and is to give us information and wisdom so that we can find our way along life's journey. The knowledge that the Spirit offers is not limited to spiritual, emotional, or psychological arenas. Verse 13 notes "all" truth, which includes every dimension and facet of truth.

You can see why Jesus responded to the leading of the Holy Spirit and obediently went into the desert to connect on a deeper level with the transitioning needs of His purpose. Every period of transition has specific needs and benefits. Christ needed to personally and publicly defeat the devil's temptations, which we will discuss in detail over the next three days. Luke recorded a benefit of the 40-day Transforming Interval: Immediately following Jesus' praying and fasting in the desert, "Jesus returned to Galilee in the power of the Spirit, and news about him spread through the whole countryside" (Luke 4:14). The Holy Spirit empowered Jesus to execute His purpose.

Likewise, if you are led by the Holy Spirit and you stay true to the course, you will receive the empowering of the Spirit to perfect your purpose. To be led by the Holy Spirit simply means to follow the Holy Spirit's gentle nudges. I once asked a friend, a Christian attorney who practices law in Washington, D.C., why he had chosen to work in our nation's capital rather than Georgia or Illinois. His response was: "When I completed law school, it felt as if the Holy Spirit's hands were on my shoulders, stirring me toward Washington, D.C. The desire to come to the nation's capital became greater and greater within me. So I knew that it was the Holy Spirit leading me to Washington, D.C."

The Holy Spirit led Jesus to the desert to commune with God through fasting and prayer. How is the Holy Spirit leading you to gain clarity on your assignment? If you are not totally aware, let me suggest a way to help you discover this most powerful benefit of walking with God.

To be led by the Holy Spirit, you must first value the Holy Spirit's leadership in your life. In other words, you take the posture of a student in relating to the Holy Spirit. You become submissive, not a know-it-all. The Holy Spirit is the third person of the triune

Godhead, which means as the Spirit of God, the Holy Spirit knows all things. If you recognize that the Holy Spirit is omniscient, you will take a receptive posture during your prayer times. This position will enable you to listen for the Holy Spirit's guidance. This does not require that you earn a doctorate in theology or that you become someone who is mistaken for the prophet Elijah because of your exceptional spirituality. To listen to the Holy Spirit, you simply have to know that the Holy Spirit knows your home address and that He will get hold of you whenever He wants you to be guided in a certain direction. Just relax. The Holy Spirit understands that human beings are not clever enough to understand divine guidance issues, so He lovingly takes on the responsibility to lead us and guide us into all truth.

Since the duty of leading is the obligation of the Holy Spirit, sit back and maintain a keen receptivity to Him. I have learned over the years that the more I obey the Holy Spirit, the more He speaks to me and the more expansive His guidance becomes. I've also learned that when I ignore the leading of the Holy Spirit, He offers me less and less guidance. Take a moment and think about whether you have heard the voice of the Lord or been aware of the leading of the Holy Spirit in your life lately. When was the last time the Holy Spirit tried to give you guidance? Did you listen? Or did you shrug your shoulder as if to say: "No way, I'm going to do my own thing"? If so, you need to ask the Lord to forgive you for your disobedience. Repentance opens the channel to the Holy Spirit's leading.

I liken the inability to discern and receive the Holy Spirit's guidance to having a telemarketer's telephone number blocked from your phone. Once you put the block on your telephone, the telemarketer can no longer get a call through to you using that number. Similarly, if you have ignored the leading of the Holy Spirit in the past, you have essentially put a block on the Holy Spirit's calls to you. To remove the blocked signal, ask the Lord to forgive you for the times you ignored or disobeyed the leadings of the Holy Spirit. That prayer of repentance will position you to receive promptings from the Holy Spirit once again.

2. Going into Isolation

Once Jesus recognized that the Holy Spirit was leading Him to the desert, He immediately obeyed and went to the secluded place for 40 days and 40 nights. Jesus was not in the desert because His budget forced Him to choose the most inexpensive route of isolation. Jesus chose to shut Himself away with God. The desert (some Bible translations use the word *wilderness*) is a depopulated place that offers few creature comforts. You are surrounded by nature, which fosters thoughts about God and communication with Him. If Jesus, the Son of God, saw the need to commune with His heavenly Father, what excuse can you have to start your life's purpose without obtaining God's blessings or full assurance? It would be unwise to presume that you are fully equipped for your journey toward perfecting your purpose when you have not given the Author of life the opportunity to bestow His blessings.

As our older daughter, Danielle, prepared for her high school graduation prom, Marlinda and I were pleased that she sought our blessings on the important transition points in her life's journey. We desperately wanted to give our blessings, even if she had not sought us out. It was a hallmark moment, touching and memorable, as we pinned on a corsage, prayed with her, and talked with her about God's promises for her life.

Communing with God is about getting confirmation that God sanctioned and approved the journey you are about to take. Jesus' mission to preach the kingdom of God, to demonstrate its power, and to go to the cross for the redemption of the world needed God's blessing and total approval. If any unanswered questions were in Jesus' heart—and I don't believe that there were any—that was the time to pose them to God. If He had any feelings of ambivalence about how to execute His mission—and I don't believe that there were—that was the time to gain clarity. During His 40-day period of communing with God, Jesus had to settle the answers to all His questions.

Similarly, before embarking on the journey of perfecting your purpose, you must pose your questions to God. In your time of prayer, ask the Lord, "Is there anything else that I need to know or settle in my heart?" This question targets the mixed emotions that may be involved in making your transition. Change is always intimidating because uncertainty clouds the emotions and threatens to hold you in your present situation. But if you want to perfect your purpose, change is inevitable. Robert Kemper, coauthor of *Mastering Transitions*, comforts pastors who are caught in a web of emotions as they seek to transition from one church to another:

> *It's difficult to live back and forth between contrary emotions. For one thing, it wears me out. But if I try to fight these emotions, or simply suppress the negative in favor of the positive, I simply complicate the already complex situation and make myself more exhausted still. Consequently, I've found it better to let such emotions weave their way in my life, and let God, in his own time, resolve the tensions.*[1]

One way to seek God's help in settling the emotions surrounding your transition is to commune with Him. Getting alone to seek God's input, however, must be an intentional action. You have to sit down with your calendar and place the dates in your schedule so that you receive God's input. In your place of isolation from people you can pose questions about confirming your purpose, God's timing to begin your purpose, and so on. The prolific author Max Lucado writes,

> *The cross was no accident. Jesus' death was not the result of a panicking cosmological engineer. The cross was not a tragic surprise. Calvary was not a knee-jerk response to a world plummeting toward destruction. It was not a patch-up job or a stopgap measure. The death of the Son of God was anything but an unexpected peril. No, it was part of an incredible plan. A calculated choice.*[2]

If the most important act of history—Jesus' going to the cross to secure salvation for humanity—was intentional, shouldn't you follow suit? Find a place of solitude and seek God to make a smooth transition into your purpose.

DAY 13 Points to Reflect Upon

To make a smooth transition into your purpose, begin the journey by reflecting on these subjects:

1. Are you sure that you are being led by the Holy Spirit as you transition into your purpose? Take a few minutes to journal any insecurities or uneasiness concerning your transition. Capturing these emotions can be therapeutic.

2. Once you've identified some of the negative emotions surrounding your transition, solicit God's help through prayer. Take a moment and pray this prayer:

   Heavenly Father, please confirm Your will and direction in my life's purpose. I want to be led totally by You in every facet of my journey. Speak to my heart, Lord, over the next few days, and I will obey Your word. I ask You these things in Jesus' name. Amen.

3. Renew your commitment to have a daily time of communing with God, even if it is just for thirty minutes.

DAY 14

Overcome Fleshly Appetites

Can you imagine fasting for 40 consecutive days and nights while in a desert? This kind of fast is not for the fainthearted. In fact, fasting for one or two days is no easy task. You have to be extremely passionate about getting God's blessings or insights to stay the course. Your body will quickly begin to cry out: "Feed me! I want pizza. Take me to McDonald's! I want a Happy Meal." Our bodies crave food. It's what our bodies need in order to stay alive. On the other hand, this natural craving works against spiritual growth. If you are going to grow in your relationship with God, which is a vital ingredient to perfecting your purpose, emulating Jesus' approach to overcoming fleshly appetites should be a part of the process.

Fleshly or carnal appetites are the desires that bring pleasure to your body, not necessarily to your soul. And they usually don't honor God. The Bible uses the word *flesh* to reference evil desires or a sinful nature that is diametrically opposed to a life controlled by the Holy Spirit. The apostle Paul describes carnal appetite this way:

> This *I say then, Walk in the Spirit, and ye shall not fulfill the lust of the flesh. For the flesh lusteth against the Spirit, and the Spirit against the flesh: and these are contrary the one to the other: so that ye cannot do the things that ye would. But if ye be led of the Spirit, ye are not under the law. Now the works of the flesh are manifest, which are these; Adultery, fornication, uncleanness, lasciviousness, idolatry, witchcraft, hatred, variance, emulations, wrath, strife, seditions, heresies, envyings, murders, drunkenness, revellings, and such like: of the which I*

*tell you before, as I have also told you in time past, that they which
do such things shall not inherit the kingdom of God.*

(Gal. 5:16–21, KJV)

As you can see, the works of the flesh are self-centered and plea-
surable to someone who lives apart from God's leadership. However, to live a victorious life—one that honors God—a person must
overcome carnal appetites. Although we can do many things to
bring the flesh under the control of the new mind—one that has
been transformed by salvation through Jesus Christ—Jesus used a
40-day fast to signal His victory over fleshly desires.

I had the opportunity of leading a fellow engineering student to
Christ while I was in graduate school. I had accepted Christ only a
year earlier, but I took my role of discipling him very seriously. I
visited his dorm twice a week to answer his questions and to fellowship with him. On one visit, I walked into my friend's dorm
room to find him sitting by the open window wearing only a pair
of shorts. It was January, and the outside temperature was no
warmer than fifteen degrees above zero. It was freezing cold. I asked
him why he was sitting by the open window practically naked. I
will never forget his youthful reply: "I'm trying to crucify my flesh
so that I can serve God more effectively."

I burst out with such a loud laugh that the guys at the other end
of the hall could hear me. But the look on my friend's face showed
that my laughter had hurt him. He was serious about his desire to
gain victory over his flesh. After he closed the window and got
dressed, I sat down with him and gave him a lesson on the process
of living a Spirit-controlled life. I'm sure I didn't understand the full
biblical teaching back then, but I did understand that he would not
attain his desire to live a holy life through self-torturing.

The apostle Paul explains that a Spirit-controlled life is one in
which the fruit of the Holy Spirit's active leadership is reflected in
one's character and lifestyle. You overcome carnal appetites by constantly submitting to the Holy Spirit's influence and judgment.
When this occurs, Paul says that you can expect this result:

*The fruit of the Spirit is love, joy, peace, longsuffering, gentleness,
goodness, faith, meekness, temperance: against such there is no law.*

And they that are Christ's have crucified the flesh with the affections
and lusts. If we live in the Spirit, let us also walk in the Spirit.

(Gal. 5:22–25, KJV)

To walk in the Spirit is to regard the Word of God, the ways of
God, and the will of God as standards to maintain. Fasting is one spiritual activity that helps to curb the carnal appetites while seeking godliness. The nine dimensions of the fruit of the Spirit (i.e., love, joy,
peace, etc.) are signs that a person has actively overcome the impulses
and appetites of the flesh. Fruit has to be seen and tasted in order to
validate its presence. Similarly, if we bring our fleshly desires under the
dominion of Christ, our families and friends must see the fruitfulness
of our lives. We cannot hide behind words or thoughts of fruitfulness;
our deeds and actions must be the fruit that people experience.

Passing the Test

During Jesus' 40-day fast, Satan threw three temptations at Him in
an attempt to cause Jesus to dishonor God by thwarting His purpose on the earth. Remember, a primary goal of overcoming fleshly
appetites is perfecting your purpose without being sidetracked by
sinful living. The biblical account of the first temptation by the
devil was this:

The tempter came to him and said, "If you are the Son of God, tell
these stones to become bread." Jesus answered, "It is written: 'Man
does not live on bread alone, but on every word that comes from the
mouth of God.'"

(Matt. 4:3–4)

The tempter was not some force conjured up by Jesus' imagination because of His extended fast. The tempter was Satan—a powerful fallen angel whose intent was to destroy God's plan of
redeeming humanity by the atoning death of Jesus on the cross.
Hence, the tempter's solicitation of Jesus to turn stones into bread
was a test to see if Jesus would control His carnal appetites or succumb to dishonoring God's plan. Although hunger is morally neutral and eating is not scripturally wrong, Jesus' response to the

tempter's suggestion sheds light on the improper motive behind the suggestion to turn stones into bread.

I offer two reasons for your consideration. First, eating bread at that point would have conveyed that God's word, or an intimate relationship with God, was inadequate to satisfy His needs during the prolonged fast. Second, the tempter's plan was to force Jesus to provide for Himself in a way that was not available to Him in His incarnation. In other words, the work of salvation required a man who was exposed to all the sensations of manhood to live a sin-free life and go to the cross to pay a debt that sinful man owed God. If Jesus had used His divine powers to turn stones into bread, He would have been providing for Himself in a way that was unavailable to other human beings. He would not do that. The purpose of the cross was clear, and Jesus had to take and pass the test of overcoming carnal appetites. Jesus was successful!

What about you? The path to your purpose must meet the test of carnal appetites. Certainly, you do not have to fast 40 days and nights, or any time at all. Some people are unable to fast because of medical issues or physical limitations. But engaging in an exercise that demonstrates you are able to overcome fleshly appetites is necessary. If you are not able to control godless urges, you will not be able to perfect your purpose. Untamed carnal appetites will always crop up as stumbling blocks along the road to your purpose.

Do you remember the story about Samson? God gifted him with such strength and courage that he was a one-man army against the Philistines. His one flaw: he could not keep his hands off prostitutes. His tryst with the seductive and treacherous Delilah cost him his freedom, strength, eyesight, and most of all, ability to fulfill God's plan because he died prematurely (Judg. 16). The lesson he taught all of us is this: walk with God and bring your carnal appetite under control, or face a disgraceful, untimely death.

Consider Fasting

You have to really want to accomplish something extremely important or on a deep personal level when contemplating a spiritual fast. When Jesus engaged in His 40-day fast, He demonstrated mastery over physical and fleshly appetites. But you may still be thinking: *Jesus was a divine being in a human body, so engaging in an extended fast was an easy feat for Him.* Not true. Yes, He was God in flesh, but He was also what scholars refer to as "very man." In other words, Jesus was also a whole man, having all the desires and needs of a human being. Luke captured the humanity of Christ's 40-day fast when he wrote, "He [Jesus] ate nothing during those days [40 days of fasting], and at the end of them he was hungry" (4:2). If Jesus was not an ordinary man with an ordinary need for food, why would He be hungry?

I am convinced that more Christians don't fast because they remain unaware of the need for the energizing presence of Jesus in their lives if they are to perfect their purpose. Fasting cultivates the presence of God in our lives and gives us victory over carnal appetites. We should expect this outcome, especially since Jesus specifically predicted that we *would* fast after He was taken up from the earth, leaving us to run the race without His physical presence.

Fasting was popular in Jesus' day. Greek philosophers such as Socrates and Plato, who lived in the fourth and fifth centuries before Christ, recommended fasting for increased mental and physical effectiveness. The ancient physician Hippocrates advocated fasting for treating a wide range of illnesses. Among the Jews, the Pharisees emphasized fasting. John the Baptist's disciples fasted, and a question they asked Jesus prompted an important statement from Him on the subject.

John's followers asked, "How is it that we and the Pharisees fast, but your disciples do not fast?" (Matt. 9:14). Jesus answered,

> *How can the guests of the bridegroom mourn while he is with them? The time will come when the bridegroom will be taken from them; then they will fast. No one sews a patch of unshrunk cloth on an old garment, for the patch will pull away from the garment, making the tear worse. Neither do men pour new wine into old wineskins. If they do, the skins will burst, the wine will run out and the wineskins will*

*be ruined. No, they pour new wine into new wineskins, and both are
preserved.*

(Matt. 9:15–17)

John's disciples knew the spiritual benefits of fasting. In explaining why His own disciples were not fasting, Jesus indicated that they would one day engage in this spiritual discipline, and His statement implied that the benefit of fasting would be the realization of His spiritual presence after He returned to the Father. It would be a form of denying self and conquering one's flesh in order to experience His presence.

President Abraham Lincoln understood this dimension of fasting. During the crisis of the Civil War, on March 30, 1863, Lincoln issued "a proclamation for a day of national humiliation, fasting, and praying." Lincoln mourned the absence of peace, and he was willing to fast as a means of praying for its presence.

Yet many Christians these days have little sense of the agony of living apart from the presence of Christ or having victory over the appetite of the flesh. Too often there is little room in our lives for the feeling that we miss our times with the Lord, times that used to be so passionate, times when hot tears would flow in sorrow for our sins, times when we realized our desperate need for cleansing and for His presence.

I understand that we could hardly sustain this intensity on an everyday basis. Yet there should be *seasons* of fasting, special periods when we give particular attention to our need for Christ's presence as we run the race. A sign of the spiritual lethargy that keeps us from being spiritual champions is our unwillingness to plan times of fasting. My prayer for you is that God will would lead you into a period of fasting so that you may grow in your relationship with Christ and overcome the appetites of the flesh.

DAY 14 Points to Reflect Upon

To overcome the appetites of your flesh, complete the following exercises:

1. Write a list of the sins in your life. Afterward, go to God in prayer, and ask Him to forgive each one. Doing this will give you a sense of deep conviction and a feeling of purity as you allow God to wash your life and heart.

2. Destroy the list you've just prayed over so that no one may read it accidentally.

3. Decide to begin a one-day partial fast, and eventually build up to more days. Under the one-day partial fast, eat one meal while drinking water throughout the day. Turn the other two regular mealtimes into prayer moments. This spiritual activity will ignite passion and power in your life for the things of God.

Overcome Worldly Appetites

S ometimes we humans boast about our internal forti-
tude—what we will or will not do. But too many people
easily fall prey to the very thing they never thought they would do.
Jesus' 40-day fast in the desert was laced with trials that called for
proof of His victory over earthly ambitions that ordinary human
beings crave. Don't get me wrong. There is no place in Scripture
where Christ's susceptibility for Satan's toys is questioned, either on
a human or a divine level. But for the sake of demonstrating His
power over sin and its appealing nature, Jesus had to pass through
the way of all human beings, since He walked the earth as a man.

A few years ago James Patterson and Peter Kim coauthored the
book *The Day America Told the Truth*. The book was the result of sur-
veys given to one thousand people who were to answer moral and
ethical questions in complete honesty—with a guarantee of absolute anonymity. One question was: "What would you be willing
to do for ten million dollars?" Here is how they responded:

- 25 percent would abandon their families (spouses, children,
  or parents) for ten million dollars.

- 23 percent said they would become a prostitute for a week
  for ten million dollars.

- 7 percent said they would be willing to kill a stranger for
  ten million dollars.[1]

This is an example of the pull that money has on people. When
worldly ambition forms people's values and their approach to their
life's purpose, it is amazing what they will do for money.

Jesus offered another approach to readying Himself to embark on a public ministry aimed at declaring the good news of His kingdom. This ministry purpose would eventually culminate in His sacrificial death on the cross. The tempter approached Jesus with another proposition:

> *Again, the devil took him to a very high mountain and showed him all the kingdoms of the world and their splendor. "All this I will give you," he said, "if you will bow down and worship me." Jesus said to him, "Away from me, Satan! For it is written: 'Worship the Lord your God, and serve him only.'" Then the devil left him, and angels came and attended him.*
>
> (Matt. 4:8–11)

The earth is a majestic planet, full of splendor and grandeur. Satan offered Jesus the kingdoms of this world and their magnificence if He performed *one* simple act—if He would bow down and worship Satan. The tempter was trying his best to see if Jesus' inner cravings were aimed at earning worldly success—fame, notoriety, power over other people, and popularity. Jesus was faced with demonstrating mastery over worldly appetites. This test included His willingness to bypass physical sufferings, verbal mockery, public rejection by the Jews, and ultimately, the cross in lieu of one quick bow to God's rival—Satan.

Satan's tempting Jesus to bow down and worship him captured two actions. First, the tempter wanted Jesus to worship him in exchange for immediate rule over the earth. Second, Satan's offering of the "kingdoms of the world and their splendor" was an appealing way of using worldly appetites to tempt Jesus. Worldly temptation includes one's unwillingness to take the high road. Without any hesitation, Jesus gave His response to this two-pronged test: "Away from me, Satan! For it is written: 'Worship the Lord your God, and serve him only'" (Matt. 4:10).

Jesus had to overcome two issues laden in the tempter's proposition: (1) immediate kingship and worldly success; and (2) the worship of God. We will discuss the second issue in Day 16 and concentrate on the first point in today's study.

From this incident, we learn that worldly appetites have to do with the temptation to accomplish a plan that has a cockeyed resemblance to God's plan. Jesus came to die on a cross for the sins of humankind. This act was designed to demonstrate His true nature as the King of kings, but the tempter wanted to make Him an earthly king. And this coronation, mind you, would have been quick and painless. No cross. No suffering. No Judas. No repudiation from religious know–it–alls. The tempter was basically saying, "You can have all these kingdoms of the world in exchange for a quick little bow."

Jesus vehemently refused Satan's offer and took the high road to the cross. How about you? What worldly prize is the tempter offering you? Whatever it is, don't accept it! It is not worth the value of perfecting your life's purpose. Escape the allure of worldly appetites by staying true to God's methods and to His course for your life, even if it takes longer. Be patient!

Taking the Worldly Appetite Test

Here is a test to assess the size of your worldly appetites:

1. Am I angry when recognition of my efforts and hard work doesn't come (or doesn't come quickly) from the people around me?

2. Am I driven by public signs (i.e., cars, houses, clothing, etc.) advertising my financial status?

3. Do I purchase costly items and *then* ask God for His advice and blessings?

4. Do I socialize more with my non–Christian friends than my Christian friends?

5. Do I dress in a way that draws attention to me? Or is my focus on my sex appeal driving the way I dress?

6. Do I think that my lifestyle is my own business and that my family, friends, and classmates don't need me to help them to develop a relationship with Jesus Christ?

7. Am I disorganized about my spiritual development?

8. Do I let my thoughts and feelings more than the Bible or God's will lead me in making decisions?

9. Do I make excuses for the areas of my life that don't reflect holiness and Christlikeness?

10. Do I listen to music that moves me to sensual thoughts and struggles?

If you answered yes to five or more questions, you have a worldly appetite. If your score was under five but more than two, you have to be cautious, you need to go on a diet from worldly foods. If truth be told, all of us have to guard against the allure of worldliness. Throughout the history of the church, even from its first-century inception, believers have had to struggle to stay free from the world's grip. We cannot escape from the world, but we can avoid worldliness. Jesus prayed for us to overcome worldliness, although He was consciously aware of our habitation *in* the world. He prayed to the Father: "My prayer is not that you [God] take them out of the world but that you protect them from the evil one" (John 17:15).

The apostle Paul expressed his concern that the church remain unspotted by the world when he wrote to the Roman Christians:

Here's what I want you to do, God helping you: Take your everyday, ordinary life—your sleeping, eating, going-to-work, and walking-around life—and place it before God as an offering. Embracing what God does for you is the best thing you can do for him. Don't become so well-adjusted to your culture that you fit into it without even thinking. Instead, fix your attention on God. You'll be changed from the inside out. Readily recognize what he wants from you, and quickly respond to it. Unlike the culture around you, always dragging you down to its level of immaturity, God brings the best out of you, develops well-formed maturity in you.

(Rom. 12:1–2, The Message)

Every generation has to battle against conforming to the values, ethics, and preferences of the world's culture, which is bent on dragging you down to its level of immaturity. God's intention is just the opposite. He is focused on bringing the best out of you, developing a well-formed maturity in you. God's heart in achieving this goal includes the perfecting of your purpose.

Changing Perspectives

At age thirty, I became lactose intolerant. No more dairy products for me. I discovered that after thirty years of eating pizza, ice cream, and cheesecake—and enjoying all of it—my body no longer was able to properly process the lactose. News of this diagnosis was hard to swallow (no pun intended). Prior to the change, my favorite food was Italian. I mean, I could put away tons of lasagna, baked ziti, and chicken Parmesan. Initially, it was hard to pass up a plate of eggplant Parmesan. Although I couldn't eat it, I craved it. Craving something that you can't have is like being a caged rabbit and seeing a carrot outside the cage. No matter how much the rabbit attempts to get at the carrot, he cannot because of his physical confinement.

Something had to give. The only answer was that I had to learn to adjust my appetites since medication did not help any. In essence, I had to change my cravings. It took some time, but when it finally happened, I was able to look back over my journey and recognize two key changes. First, I had to accept my new dietary restrictions, and second, I had to make a paradigm shift in my thinking and cravings. Transitioning from a worldly perspective to a godly one is a similar process. How much time the process takes is entirely up to you, but it is a reflection of your willingness to be shaped in two areas. Recognizing your need is the first step, and changing your thinking and cravings is the second step.

A man living in Southern California was on his way to work one morning in his brand-new BMW. Suddenly, the "big one" hit: the earth began to tremble under his wheels, and then the earth swallowed his car. The man was seriously injured, but as he climbed out of the wreckage he didn't even notice that his left arm had been cut off at the elbow. He just stood by the side of the road, viewing the wreckage and crying out, "Oh, no, my Beemer, my Beemer!" A man who witnessed the disaster said to him, "How can you be crying about your car? Don't you realize that your arm has been cut off?" The man looked down in horror at his missing limb and said, "Oh, no! My Rolex! My Rolex!" This Californian just did not get it. He was worldly but couldn't see it. How about you? Are you seeing the need to move away from worldliness and toward godly values?

Recognizing the need to live counterculturally must be intentionally acknowledged. Paul stated that the way to live above this world's culture is to "place your life before God as an offering." Do that right now. Find a quiet spot wherever you are and get ready to give your life to God as an offering. Please pray this prayer:

> *Father, I realize that I have to live in this world,*
> *but I no longer want to live with the world's values and culture.*
> *Take away my cravings to judge my quality of life*
> *based on the immature standards and values of this society.*
> *I ask for Your forgiveness and power to live in a way that honors You.*
> *I give You my life as an offering. Please accept it.*
> *I ask You these things in Jesus' name. Amen.*

DAY 15 Points to Reflect Upon

To advance the process of overcoming worldly appetites, contemplate the following points:

1. Make a list of the areas in your life where worldliness abounds.

2. Determine to eliminate several worldly habits or appetites each week for the next several weeks. Watch the cravings disappear as you meditate on Romans 12:1–2.

3. Review the 10-point test on worldliness.

DAY 16

Determine How God Wants to
Be Worshiped

J esus spent 40 days and nights fasting prior to launching His
purpose. This Transforming Interval powerfully portrays
the need to get into a quiet place, connect with your heart through
introspection, and connect with God through worship. And as if
fasting in a desert weren't hard enough, add Satan's three-pronged
test to the mix of Jesus' dilemma. The tempter first tested Jesus to
sin against God by turning stones into bread. This appeal was designed to cause Jesus to succumb to fleshly appetites. The second
test was the call for Jesus to throw Himself off a high point of the
temple in order for God's angels to rescue Him. Jesus said that such
behavior must be shunned because it was testing God. This second
test was also an appeal for Jesus to succumb to a worldly appetite—
one that assumes God should bail us out of self-induced jams. The
third test was the promise of earthly kingdoms or worldly success
in exchange for Jesus' worship of Satan. This test highlighted two
dimensions: worldly appetites, and improper worship. Overcoming
worldly appetites was yesterday's focus, while today's spotlight is on
how the worship of God helps you perfect your purpose.

To fully understand our need to worship God, we must look
once again to the tempter's words to Jesus in the desert. This time,
let's look at the verses as they are presented in The Message, a modern rendering of the Bible by Dr. Eugene Peterson, a professor of
theology.

*For the third test, the Devil took him on the peak of a huge moun-
tain. He gestured expansively, pointing out all the earth's kingdoms,
how glorious they all were. Then he said, "They're yours—lock,
stock, and barrel. Just go down on your knees and worship me, and
they're yours."*

*Jesus' refusal was curt: "Beat it, Satan!" He backed his rebuke
with a third quotation from Deuteronomy: "Worship the Lord your
God, and only him. Serve him with absolute single-heartedness."*

*The Test was over. The Devil left. And in his place, angels! Angels
came and took care of Jesus' needs.*

(Matt. 4:8–11)

The Power of True Worship

Reading the Scriptures in this modernized language provides a refreshing perspective to the subject of worship. We glean three lessons from Jesus' bout with Satan: (1) worship is valuable; (2) worship
belongs to God; and (3) worship is connected with serving. Let's
explore these ideas since our ability to successfully venture into our
purpose hinges on our willingness to worship God.

1. Worship Is Valuable

Just imagine: Satan was willing to give up *all* the kingdoms of
this world and *their* splendor if Jesus would just bow and worship
him. The tempter did not try to negotiate for two, three, or fifty
kingdoms in exchange for Jesus' worship. He went right to the
upper limit and bargained with all the kingdoms and their entire
splendor in the hope that he would be worshiped. Worship must be
extremely valuable.

The word *worship* stems from the Old English word *worth-ship*,
which means "the adoring response to God as the center of value,
to God understood as intrinsic worth."[1] Since worship is our honest and highest expression of thankfulness to God's worthiness, it requires an assessment, an evaluation, or a reporting back to God what
we have observed about Him. This reporting back to God occurs
in the form of a praise report. We verbally, with gestures, and in

every other form of communication known to humanity convey to God that we honor and magnify Him because of His love and greatness. Only someone who is totally unobservant and unappreciative of God's provision and person can live without worshiping God. Such a person will most likely fail to acknowledge the value of others since he is unable to recognize God's worth.

Noted author Robert E. Webber writes, "Worship lifts the worshiper out of the drudgery and brings meaning to life. Worship links the worshiper with that common set of memories belonging to the Christian family. The memory of Christ and the connection with Christian people throughout history and around the world is made through the celebration of those sacred events of the church year."[2] Webber acknowledges that worship is comprised of sacred memories of events that point to God's involvement in our lives. Therefore, the value of worship is beyond human assessment because we have no other commodity that we can give to God in addition to ourselves as an expression of our personal gratitude for how He cares for us.

No wonder Jesus' response to Satan's request for worship was curt. Worship is too valuable; it belongs to God and God alone.

2. Worship Belongs to God

The devil's request to have Jesus worship him was a feeble attempt to launch an attack against God's inherent value by going through Jesus. Worship should be directed to your Creator—the One who gives you life. Satan wanted worship in exchange for *things*—giving Jesus the kingdoms of this world and their splendor. Jesus put an abrupt stop to the tempter's ploy. Worship belongs only to God.

If Jesus accepted the tempter's proposition, not only would He violate the biblical order regarding worship, but He would also abort God's purpose for His life and ministry. To stay true to His purpose, Jesus passed the tempter's test when He stated, "Worship the Lord your God, and only him." The worship of God is connected to the success of your purpose. And the converse is equally true: the lack of the worship of God is a surefire way to abort your purpose.

Have you ever seen the movie *Chariots of Fire*? In one scene, Eric Liddell, a track star who participated periodically in Christian missions, though his family served the Lord full-time, was asked by his sister: "How come you don't spend more time on the mission field? And why are you always competing in races?" Eric's response was: "God made me for a purpose, but He also made me fast. And when I run, I feel His pleasure." This memorable response points to yet another definition of worship. Worship occurs when the created thing does what he or she has been created to do. God is the Creator of all things and all people. When the created thing does what the Creator designed it to do or to be, that is the highest form of appreciation and worship.

3. Worship Is Connected with Serving

In reply to the tempter's desire for worship, Jesus answered, "Worship the Lord your God, and only him. Serve him with absolute single-heartedness." Jesus quoted the Old Testament passage (Deut. 6:13) that made God's commandment clear: He is the only One to be worshiped. Jesus further explained that the worship of God should occur through absolute service. This is where the term *servant of God* arose. For example, when Paul referred to himself as a servant of Jesus Christ (Rom. 1:1), he acknowledged that he was a worshiper who sought to serve *all* of God's interest. The English word *servant* is the Greek word *doulos*, which has a threefold meaning for a person born into slavery. Such a person is (1) one who is in permanent relationship with his master; (2) one whose will is swallowed up in the will of his master; and (3) one who serves to the extent that he disregards his own interests. To consider yourself a worshiper of God—a servant of God—you must show these three traits in your lifestyle.

What Satan desired from Jesus was not a simple bow of reverence. He sought a permanent relationship in which Jesus' will would have been swallowed up by the will of the tempter. The total abandonment of Jesus' mission and purpose in exchange for a convoluted plan was the deal the tempter was putting on the table. Most people assume that it is a small matter when they abandon the sole worship of God. Not so! Satan demands total obedience to him, although his offer appears subtle. Satan tried to seize a moment when he thought Jesus had dropped His guard due to a 40-day fast. But he was sadly mistaken. Jesus would never compromise His allegiance to the worship and service of God's plan, especially in exchange for Satan's plan.

In the same matter-of-fact way that Jesus handled it, you cannot compromise your obedience and service to God because of a subtle request for your submission to the tempter's plan. Worship is about submission. Whom you worship expresses ultimately where you get your life's orders. Whom you worship also dictates where you get your focus and priority of purpose. The tempter's ploy is always laden with subtlety. That is why you must not be consumed with busyness or be eager to grasp at all opportunities that come your way. Sometimes opportunities, as good as they may appear, are designed to pull you away from the worship of God and the pathway to your purpose.

One way to maintain keen discernment and vigilance in the pursuit of your purpose is to establish and maintain an unbroken worship of God. Since worship declares the direction of your allegiance, it also demonstrates the direction of your service. Keeping your worship pure toward God also results in a pure service to God.

Similarly, living only partially devoted to God will also result in a partially devoted service to God, which will adversely impact the pursuit of your purpose. A partially devoted service to God reflects a worship pattern interwoven with practices that question the purity and direction of your allegiance. Your focus and allegiance volleys from serving God to serving yourself, depicting your misunderstanding of the absoluteness of your service to and worship of God. The Lord requires total allegiance. He deserves complete worship because of His complete "worth-ship." Being devoted to God through worship and service communicates complete allegiance to the pursuit of God's purpose for your life.

DAY 16 Points to Reflect Upon

The journey in perfecting your purpose must include the worship of God. Worship is all about how you declare God's "worthship" through your service and submission to His plans and purposes. Reflect on the following points:

1. Contemplate the value of worship by remembering how Jesus changed your life.

2. Review your purpose in light of the question: Is there any mixture in my service of God? Your service should have three distinctions if it contains no mixture. It should reflect (a) one who is in permanent relationship with his master; (b) one whose will is swallowed up in the will of his master; and (c) one who served to the extent that he disregarded his own interests. If a mixture is present, ask God to forgive you, and move toward living in light of these three qualities of service.

3. Identify five specific things you do that demonstrate your service of God. Worship without service is no worship at all.

Live By a Code

Post a guard at my mouth, GOD,
set a watch at the door of my lips.
Don't let me so much as dream of evil
or thoughtlessly fall into bad company.
And these people who only do wrong—
don't let them lure me with their sweet talk!
Psalm 141:3–4, The Message

DAY **17**

Live By a Moral Code

In the movie *A Few Good Men* one of the principal characters, Lance Corporal Harold Dawson (played by Wolfgang
Bodison), was arrested for the accidental murder of a weaker marine. His defense attorney, Lieutenant Daniel Kaffee (played by Tom
Cruise), wanted him to accept a guilty plea that would lead to a dis-
honorable discharge from the Corps. Dawson's memorable response
was: "We joined the marines because we wanted to live our lives by
a certain code, and we found it in the Corps." In essence Corporal
Dawson was asking his attorney: What code will I have to live by if
I'm no longer in the marines? Returning to civilian life would remove him from the strength, safety, and clarity he found in the
United States Marine Corps codes. This young soldier sought a
solid moral code to guide him in daily living.

The Ten Commandments—God's moral code for humanity—
were handed to Moses following his 40 days of fasting and communion with God. The Ten Commandments offer us four areas in
which we should act ethically for a lifetime. They establish a moral
compass that guides us on how we ought to (1) live by a code; (2)
treat God; (3) treat ourselves and our families; and (4) treat others
and behave in society. Each of the next four days will be dedicated
to discussing one of these areas. Let's begin with the first discussion:
living by a code.

Living By a Code

The cry of the human heart is: oh, how I wish there was a code,
some system to live by, that would help me choose right from

wrong. I wish there was some constant in my life that would guide me when my emotions are all over the place, when I hear conflicting perspectives from my counselors, or when I cannot discern between opportunity and mistake. I wish this code was intelligent and took into consideration my moods: the days when I'm sad and need to be cheered up; or the times when I'm confused and need life to be explained in order to sort out conflicting issues. I need such a code to teach my children, help me work through my conflicts with other people—friends and strangers alike—and leave a lasting legacy to the generations that will follow me.

Look no farther. God thought about the needs of the human heart before we were even aware of our needs. He provided the Bible—a code for us to live by that remains constant when we are fickle. Built on the foundation of the Ten Commandments, the moral codes outlined throughout the Scriptures did not evolve from God's knee-jerk reactions to humanity's needs. Neither did the Bible arise because it was a secondary or tertiary code that God cooked up since His first code did not work. The Bible is the one and only code that God has given us to live by.

The pop diva Madonna, who has made tens of millions of dollars from a career built on rebellion, irreverence, and sexually charged performances, told ABC News' *20/20*, "I brought a lot of chaos to people's lives, because of my selfish behavior." She further admitted that while she promoted this lewd and selfish behavior bent on knocking society's values, she was not offering any other form of life in return.[1] Madonna saw herself as hypocritical. Thankfully, confusion does not have to prevail for Madonna or for any one of us about finding a code to live by. God has provided one for us.

In the book of Exodus we read of a second 40-day Transforming Interval with Moses. This humble man was the principal leader of the one million-plus Israelites who were miraculously led out of 430 years of Egyptian slavery. While they were en route to the Promised Land, God decided to provide them with a moral code. Prior to the 40-day period and the issuance of the system of moral expectation and guidance, God told Moses to tell the people of Israel these things:

Moses went up to God, and the LORD called to him from the moun-
tain and said, "This is what you are to say to the house of Jacob and
what you are to tell the people of Israel: 'You yourselves have seen
what I did to Egypt, and how I carried you on eagles' wings and
brought you to myself. Now if you obey me fully and keep my
covenant, then out of all nations you will be my treasured possession.
Although the whole earth is mine, you will be for me a kingdom of
priests and a holy nation.' These are the words you are to speak to
the Israelites."

(Exod. 19:3–6)

God wanted the Israelites to be aware of three things that should
frame their perspective of the forthcoming code. Moses was to (1)
remind them that God delivered them from the Egyptians; (2) convey how God wanted their full obedience in the keeping of the
covenant—His moral code; and (3) explain that in response to their
obedience, they ought to expect to be God's treasured possession—
a kingdom of priests and a holy nation. In short, God was preparing the Israelites for His forthcoming covenant (moral code) by
telling them that He loved them.

To be loved by God is an invaluable prize. To be loved by God
is to be rescued from the clutches of sin, placed in a land of promise, and given a moral code to live by. God wanted to do all of that
for the Israelites. He rescued them from the pain of Egyptian
bondage, prepared them for a new life in a Promised Land, and gave
them the Ten Commandments to guide their behavioral choices so
that they could experience a heavenly community on earth. Living
by His code would result in a maximized relationship with God.
This threefold agenda foretold the essence of the salvation that Jesus
Christ offers through the Cross.

In our modern day, to be loved by God is to recognize that God
has rescued us from a life of sin, aimlessness, and confusion. God has
prepared and communicated a divine purpose for your life, and He
offers you a moral code—the Holy Bible—as a means of accomplishing that purpose in you. All God wants in return is loyalty to
His love for you.

The renowned Bible teacher and author R. C. Sproul writes,

"The call to *hesed* [Hebrew word that means 'to love loyally'] is a call to Israel to mirror and reflect the character of God Himself. He is the author of loyal love, a love of mercy and kindness. Since He has shown His people this kind of love, He now commands them to display this kind of love in their dealings with one another."[2] Hence, the Ten Commandments are a moral code created by God's love that helps govern and guide the behavior and expectations of the Israelite community.

Learning the Code

My family and I recently brought home a new addition: a three-month-old Yorkshire terrier. My daughters named her Star Mocha Ireland. She now weighs three pounds, and according to the scientific data on her species, she will never weigh beyond four to seven pounds. You've figured it out; she is a lapdog. Star, like any other puppy, has lots of energy. She thinks the whole house is hers to do whatever she wants, whenever she wants, and wherever she wants. And this thinking encompasses playing, nipping, and even eliminating at will. We quickly realized that Star Mocha had to learn the code of how to live in the Ireland household. Armed with the book *Puppies for Dummies*, I took up the task of teaching Star our moral code—the limits of behavior that will be tolerated in our home.

Star has no choice but to live by our code if she wants to live with us. We human beings, on the other hand, can willfully reject God's moral code, though it was created by His love for us and outlines the best way we ought to live. God's love is not invalidated by our free will to reject His moral code in lieu of some other system of living, however.

God expressed this love by handing His code to Moses following 40 days of fasting. The Bible declares, "When the LORD finished speaking to Moses on Mount Sinai, he gave him the two tablets of the Testimony, the tablets of stone inscribed by the finger of God" (Exod. 31:18). Amidst all of the laws related to ceremonial cleansing, justice, social responsibility, and Sabbath laws that were given to Moses to institute among the Hebrews, the Ten Commandments were the central code to guide their moral actions.

In Exodus 20, the Ten Commandments appear in the first seventeen verses, and I've listed them in the order they were spoken to Moses:

1. You shall have no other gods before Me.

2. You shall not make for yourself an idol.

3. You shall not misuse the name of the Lord your God.

4. Remember the Sabbath day by keeping it holy.

5. Honor your father and your mother.

6. You shall not commit murder.

7. You shall not commit adultery.

8. You shall not steal.

9. You shall not give false testimony against your neighbor.

10. You shall not covet your neighbor's house or wife, or anything that belongs to your neighbor.

These Ten Commandments were distinguished from the rest of the law of God since they were audibly delivered to Moses and later written by God on two stone tablets. Old Testament scholar Walter C. Kaiser Jr. writes,

The purpose of the law of God was to show (1) man's awful sinfulness in his moral distance from God, (2) man's need for a mediator if he ever was to approach God (which mediatorial work Israel promptly assigned to Moses, but which became the occasion for God to give the promise about "that prophet" who was to come in Deut. 18:15–19), and (3) man how to live more abundantly by using the unchangeable perfections of the nature of God as revealed in the moral law as his guide.[3]

Today we live in the strict guidance of the New Testament, which conveys that Jesus was the prophet foretold in Deuteronomy 18, who had come to fulfill the teachings of the Old Testament. We can fulfill the requirements of the law only through Jesus' grace and enablement. Jesus reduced the entire Old Testament law and the Ten Commandments to two essential codes: " 'Hear, O Israel, the Lord our God, the Lord is one. Love the Lord your God with all your heart and with all your soul and with all your mind and with all your strength.' The second is this: 'Love your neighbor as yourself.' There is no commandment greater than these" (Mark 12:29–31).

Trusting the Code

If you are going to perfect your purpose, you must embrace these two codes while acknowledging that they do not invalidate the Ten Commandments as the moral underpinning of your life. Without a moral code, you have no reliable compass to direct you toward your life's destination. For this reason, the psalmist wrote, "How sweet are your words to my taste, sweeter than honey to my mouth! I gain understanding from your precepts; therefore I hate every wrong path. Your word is a lamp to my feet and a light for my path" (Ps. 119:103–5).

At the height of her fame as the other woman in the Ivana and Donald Trump breakup, Marla Maples spoke of her religious roots. She told interviewers that she believed in the Bible, then added the disclaimer, "But you can't always take [it] literally and be happy."[4] If Marla Maples and others who hold to the same questionable approach to God's word had a chance to rewrite the Ten Commandments, it would probably read like this:[5]

1. You shall have no other gods before Me . . . *unless it makes you unhappy.*

2. You shall not make for yourself an idol . . . *unless it makes you unhappy.*

3. You shall not misuse the name of the Lord your God . . . *unless it makes you unhappy.*

4. Remember the Sabbath day by keeping it holy . . . *unless it makes you unhappy.*

5. Honor your father and your mother . . . *unless it makes you unhappy.*

6. You shall not commit murder . . . *unless it makes you unhappy.*

7. You shall not commit adultery . . . *unless it makes you unhappy.*

8. You shall not steal . . . *unless it makes you unhappy.*

9. You shall not give false testimony against your neighbor . . . *unless it makes you unhappy.*

10. You shall not covet your neighbor's house or wife, or anything that belongs to your neighbor . . . *unless it makes you unhappy.*

God is not a killjoy. He is not opposed to our personal happiness. The sole reason for the provision of the Ten Commandments as a moral code was to ensure our very happiness. God wants us to attain our purpose in life, and a moral code clears the path so that we are not encumbered by unnecessary baggage that can accumulate from improper moral choices.

DAY 17 Points to Reflect Upon

Morality is a vital ingredient to perfecting your purpose. Without a solid reliable moral code to live by, you would often lose your direction.

1. Read and meditate on the Ten Commandments (Exod. 20).

2. Read Psalm 119:97–112 and focus on the psalmist's view of God's Word as a source of life, light, and wisdom in daily living.

3. Use the top two important commandments to guide your decisions today. Remember they read like this: " 'Hear, O Is-

rael, the Lord our God, the Lord is one. Love the Lord your God with all your heart and with all your soul and with all your mind and with all your strength.' The second is this: 'Love your neighbor as yourself'" (Mark 12:29–31).

DAY 18

Understand How to Treat God

Our lives need a center—a core from which our behavior, laws, society, and families can find guidance and acceptance. Moses had the daunting task of leading the Israelites out of Egypt, away from a life of bondage and slavery. In the wilderness, God handed him a moral code—the Ten Commandments—which formed the core of their new society. Moses received two stone tablets following a 40-day period of communing with God through fasting. This code replaced the Israelites' old code of pain and fear that resulted from being enslaved. After 430 years of brutality under the domination of Egypt, the Hebrews were now given a system to live by.

A society built on pain or the avoidance of pain can never enter into a better promise or perfect its purpose until this core is replaced by a healthier one. The Israelites were emotionally and psychologically paralyzed by their harsh treatment in Egypt. So debilitating was their management that when the notion of launching an attack against the people who occupied their Promised Land was announced, the fearful bunch of ex-slaves declared, " 'Wouldn't it be better for us to go back to Egypt?' And they said to each other, 'We should choose a leader and go back to Egypt' " (Num. 14:3–4). Fearful thinking had permeated the people. Although they were no longer living in Egypt, the mind-set of slaves still controlled their behavior and view of themselves. God had to transform them from the inside out or they would not know how to treat Him and enter into the promises He had outlined for them.

Their poor treatment of God was already evident in their disbelief of His pledge to give them a Promised Land. Slavery had so overwhelmed them that God's word had no positive impact on them. The writer of Hebrews puts it this way: "We [New Testament believers] also have had the gospel preached to us, just as they [Israelites en route to the Promised Land] did; but the message they heard was of no value to them, because those who heard did not combine it with faith" (4:2). The Israelites saw themselves based on their former days in Egypt and not based on God's freshly stated promises to them. They had to learn that God was interested not in harming them but in displaying His love and care for them. In addition to acknowledging God's love toward them, God wanted them to please Him, to honor Him, and to be true to Him in their devotion.

In Day 17, we explored how God painstakingly conveyed His love to the Israelites when He gave them the Ten Commandments. Now it was His turn to let them know how to please Him. God invited Moses up to the mountain to commune with Him, and the invitation turned into 40 days of fasting and dialogue:

> *When Moses went up on the mountain, the cloud covered it, and the glory of the LORD settled on Mount Sinai. For six days the cloud covered the mountain, and on the seventh day the LORD called to Moses from within the cloud. To the Israelites the glory of the LORD looked like a consuming fire on top of the mountain. Then Moses entered the cloud as he went on up the mountain. And he stayed on the mountain forty days and forty nights.*
>
> (Exod. 24:15–18)

I would have loved to tag along with Moses as he visited with God. But the next best thing is to understand the outcome of his visit. Fortunately, the Bible captures the salient points in this verse: "When the LORD finished speaking to Moses on Mount Sinai, he gave him the two tablets of the Testimony, the tablets of stone inscribed by the finger of God" (Exod. 31:18). Although eight chapters of the book of Exodus—chapters 24–31—provide details of God's conversation with Moses, the two stone tablets referenced in chapter 31 were the primary focus of the conversation. On these two stone tablets were inscribed the Ten Commandments, which captured the moral code God provided to the Israelites. This code served several purposes including being a compass to direct their personal behavior, their communal living, and their treatment of God.

Up-front Integrity

The first three commandments establish how God wants to be treated. The way you regard the Lord is vital to the success of your purpose. Without God's blessings and favor, how will you navigate the awkward circumstances that befall all of us? Rather than leaving us to stumble upon how He wants to be treated based on trial and error, God uses what I call "up-front integrity." Before the nation of Israel was formed, God outlined to the ex-slaves His expectations of how He wanted them to treat Him.

The first commandment says, "I am the LORD your God, who brought you out of Egypt, out of the land of slavery. You should have no other gods before Me" (Exod. 20:2–3). God tells us that He requires 100 percent devotion and allegiance. He is not an abstract deity who is to be viewed as a religious or political figurehead. He is the One who brought the Israelites out of the land of slavery, and no other gods should be worshiped or entertained in their hearts. Old Testament scholars Keil and Delitzsch write, "Nearly all the commandments are couched in the negative form of prohibition, because they presuppose the existence of sin and evil desires in the human heart."[1] God wanted to avert any possible polytheism and idolatry to which the human heart was susceptible.

God is pleased when He is first, and He demands being first—not because He's an egotistical despot but because He loves us so much that He wants to lead us into a fruitful life chock full of His promises. To enjoy this life, you have to place everything, even your purpose, at His feet as an offering. As I shared earlier, your purpose stems from God. He is the fountainhead of life once you have committed to walk with Jesus Christ. He has given you a purpose, and He will help you to perfect that purpose. But you must place your purpose, along with all other gifts that come from His hand, on the altar with the prayer:

God, all that I have and all that I am, I freely give it to You. Nothing that I have, including my purpose and my gifts, will take the prime place in my life. You are first, and You'll always be first. Amen.

The ability to pray that prayer and mean it will reflect allegiance to the first commandment.

The second commandment cautioned:

You shall not make for yourself an idol in the form of anything in heaven above or on the earth beneath or in the waters below. You shall not bow down to them or worship them; for I, the LORD your God, am a jealous God, punishing the children for the sin of the fathers to the third and fourth generation of those who hate me, but showing love to a thousand generations of those who love me and keep my commandments.

(Exod. 20:4–6)

God communicated that He would be pleased if the Israelites did not practice any form of idolatry. At its core, idolatry negates the existence of God and removes every acknowledgment of His works. For the Israelites to ignore what God had done for them historically and to be unappreciative of His loving consideration of their plight in a land of slavery would be an act of unparalleled indignity. God would not be pleased if such idolatrous behavior occurred.

In applying this commandment to our twenty-first century society, God would be similarly displeased if we were to show gratitude to anyone other than Him after achieving our accomplishments. Even the rankest sinners understand this commandment. You hear them say, "I thank God," while holding their crotch or while displaying too much of their breasts as they parade across the stage to pick up their Oscar or Grammy Awards. Without sounding cynical or disingenuous, I am thankful that they have a general knowledge of God, though their lifestyle and personal values are wanting. But the point is clear. God is pleased if you abstain from idolatry, and if you worship Him because of His ongoing goodness and greatness.

The third commandment is expressed in this language: "You shall not misuse the name of the LORD your God, for the LORD will not hold anyone guiltless who misuses his name" (Exod. 20:7). Peppered in many of Hollywood scripts is the "G-D" curse word. It's spoken in our society so glibly that if you're not careful, it may seem an acceptable form of contemporary speech.

A few months after I became a Christian, I almost got into a fist-fight with a total stranger as we walked into a convenience store. Apparently, he had forgotten something in his car so he blurted out loudly that curse word. In my zeal for the Lord, I immediately responded, "God is not damned, but you will be!" My retort hit him like a ton of bricks. He was speechless for a moment. In a few minutes we met near the freezer in the back of the store as I was reaching for a bottle of water. He was obviously angry. "What I said earlier is an innocent expression," he said. I noted that he was poised to take our discussion to another level if I was up for the challenge. I smiled and said, "It's not a true expression," and then we parted ways.

This third commandment is like the other two in that God wants to be treated honorably. Using His name in a careless or irreverent way is not to be condoned or practiced.

These first three commandments capture God's up-front integrity. He urged the Israelites—and us—to *please Me*. God promises that "when a man's ways are pleasing to the LORD, he makes even his enemies live at peace with him" (Prov. 16:7). Do you have any enemies—anyone standing in the path of your purpose? Labor to please God, and even those people or things will be moved out of the way of your success.

DAY 18 Points to Reflect Upon

God has identified specific ways in which you can please Him. Pleasing Him shows gratitude for His love and grace toward you. Pleasing Him also releases blessings upon you.

1. Read Exodus 22 and pay attention to the specific nature of

the instructions. Doesn't this tell you how He is particular about your pleasing Him?

2. Meditate on God's explanation *up front* about how we can please Him. Contemplate His love as He did this.

3. If you had to write three statements to give to family and friends on how to please you, what would they be? Consider writing these statements.

Understand How to Treat Yourself and Your Family

When my younger daughter, Jessica, was six years old, she requested a pet. After we discussed the family schedule and her responsibility to help care for a pet, the options boiled down to one thing: tropical fish. So off we went to the neighborhood pet shop in search of tropical fish. As we passed one aquarium stand, the shopkeeper pointed to a series of twelve-ounce jars, each of which contained a beautifully colored fish, and he asked if we wanted to buy some "family fish." With a quizzical look on my face, my response was: "Family fish? I have never heard of that type of fish before." "Yeah," he said, "this is the type of fish that you have to keep in separate jars or they will kill each other." This species is known as the Siamese fighting fish, and no more than one male can be kept in the same container. Placed together, the males will fight each other until one dies.

I will never forget that day in the pet shop because of the salesperson's description of the "family fish." If even tropical fish face a challenge in achieving family harmony, we human beings must work harder at building successful families. God was keenly aware of this need during the infancy of the Israelite nation, as He is in our modern society. It is as if nothing has changed. Yet God's solution is the same for both audiences.

The Ten Commandments—the moral code—were handed to the Israelites after Moses had a Transforming Interval with God. Moses communed with God in fasting and dialogue for forty days and nights on Mount Sinai. Afterward, God issued the Ten Commandments.

Get Some Rest!

While the first three commandments guide us in how to treat God, commandments four and five teach us how to treat ourselves and our families. Apparently, God thought the whole idea of living by a moral code was critical to the perfecting of one's purpose. You would think that God would have just snapped His fingers, and presto, Moses and the rest of the ex-slaves would have fulfilled their purpose. But God desired to build each person wholly. He wanted the Israelites to learn how to care for themselves and for their families in a way that brought honor to His name. So, God put first things first. When He wrote the fourth commandment, He wanted His people to learn and experience the power of a Sabbath—a day of rest.

In commenting on this commandment, Old Testament scholars Keil and Delitzsch write, "In order therefore that His people might rest from toil so oppressive to both body and soul, and be refreshed, God prescribed the keeping of the Sabbath, that they might thus possess a day for the repose and elevation of their spirits, and a foretaste of the blessedness into which the people of God are at last to enter [the completion of salvation in heaven]."[1]

When you cut through all of the theological meaning of keeping the Sabbath holy, you hear God telling you to take a day off regularly from your work or else you'll be no good to yourself, to your purpose, or to the people you love. Not only are you to set apart a day for rejuvenating yourself spiritually and naturally, but you are to regard it with a significant measure of sacredness. It is holy!

One day a man challenged another to an all-day wood-chopping contest. The challenger worked very hard, stopping only for a brief lunch break. The other man had a leisurely lunch and took several breaks during the day. At the end of the day, the challenger was surprised and annoyed to find that the other fellow had chopped substantially more wood than he had. "I don't get it," he said. "Every time I checked, you were taking a rest, yet you chopped more wood than I did." "But you didn't notice," said the winning woodsman, "that when I sat down to rest, I was sharpening my ax."

This is what the Sabbath day is all about. It is sharpening your ax spiritually, emotionally, and physically so that you can have enough energy to honor God and perfect your purpose. As a society, we're too busy! We're not focused, purpose-driven, or eternity minded. We don't need more time. Time is sufficient to perfect your purpose. Perfecting your purpose is defined as doing the will of God. There's always time to accomplish the will of God. It is God's will that you keep the Sabbath day holy. In so doing, you must use 24 of the 168 hours in every week to rejuvenate your soul so that you can have the emotional and physical strength to serve Him and enjoy the family He has given to you.

Enjoy Your Family!

The children in a prominent family decided to give their father a book of the family's history for his birthday present. They commissioned a professional biographer to do the work, carefully warning him of the family's "black sheep" problem. Uncle George had been executed in the electric chair for murder. The biographer assured the children, "I can handle that situation so that there will be no embarrassment. I'll merely say that Uncle George occupied a chair of applied electronics at an important government institution. He was attached to his position by the strongest ties and his death came as a real shock."[2]

Sometimes, it is tough to honor people in our families because of all of the shocking (no pun intended) things they do. Yet since we are covenant-keepers, we must adhere to the fifth commandment. The commandment says, "Honor your father and your mother, so that you may live long in the land the LORD your God is giving you" (Exod. 20:12). The word *honor* means "to carry a lot of weight, noteworthy." In the New Testament, Paul provides us with an interpretation that reads: "Children, obey your parents in the Lord, for this is right. 'Honor your father and mother'—which is the first commandment with a promise—'that it may go well with you and that you may enjoy long life on the earth' " (Eph.

6:1–3). God highlighted to Moses the importance of building familial ties that valued parents. Thousands of years later Paul highlighted this very commandment in an effort to teach Christians to similarly esteem their parents.

On both occasions, the commandment is presented with a promise: if you honor your parents, "it may go well with you" and "you may enjoy long life on the earth." There is a correlation between valuing parents and having success and longevity of life. *Correlation* is a statistical term that means "the interdependence of two or more elements." To save us the trouble of plugging in years of data and performing a correlational analysis on the relationship between honoring parents and succeeding at one's life's purpose, God simply challenges us to live in accordance with the fifth commandment.

When parents are undeserving of honor because of their brokenness and poor choices, God circumvents that correlation and pronounces long life and success upon those children. This outcome is usually the case when people apply God's laws of forgiveness toward their delinquent parents, surrender their anger and bitterness to the lordship of Jesus Christ, and maintain true devotion toward God and His purposes.

Once, three women were bragging about their grown sons. The first said, "You should have seen what my boy did for me on my birthday! He threw a big party at a fancy restaurant—he even hired a big band to play." The second woman said, "That's nice, but listen to what my son did. Last winter he gave me an all-expense-paid cruise to the Greek islands—all first class." The third woman said, "That's nothing! For the last three years my son has been paying a psychiatrist $150 an hour two times a week—and the whole time he talks about nothing but me!"

According to a study of more than 3000 families, the following six qualities are typical of successful families:[3]

1. They are committed to make the family work.

2. They spend a quantity of and quality time together.

3. They have effective communication.

4. They express appreciation of each other.

5. Successful families are able to solve problems in a crisis.

6. They have a strong spiritual commitment.

The beauty of these six practices is that any family can choose to live this way. Whatever may have transpired in the past, decide to align yourself with God's fourth and fifth commandments in order to build a successful family. The outworking of this alignment will be the institution of these six traits, which embody successful families.

DAY 19 Points to Reflect Upon

You must embrace foundational values on a personal level to attain your purpose while maintaining a healthy personal and family life. Review what you've learned:

1. What day is your Sabbath? Make a commitment to guard it because it is holy—sacred before God *and* you.

2. In a gesture of honoring your father and your mother, take a moment to drop a few lines conveying your appreciation to your parent(s) or the one who influenced you like a parent. There is nothing like a surprise to warm the heart.

3. Of the six traits practiced in healthy families, which ones have you mastered? Conversely, which ones will you commit to improving?

DAY **20**

Understand How to Treat Others

W hen the Israelites camped in front of Mount Sinai, they likely were thinking that the toughest part of the journey toward their purpose was behind them (Exod. 19:1–2). Little did they know that they had to forcefully seize their Promised Land from people who lived in the land, and they had to build a community demonstrating justice, equity, love, and a deep devotion to God. Fighting your enemy is one thing, but learning to build a loving community is quite another. The latter goal is an especially difficult task when the people with whom you're called to walk out this love are a bunch of ex-slaves who know only how to take orders, hide their emotions so that their oppressors can't play with their feelings, and protect the little dignity that they have left. Fortunately, God outlined a plan to help them usher in a prototype community illustrating how people ought to be treated.

In Exodus 20, the Ten Commandments are listed in response to Moses' 40-day fasting and communion with God. They are as follows:

1. You shall have no other gods before Me.

2. You shall not make for yourself an idol.

3. You shall not misuse the name of the Lord your God.

4. Remember the Sabbath day by keeping it holy.

5. Honor your father and your mother.

6. You shall not commit murder.

7. You shall not commit adultery.

8. You shall not steal.

9. You shall not give false testimony against your neighbor.

10. You shall not covet your neighbor's house or wife, or anything that belongs to your neighbor.

While the first three commandments instruct us in how God desires to be treated, commandments four and five guide us in how to treat ourselves and our families. The last five commandments outline God's prescription for our interaction with and treatment of others in our society. Moses' purpose was not just to lead the children of Israel out of Egypt and into a Promised Land; he was to build a community where God ruled. Imagine a community where everyone sought God's purpose for his or her life, lived in holiness before God, and lived for the sole reason of honoring God. Such a community would be a theocratic (God rules the people) society that would be unparalleled.

We Need to Get Angry!

What we have today is the opposite of a theocracy. According to the Bible, when a belief in and a personal commitment to God, through the person of Jesus Christ, are absent from society, the infrastructure of that society crumbles. The apostle Paul writes, "Although they knew God, they neither glorified him as God nor gave thanks to him, but their thinking became futile and their foolish hearts were darkened. . . . Therefore God gave them over in the sinful desires of their hearts to sexual impurity for the degrading of their bodies with one another" (Rom. 1:21, 24). Without a desire to interact with God, human beings lose the ability to conduct themselves in a respectful, accommodating, and loving manner toward others. Consequently, the removal of a moral code—and the reliance on such quick fixes as political correctness and postmodernism (the belief that truth is personal and private)—is a basic reason for America's crisis.

As in most crises, people look out for themselves and not the society at large. This is one meaning behind Paul's statement: "Their foolish hearts were darkened." Modern-day social architects refer to this self-perpetuating erosion of society's values as the "culture of poverty." To effect change in our crumbling culture, Christians and other people seeking truth, justice, and a godly culture must model—on an individual level—the qualities that bring about societal reformation. Thus, the church must become a community of salt and light in a more radical and effective sense. One way to build these communities is to personally embrace the last five commandments as God's word. Although we live in the New Testament era, where God rules through grace and not through the law, we must continue to respect and uphold these five commandments.

Building a Just Community

The forming of an exemplary community was in God's heart when He invited Moses to "come up to me on the mountain and stay here, and I will give you the tablets of stone, with the law and commands I have written for their [the Israelites'] instruction" (Exod. 24:12). Community is not so much a place as it is a shared experience among a certain group of people. Experiencing community means experiencing a sense of belonging. True community practices inclusivity, realism, and commitment to one another. It is a safe place; it is a group that can fight gracefully against common foes. To build a theocratic community, people must answer two questions: (1) Why are we together? and (2) How are we to be together?

The first question (Why are we together?) speaks of a common vision that should grip the hearts of the members of the community in such a way that they share their lives with one another. The answer to this fundamental question forms the bedrock of a theocratic society that says, "When I pursue a vital relationship with my God, I simultaneously pursue a vital relationship with all those who serve my God." We are together to build a community that honors the Lord Jesus Christ. We are together to demonstrate how to love one another. We are together because we have experienced the common salvation established by Jesus' death, burial, and resurrection. The question of why we are together must move each member of the community to the core.

The second question (How are we to be together?) speaks to the issue of justice, laws, equity, and treatment of each member of the community. The English scholar C. S. Lewis accepted Jesus as his Savior after many years of searching through philosophical and intellectual studies for the truth about God. Once he was born again, Lewis was able to look back and recognize that people make moral judgments about other people's behavior all the time. In his book *Mere Christianity* Lewis argues that there must be a strong foundation, however, from which to pass judgment on a person's behavior, whether *better* or *worse*. He defends the universal concept of fairness. In other words, if a universally acceptable standard of fairness can be employed across generational and national lines, societal behavior could be judged.[1] God presented this premise of fairness to Moses.

The Israelites were to live according to the Ten Commandments. This commitment to God's moral code would ensure fairness, justice, equity, and fulfillment for each member of the community. As is the case with any community, individualism is the greatest enemy. Individualism is the preoccupation with the freedom of individuals to make their own decisions, live the way they want to live, and believe that anything that violates this view of life is wrong. A life based on individualism can never create a joyous family, a loving community, or a just society. This life is only after the things that bring pleasure to "number one," even if it means death and displeasure for everyone else. A life based on individualism can never honor God.

A man named Max Jukes lived in New York. He did not believe in Christ or in Christian training. He refused to take his children to church, even when they asked to go. He has had 1,026 descendants; 300 were sent to prison for an average term of thirteen years; 190 were known prostitutes; 680 were admitted alcoholics. His family, thus far, has cost the state in excess of $420,000. They made no contribution to society.

A man named Jonathan Edwards lived in the same state, at the same time as Jukes. He loved the Lord and saw that his children were in church every Sunday. He has had 929 descendants, and of them, 430 were ministers; 86 became university professors; 13 became university presidents; 75 authored good books; 7 were elected to the United States Congress; and 1 was vice president of his nation. His family never cost the state one cent but has contributed immeasurably to the life of plenty in this land today.[2]

Many salvation-related principles taught in the Bible can bring about the "good society" if they are embraced as a lifestyle. Jesus taught what is known as the golden rule: "In everything, do to others what you would have them do to you" (Matt. 7:12). This principle is the summation of the entirety of the teaching of the Law and the Prophets (Matt. 7:12), which is systemic of how salvation relates to the improved treatment of God, of other human beings, and of oneself. The purification of the human heart is at the core of biblical salvation, yet many of its principles directed at individual change have societal ramifications. For example, Jesus taught, "Love your neighbor as yourself" (Luke 10:27). Although this principle is articulated within a biblical manner, it is nonetheless a natural truth. Who would not want his neighbor to love him as he loves himself?

Experiencing community should then allow a heart-to-heart connection with all those within the community. In essence, community will become an experience where the deepest thing in you connects with the deepest thing in me. Once this dynamic is at work, I will not commit murder, I will not commit adultery, I will not steal, I will not give false testimony against my neighbor, and I will not covet my neighbor's house or wife, or anything that belongs to my neighbor. I will be too fulfilled to think about violating these commandments. And so will my neighbor.

DAY 20 Points to Reflect Upon

How do we live in a broken society? The last five of the Ten Commandments point us to a lifestyle pattern that reflects fairness, equity, and justice.

1. Two questions must be answered in order to experience true

community: Why are we together? And how are we to be together?

2. Pray and ask God to keep you from violating any of the Ten Commandments. Be especially mindful about the last five, which focus on how to treat others.

3. Are you engaged in building community in your life (that is, forming relationships where the deepest thing in you connects with the deepest thing in others)? In a practical sense, share what Christ means to you with someone who has experienced a similar faith.

Step #6

Bury the Past

It was only when I lay there on rotting prison straw that I sensed within myself the first stirrings of good. Gradually, it was disclosed to me that the line separating good and evil passes not through states, nor between classes, nor between political parties either—but right through every human heart—and through human hearts . . . I nourished my soul there, and I say without hesitation: Bless you, prison, for having been in my life.

Aleksandr Solzhenitsyn
Gulag Archipelago

DAY 21

Survive the Loss of a Significant Relationship

To embrace your life's purpose by practicing lifelong habits, you have to bury the pain of the past. Joseph—an exciting Old Testament character—gave orders for his deceased father, Jacob, to be embalmed over the span of 40 days. Although the actual time of embalming—the process of preserving someone's body through the use of aromatics—took only a few days, Joseph authorized the Egyptian physicians to use 40 days.

In the biblical narrative, 40 days mean "completion, wholeness, and the fulfillment of one's entire course." When Joseph affirmed the 40-day embalming of his father, he was communicating two significant victories. First, the extended embalming period was an external communiqué that Jacob had completed his life. He had fulfilled his entire course. He had finished well. Many people start their lives with hoopla, meandering through business and family endeavors, only to stumble into their grace. Not so with Jacob. He had successful children, he passed on a spiritual legacy to his grandchildren, and he lived to see his favorite son, Joseph, sit as a world leader.

Second, the 40-day embalming triggered an internal message to Joseph: he had overcome a painful past that also needed to be buried. Over the course of the next four days we will examine the value of breaking free from past hurts and burying them by studying what Joseph did to (1) overcome the loss of a significant relationship; (2) break free from painful memories; (3) practice the

| 143

habit of letting go; and (4) focus on the portion of his life yet to be lived (Gen. 50:1–2).

Reviewing the Past

To understand and appreciate Joseph's triumphs, especially in relationships, let's take a look at the enormous hurdles from his past he had to circumvent:

- At seventeen he was known as his father's favored child (Gen. 37:3), which enraged his ten older brothers to the point of intense jealousy and hatred (Gen. 37:4). They could not even speak to him peacefully, especially when they learned of the dreams he received from God. These dreams forecasted his rise to prominence that would result in his brothers' honoring him openly.

- Malicious hatred drove Joseph's brothers to throw him into an empty pit only later to sell him as a slave to Midianite merchants for twenty pieces of silver (Gen. 37:28).

- Joseph's brothers lied to their dad, Jacob, saying a wild animal devoured Joseph. Having soaked Joseph's multicolored coat in animal's blood, they gave it to Jacob as proof of his son's tragic death. Jacob mourned so vehemently that "all his sons and daughters came to comfort him, but he refused to be comforted. 'No,' he said, 'in mourning will I go down to the grave to my son.' So his father wept for him" (Gen. 37:35).

- Joseph was sold a second time. The Midianites put him up for sale in Egypt. Potiphar, the captain of Pharaoh's guards, purchased Joseph to work as a slave on his estate, which was also the location of the jailhouse of the king's prisoners (Gen. 39:1–6).

- Joseph served Potiphar faithfully, climbing to the rank of chief of staff and overseeing all of his business and household affairs. This clever Hebrew slave fascinated and earned the attention of Potiphar's wife, who made numerous sexual advances toward the handsome and physically attractive Joseph. One day her advances resulted in Joseph tearing away from her hold, leaving his clothing in her hands while he made a naked dash for safety. Embarrassed because her flirtatious behavior was not welcomed or reciprocated, Potiphar's wife leveled an accusation of aggravated sexual misconduct against Joseph to her husband. Potiphar had no alternative but to imprison Joseph (Gen. 39:6–20).

- Joseph was placed in the same prison as the rest of Pharaoh's prisoners, which was the very house of the captain of the guard, Potiphar, where Joseph formerly functioned as chief of staff (Gen. 40:1–3).

- The consensus of Old Testament scholars is that Joseph spent more than ten years in prison for a crime he never committed or was tempted to commit. This time frame could be derived from the fact that Joseph was released from prison at age thirty (Gen. 41:46).

- After summoning Joseph from the jail cell to interpret his troubling dream, Pharaoh released Joseph from prison and placed him as second in command of Egypt, the most powerful nation of the world in those days (Gen. 41:39–40).

Some people can't walk forward, can't live their lives in the present, can't perfect their purpose because they are unwilling to let go of painful past experiences. Whether you've faced incredible hurts from the fragmenting of a valued relationship, financial losses from business risks, or even victimization at the hands of cruel people, you must bury the past in order to perfect your purpose.

Joseph was a virtuous Old Testament character who faced incredible pain from age seventeen through thirty, but was able to overcome all of his adversities. Joseph's climb from the pit, down into the prison, and up into the palace did not come as a result of his ingenuity. Rather, he maintained a divine connection, a life of walking with God through these minefields of tragedies. This relationship with God preserved his destiny. At age thirty, all of the bad days were behind him. Because of a famine in Canaan, Joseph's dad, Jacob, was forced to come to Egypt for sustenance and short-term relocation. As Providence would have it, Jacob met up with his son Joseph—the man who functioned as second in command of Egypt. The relationship of father and son was rekindled for another seventeen years (Gen. 47:28), only to end with Jacob's death.

Losing a Relationship

Relational pain occurs because you're with someone too long or too short a time. If you are in a relationship that you feel has lasted too long, I'm sure that you want out because the relationship is painful and dysfunctional. Joseph's problem was that his relationship with his father ended too soon.

Joseph loved his dad, and the feelings were mutually evident in Jacob's willingness to utter his last words to him without worrying about their fulfillment. When the time drew near for Israel to die, he called for his son Joseph and said to him,

> *"If I have found favor in your eyes, put your hand under my thigh and promise that you will show me kindness and faithfulness. Do not bury me in Egypt, but when I rest with my fathers, carry me out of Egypt and bury me where they are buried." "I will do as you say," he said. "Swear to me," he said. Then Joseph swore to him, and Israel worshiped as he leaned on the top of his staff.*
>
> (Gen. 47:29–31)

God's words to Jacob make note of the love relationship between father and son. To gain victory over the pain of his loss, Joseph (1) instituted his father's wishes and (2) fulfilled his father's unfulfilled vision.

1. Joseph Instituted His Father's Wishes

After Jacob died, Joseph said to Pharaoh's officials: "My father made me swear an oath and said, 'I am about to die; bury me in the tomb I dug for myself in the land of Canaan.' Now let me go up and bury my father; then I will return" (Gen. 50:5). The meaningfulness of a relationship is that you fulfill the wishes and dreams of the other person to the best of your ability. A significant relationship offers a lot to both parties. Your closeness to the other person allows you to understand the other's feelings, hopes, dreams, and even fears. Jacob opened his heart to his son and asked for his body to be buried in the land of promise—Canaan. Having requested a short-term leave from Pharaoh's court, Joseph was easing his pain by fulfilling his dad's deathbed wish.

Perfecting your purpose cannot occur if you are burdened with the pain of lost relationships. Dealing with a lost relationship is like dealing with an open sore; it is irritated constantly by any little touch. You have to find a way to remove this proverbial monkey from your back so that your purpose is not hampered or hindered in any way.

When my paternal grandfather was on his deathbed, my three siblings and I were summoned to him. I was a stranger to my grandfather. At twelve years of age I knew nothing of real sickness or death. But I knew enough to recognize that the call was solemn, sobering, and must be obeyed without question. I remember my grandfather, Cecil Ireland, lying in bed with half his body paralyzed from a stroke. He used his mobile hand to motion for one of the aides to pass him a particular Bible lying on the table. When he received it, he opened it to make sure it was the correct one. In a moment, this weakened figure of a man handed me a Bible in which he had personally written the words: "To David from grandfather."

My grandfather did not leave me money, property, or personal experiences other than a wish captured by a gift: know the God of the Bible and find true salvation. Years later, at age twenty, I fulfilled his wish. I found salvation. I will be forever grateful! Looking back, I learned that fulfilling my grandfather's wishes to know Christ became medicine to my life's pain. Try it! You'll find that while you're laboring to fulfill the precious wishes of someone important to you, your pain will dissipate, clearing the pathway to perfect your purpose.

2. Joseph Fulfilled His Father's Unfulfilled Vision

You don't necessarily go to school to learn your life's purpose. The preferred approach is to attend school to hone and develop your purpose *after* you've found out what it is. But most of us don't take this approach. Rather, we drift through life—whether young or old—and suddenly something or someone comes along that makes us yearn to live a certain way, with a certain purpose and aspiration in mind. Noted author and church statesman Chuck Colson revealed that "the real legacy of my life was my biggest failure—that I was an ex-convict. My greatest humiliation—being sent to prison—was the beginning of God's greatest use of my life; He chose the one experience in which I could not glory for His glory."[1] His purpose was birthed in prison.

A life purpose originating from God is usually greater than you. It summons resources beyond your possession. This purpose calls for the help of coming generations. If passed on to your descendants, it will outlive them. Purpose is a cause worth fighting for. Senator John McCain says, "Nothing is more liberating than to fight for a cause larger than yourself, something that encompasses you, but is not defined by your existence alone."[2]

Such was the case with Jacob and Joseph. God handed Jacob a life purpose that would outlive him. God reminded him of this goal as he proceeded for an indefinite sojourn in Egypt due to the devastating famine in the land of Canaan.

> *God spoke to Israel [Jacob] in a vision at night and said, "Jacob! Jacob!"*
>
> *"Here I am," he replied.*
>
> *"I am God, the God of your father," he said. "Do not be afraid to go down to Egypt, for I will make you into a great nation there. I will go down to Egypt with you, and I will surely bring you back again. And Joseph's own hand will close your eyes."*
>
> (Gen. 46:2–4)

Joseph embraced Jacob's vision to become a great nation and live in Canaan—the Promised Land for God's people. When he was up in years, Joseph said to his brothers: " 'I am about to die. But God will surely come to your aid and take you up out of this land to the land he promised on oath to Abraham, Isaac and Jacob.' And Joseph made the sons of Israel swear an oath and said, 'God will surely come to your aid, and then you must carry my bones up from this place' " (Gen. 50:25). The practice of this truth—*you must fulfill the unfulfilled vision of your forefathers*—was so real to the Israelites that 430 years later when Moses was leading them out of Egyptian bondage, he "took the bones of Joseph with him because Joseph had made the sons of Israel swear an oath. He had said, 'God will surely come to your aid, and then you must carry my bones up with you from this place' " (Exod. 13:19).

When God instills a truth or a promise into your heart, you must instill that same promise into your descendants' hearts. Be they spiritual or natural descendants, you have a responsibility to fulfill God's vision, even if it outlives you. Acknowledging the possibility that your life can be cut short, you must be preemptive and pass on the legacy of spiritual pursuits that God planted in your heart in earlier days. Jacob realized that the unfulfilled aspect of his purpose was his responsibility, both as a natural and a spiritual father, to be passed on to his son Joseph. In earlier days, God made Abraham's purpose quite clear to him:

> The LORD had said to Abram, "Leave your country, your people and your father's household and go to the land I will show you. I will make you into a great nation and I will bless you; I will make your name great, and you will be a blessing. I will bless those who bless you, and whoever curses you I will curse; and all peoples on earth will be blessed through you."
>
> (Gen. 12:1–3)

Isaac, Abraham's son, knew the divine purpose spoken to Abraham. Seeing it was unfulfilled in his lifetime, Abraham handed the baton of purpose to Isaac. Isaac, in turn, passed the baton to Jacob because the divine purpose had outlived him. Then Jacob passed it on to Joseph.

Now it was Joseph's turn to pass the baton of purpose to his descendants because the vision for a Promised Land was still unfulfilled in his lifetime. What about you? What vision was unfulfilled by your parents or grandparents, be they spiritual, natural, or adoptive? The suggestion is not for you to ignore your personal passions or vocational dreams in order to chase the area of business your mom or dad wanted you to pursue. My point is bigger than that. The 40-day embalming of Jacob sealed Joseph's healing and reacquainted him with the very reason that God had allowed him to wind up in Egypt many years ago. Although the means of Joseph's arrival in Egypt were painful, the result was the rescuing of the people of Israel from death by starvation, and the preserving of Jacob's vision that had been handed down from two earlier generations.

Just as Jacob's vision outlived him but still called for fulfillment, the vision of precious people in your life and heritage requires your attention. Look around you. Ask your relatives penetrating questions about the passions of earlier family members. And if your family is not a good source, embrace the dream of your church. Your pastor has a dream yet to be fulfilled. Labor to see that purpose accomplished!

DAY 21 Points to Reflect Upon

How do you overcome the loss of a significant relationship? Drawing from the life of the Old Testament hero Joseph, you learn to

1. draw strength and healing by *instituting* the wishes of significant people in your life who may have passed away. Or, in some cases, these people may still be living.

2. investigate the legacy that previous members of your natural or spiritual family have left unfulfilled. Pray about their unfulfilled dreams. Ask God to raise up people who will champion the causes that are His will for our day.

3. try to fulfill the pertinent aspects of the unfulfilled dreams of important people in your life who have passed away. Do this by incorporating the godly pieces of their dreams into your life's purpose.

Overcome Painful Memories

Carol Patron is a precious member of my congregation who is extremely proud of her testimony. After she was raped at the early age of fourteen by her stepfather, she became pregnant. During that time, in the late 1960s, young women who faced such atrocities were typically rushed into seclusion. Carol was placed in a foster home and left alone with her foster family to suffer through the nine-month pregnancy and agonizing emotions associated with the birth of her unplanned child.

Carol gave birth to a healthy baby girl, who at the age of nine months was placed with an adoption agency. Carol was sent to a boarding school, away from her family. Fortunately, her abuser was sent to prison for his incestuous behavior. Without adequate counseling or any other psychological guidance, Carol learned to stuff her painful memories deep inside in the hopes that they would heal by themselves.

After high school and a troubled adulthood of dysfunctional relationships, Carol came to Christ Church (my congregation) on April 8, 2001. Following a sermon on God's grace, I gave the invitation for people to pray with me to receive forgiveness of their sins and start a brand-new life with Jesus Christ. Carol responded by repeating the prayer I offered and felt God's sweet forgiveness wash over her life. Two years went by, and Carol devoured sermons and attended Bible studies. She grew spiritually in leaps and bounds.

A New Chapter

In January 2004 Carol received a telephone call at work that changed her life. In her professional style, she answered her phone, "This is Carol Patron." On the other end, a voice said: "This is Patricia," the daughter who was placed for adoption many years ago. The phone went silent for a moment. Suddenly, the conversation exploded into tears on both ends of the phone when Carol and Patricia knew that they had indeed reconnected, mother and daughter. The silence of words continued amidst their uncontrollable sobbing. Then Patricia explained how she had tracked down Carol through a series of inquiries starting with her adoptive father. They knew that they had to meet in person. Carol drove out of state to meet her daughter and the grandchildren she never knew existed. Patricia brought her entire family, including her adoptive father (her adoptive mother had passed a year earlier), to meet her birth mother and newfound friend.

I remember the Thursday afternoon when Patricia came to New Jersey unannounced to surprise Carol. In her excitement about the miracle that God had orchestrated through all the painful memories, Carol brought Patricia to my office. They hugged as they tearfully shared the whole story with me. I rejoiced with them as I witnessed the Scripture come to life: "We know that in all things God works for the good of those who love him, who have been called according to his purpose" (Rom. 8:28). This verse provides two perspectives to help us move away from the faulty thinking that painful memories often trigger. First, all things work together for good to those who love God and are called according to His purpose. Second, if all things *don't* work together for good when God is in charge, then *nothing* works together for good. You cannot have a mixture of *some* things working together for good.

The 50/20 Principle

As we learned from Day 21 and Genesis 37–41, the life of Joseph was fraught with painful trials, though not attributed to any weakness on his part. He was sold into slavery by his jealous brothers and later accused of attempted rape by his employer's wife. This false charge led to his imprisonment for an estimated ten years. How do you face such nasty situations, one after the other, without losing hope and walking away from God and His purpose for your life? The answer is found in Genesis 50:20. I call it the 50/20 principle. These words followed the death of Jacob, Joseph's dad. His brothers were dreadfully afraid that Joseph would seek revenge for causing such painful memories. But instead of making threats or punishing them, Joseph expressed a powerful concept—the 50/20 principle that heals painful memories. After Joseph calmed their fears, he said: "You intended to harm me, but God intended it for good to accomplish what is now being done, the saving of many lives."

What a unique perspective! It is the Old Testament counterpart to the Romans 8:28 passage in the New Testament. H. C. Leupold, an Old Testament scholar, offers these thoughts on Genesis 50:20: "The proof of God's control of the situation lies in the fact that where they on their part [Joseph's brothers] did devise evil against him [Joseph], God devised it for good—a remarkable example of God's concurrence, overriding the evil consequence of the wicked deed to bring about results remarkably blessed."[1]

The 50/20 principle offers a noble perspective that includes God's involvement in our past hurts. Joseph did not attribute the authorship of his pain to God. Nor did he assign blame to God for all the grueling circumstances he had lived through. He simply said, "God brought good out of your [his brothers'] bad." Phrasing the 50/20 principle another way, Joseph was saying, "When I look at my past through the God lenses, pain has a purpose and a plan."

Joseph was not merely spouting some masculine bravado. He was quite aware that his brothers had been driven by their jealousy and hatred of him in selling him to the Midianite merchants for twenty pieces of silver (Gen. 37:28). Joseph was well aware of his pain, particularly when it culminated in a ten-year prison stint based upon the trumped up charge of attempted rape by Potiphar's loose wife. Joseph was not oblivious to the reality of his pain. He just had a heavenly perspective on how to deal with it.

Joseph invoked the 50/20 principle: "You intended to harm me, but God intended it for good to accomplish what is now being done, the saving of many lives." Think about the power of this revelation. Because Joseph was in the place where God wanted him to be, he was able to interpret Pharaoh's troubling dreams. Because he maintained intimacy with God while in the pit, while in Potiphar's household, and while in the prison, interpreting the king's dream was not beyond his level of intimacy with God. When pain is properly processed, it leads to greater intimacy with God. The apostle Paul told the Corinthian Christians:

> I am no longer sorry that I sent that letter to you, though I was very sorry for a time, realizing how painful it would be to you. But it hurt you only for a little while. Now I am glad I sent it, not because it hurt you, but because the pain turned you to God. It was a good kind of sorrow you felt, the kind of sorrow God wants his people to have.

(2 Cor. 7:8–9, TLB)

Pain turns you to God! Joseph realized that in the midst of his ordeal. The 50/20 principle was birthed in pain. The revelation is not the principle alone; it is the fact that Joseph knew that God was up to something greater. The force of the words "God intended it for good to accomplish what is now being done, the saving of many lives" is felt when you acknowledge that because Joseph was in the right place at the right time with the right attitude, more than sixty-six lives were spared from death by starvation (Gen. 46:26–27). This figure does not include the hundreds of livestock that Joseph's father and brothers owned when they migrated to Egypt from Canaan. Furthermore, Joseph's position offered more than the saving of lives; it was the saving of a life's purpose.

The patriarchal purpose was to birth a nation that would occupy a Promised Land and serve God wholeheartedly. This purpose was eventually realized because Joseph gave birth to the 50/20 principle despite the emotional ordeal of his painful past. As we've learned from Paul, pain turns you to God. Pain is like an intersection in the road. When you see the green arrow in the traffic light signaling you to proceed, make the turn and go toward God.

Narcotics Anonymous has recognized that pain is a signal to the addict that his freedom from addiction needs help that is beyond him. This philosophy of healing suggests that addicts are powerless in their ability to heal themselves and they need a Higher Power to set them free. Step number three in the Narcotics Anonymous recovery process is, "We made a decision to turn our will and our lives over to the care of God as we understood Him." Their reasoning is, "At times during our recovery, the decision to ask for God's help is our greatest source of strength and courage."[2]

How can you apply the 50/20 principle to your painful memories? Joseph did three things. First, he accepted the truth of what happened to him. He told his brothers that they intended to harm him. That was the truth.

Second, Joseph introduced the God initiative that was at work in his pain when he said, "God intended it for good." In order for you to emerge unscathed from your difficult past and perfect your purpose, the "God initiative" must become your reality. Accept the fact that God is so powerful that He can take someone else's malicious acts and intentions, and turn them around for your good. If God is all-powerful, He is powerful enough to use evil for good intentions.

Third, remember the story of Carol Patron? It is like the last statement of Joseph's 50/20 principle: "the saving of many lives." God took Carol's incestuous rape and brought wonderful children and grandchildren into her life who are now learning about the good news of Jesus. I have joined Carol in prayer and in counsel about how to share Christ with her long-lost daughter and her family. I said, "Don't push Christ on her. But let your light of godliness shine before her, look for opportunities to share the good news of Jesus' love to her, and watch God go to work and bring her and the grandkids into His kingdom."

Don't despair! Pain can become the womb from which your purpose is birthed. Adopt the 50/20 principle, and let God get glory out of your pain.

DAY 22 Points to Reflect Upon

Joseph faced numerous hurdles of painful experiences, but he was able to circumvent them and perfect his purpose. You can overcome painful memories by

1. applying the 50/20 principle to your life. Learn to say, "You intended to harm me, but God intended it for good to accomplish what is now being done, the saving of many lives" (Gen. 50:20).

2. reading about the early days of Joseph's story in Genesis 37.

3. reading about the latter days of Joseph's story in Genesis 50.

DAY 23

Practice the Habit of Letting Go

A man went back to work in a place from which he had been fired several months previously, and his work had become superior. A fellow worker remembered how inconsistent he had been in the past and asked, "What happened to make such a difference in you?" The man told this story: "When I was in college, I was part of a fraternity initiation committee. We placed the new members in the middle of a long stretch of a country road. I was to drive my car as fast as possible straight at them. The challenge was for them to stand firm until a signal was given to jump out of the way. It was a dark night. I had reached one hundred miles an hour and saw their looks of terror in the headlights. The signal was given and everyone jumped clear—except one boy. He was killed and I left college. The look on that boy's face as I drove the car into him haunted me constantly. I finally turned to alcohol to help me deal with it. Soon, I became a problem drinker.

"My wife had to work to bring in the only income we had. I was drinking at home one morning when someone rang the doorbell. I opened the door to find myself facing a woman who seemed vaguely familiar. She sat down in our living room and told me she was the mother of the boy I had killed. She said that for years she had hated me, and that she had spent agonizing nights rehearsing ways to get revenge. Then she told me of the love and forgiveness that had come when she gave her heart to Christ. She said, 'I have come to let you know that I forgive you and I want you to forgive me.' I looked into her eyes that morning and was given permission to be the kind of man I might have been had I never killed that boy. That forgiveness changed my whole life."[1]

Letting go of the past is all about exercising forgiveness, God's gift to humanity. In the opening story, unforgiveness had clogged the engine of the man's life. He was unable to properly care for his family, hold down a job, or attempt to entertain the idea of having a life's purpose. Through forgiveness, he was able to embrace these areas of his life. The sad commentary is that many people don't know the power that forgiveness brings. Not long before she died in 1988, in a moment of surprising candor on television, Marghanita Laski, one of our best-known secular humanists and novelists, said, "What I envy most about you Christians is your forgiveness; I have nobody to forgive me."[2]

I'm always intrigued when I meet people who have scaled the walls of their crises despite seemingly insurmountable odds to finally enjoy a life driven by God's purpose. That was what happened in the life of the Old Testament character Joseph. He turned the corner of rejection and hatred from his envious brothers (Gen. 37:3–11), escaped the bondage of slavery by accepting it as part of his destiny (Gen. 39:1–7), lived through an estimated ten-year prison term, though he was falsely accused of attempted rape (Gen. 39:19–23), and finally sat as second in command of the most powerful nation of the world then, Egypt (Gen. 41:39–40).

This painful drama summarizes approximately thirteen years of Joseph's life. Thirteen years of pain. What was the secret Joseph discovered that enabled him to let go of his past? In a single word: *forgiveness*. Joseph knew and invoked the power of forgiveness. He forgave his brothers. He forgave Potiphar's wife for accusing him of attempted rape. He forgave Potiphar for believing his wife's lies about him. Forgiveness was Joseph's secret weapon to staying true to God and true to his purpose.

The Gift of Forgiveness

We can answer three questions while observing Joseph's life and his habit of letting go of past hurts through forgiveness: (1) Why is forgiveness so powerful? (2) How do I exercise forgiveness? and (3) Why is my purpose safeguarded through forgiveness?

1. Why Is Forgiveness So Powerful?

In God's infinite wisdom He created a gift that uses no dynamite or explosive ingredient, yet when employed, it can stop the pain of the greatest abuse to the human heart. Forgiveness is that gift. Forgiveness works two ways: vertically and horizontally. Vertical forgiveness is the pardon that God grants humanity. We receive a release—a setting free from our sins—when we ask God to forgive us. God's view on vertical forgiveness is: "As far as the east is from the west, so far has he removed our transgressions from us" (Ps. 103:12). This distancing from our sin occurs the instant we ask God to forgive us: "You [the Lord] will again have compassion on us; you will tread our sins underfoot and hurl all our iniquities into the depths of the sea" (Mic. 7:19). Concerning this verse Corrie ten Boom said, "Even though I cannot find a Scripture for it, I believed God then places a sign out there that says, NO FISHING ALLOWED."[3]

Through vertical forgiveness, the weight of sin is lifted from our shoulders. The burdens of our hearts roll away when we ask God for His forgiveness. In a similar way, horizontal forgiveness occurs when we ask someone to forgive us. The power of horizontal forgiveness stems from the strength that exudes from vertical forgiveness.

Jesus teaches that vertical forgiveness is the foundation from which springs horizontal forgiveness: "If you forgive men when they sin against you, your heavenly Father will also forgive you. But if you do not forgive men their sins, your Father will not forgive your sins" (Matt. 6:14–15). You cannot achieve vertical forgiveness unless you *first* forgive on a horizontal level. God offers no free rides into His blessings. We must practice person-to-person forgiveness if we dare entertain the idea of experiencing vertical forgiveness from God.

2. How Do I Exercise Forgiveness?

A woman accompanied her husband to the doctor's office. After the man's checkup, the doctor called the wife into his office to speak with her privately. He said, "Your husband is suffering from a very severe disease combined with horrible stress. You must do the following, or your husband will surely die:

"Each morning, make him a healthy breakfast. Be pleasant, and make sure he is in a good mood. For lunch, make him a nutritious meal. For dinner, prepare an especially nice meal for him. Don't burden him with chores. Don't discuss your problems with him. And most important, show him lots of affection, and forgive him every time he does something foolish even if you feel he doesn't deserve it. If you can do this for the next ten to twelve months, I think your husband will regain his health completely."

On the way home, the husband asked his wife, "What did the doctor say?" "You're going to die," she replied.

Lewis B. Smedes, author of *Forgive and Forget* and *The Art of Forgiving*, says forgiveness is both a simple and a complex thing comprised of four steps: (1) the wronged party must blame the individual who caused the injury; (2) true forgiveness means "rediscovering" that the person who caused the hurt is someone with flaws; (3) forgiveness is realized only when the injured party surrenders the right to get even; and (4) the forgiver must change his or her attitude toward the person.[4]

STEP #1: ASSIGN BLAME. True forgiveness cannot occur unless you blame the person who has wronged you. If you do not level blame at someone, who would you forgive, and for what would you offer forgiveness? Hence, assigning blame must precede attaining forgiveness.

True to the four-step process of forgiveness, Joseph assigned blame to his brothers for their evil treatment and actions toward him when he said, "You intended to harm me, but God intended it for good" (Gen. 50:20). The emphasis was on *you*, which referred to his brothers. The process of forgiveness does not end there, however.

STEP #2: REALIZE THAT EVERYONE IS FLAWED. As you exercise horizontal forgiveness, you need to acknowledge that no one is perfect. In light of this reality, step two categorizes the person who wronged you as a flawed, complicated, or broken human being. This categorization is not meant to be mean-spirited; rather, it accurately depicts that such a flawed person is expected to make blunders every now and again—or quite often.

The person's need for forgiveness should not come as a surprise to you, given his or her complicated personality, flawed character, or difficult temperament. A staff member was upset because of something that I had said to her two years ago. She had stuffed down the offense, but due to a series of difficult emotional circumstances, it had risen to a point where she could not keep avoiding her pain. Apparently, she had not forgiven me, although I did not know that I had offended her. As she poured out her complaint to me, I asked to be forgiven. My plea was: pastors are complicated people who need to be forgiven of their brokenness, just like everyone else. Hearing that, she dropped her guard, her heart opened, and she forgave me. Seldom is forgiveness granted if this second step is not in place when dealing with people. People are flawed! The person who offended you, whether knowingly or unknowingly, is flawed.

STEP #3: SURRENDER YOUR RIGHT TO GET EVEN. God tells us that vengeance belongs to Him. If you seek to avenge yourself of an infraction, you will be taking the place of God. That was why Joseph asked his brothers as they feared his retaliation: "Am I in the place of God?" (Gen. 50:19). If you take the place of God in executing revenge, look out! God will take revenge against you because of your infractions against Him.

STEP #4: CHANGE YOUR ATTITUDE. Forgiveness is not to be confused with reconciliation—the reuniting of parties to the same relationship before the infraction. Don't get me wrong. Reconciliation is a biblical call to all of us, but it does not suggest that everyone who is forgiven ought to be restored to the place or position from which he fell. Forgiveness is not whitewashing a wrong, nor does it eliminate the need for healthy boundaries. It does mean that you as the forgiver must change your attitude toward the person who harmed you. Instead of hating the offender, you begin to love him and wish him well.

The story is told in Spain of a father and his teenage son who had such a strained relationship that the boy ran away from home. His father began a journey in search of his rebellious son. Finally, in a last, desperate effort to find him, the father took out an ad in the newspaper in Madrid. The ad read: "Dear Paco, meet me in front of the newspaper office at noon. All is forgiven. I love you. Your father." The next day at noon eight hundred Pacos showed up in front of the newspaper office. All sought forgiveness and love from their fathers. Everyone wants to be forgiven.

3. Why Is My Purpose Safeguarded Through Forgiveness?

Joseph's order for his dad to be embalmed for 40 days signified that Joseph had put the past behind him and that only matters of destiny and purpose ought to be the family's concern. The Egyptians were experts at embalming. This process of delaying the body's decay gave Joseph the needed time to transport Jacob's body to his preferred burial site in Canaan. It was the Promised Land that God foretold would be the home of the nation that came from the loins of Abraham, Joseph's great-grandfather. Joseph would eventually be responsible to pursue this destiny as his personal aim and life's purpose.

He could not deny forgiveness of his brothers and all others who hurt him. He needed God's favor and blessings to perfect his purpose, which comes by way of forgiveness. After Jacob's burial, Joseph said to his brothers:

> Don't be afraid. Am I in the place of God? You intended to harm me, but God intended it for good to accomplish what is now being done, the saving of many lives.
>
> (Gen. 50:19–20)

Joseph forgave his brothers, thus signifying that he had let go of the past. Using the target in archery as a metaphor for your life's purpose, forgiveness would be the arrow that hits the bull's-eye. Go ahead. Shoot the arrow. Hit the target. Invoke forgiveness and re-joice in the outcome—the perfecting of your life's destiny.

DAY 23 Points to Reflect Upon

Joseph faced numerous hurdles of painful experiences, but he was able to circumvent them and perfect his purpose. You can overcome painful memories by considering the following:

1. What past experiences do you battle? Take a moment, get in a quiet place, ask God to finally wash your heart of the stain of unforgiveness, and let His healing flow through your life.

2. The four steps of forgiveness are (1) assign blame; (2) recognize that everyone is flawed; (3) surrender your right to get even; and (4) change your attitude toward the offender.

3. Forgiveness is different from reconciliation and the elimination of injustice.

Learn to Live Again

Everyone loves a good comeback story. We spend hundreds of millions of dollars per year attending movies that Hollywood says will top the last one in entertainment value. Whether the genre is science fiction, action, comedy or suspense, we pay money to have our emotions titillated by comeback stories. I'm a lover of Westerns. Put me in front of a good Clint Eastwood Western, like *The Pale Rider*, and I'll be in another zone until the movie credits are rolling. I am such a well-known fan that my daughter Jessica downloaded the theme music of *The Good, the Bad, and the Ugly* as the ring for my cell phone. You should have seen the faces of my pastoral team the first time they heard my phone ring in the church office.

Though I can't prove it, I strongly believe that we pay money to watch movies that portray the underdog getting justice or the odd guy getting the beautiful girl because deep down we all secretly desire to be like the comeback kid. My contention is that you don't have to become a Hollywood star to be the comeback kid. Just come back! Come back from your past defeats! Come back from your past sinful patterns! Come back from your past mistakes in relationships! Just come back and you will be the story that screenwriters dramatize on the big screen. And even if that never occurs, your comeback story will leave a lasting legacy for your family.

When a child fails her tryout for a high school basketball team, it usually marks the end of her career. Michael Jordan got cut from his high school varsity basketball team as a sophomore, but is now considered one of the greatest basketball players of all time. He said of himself: "I've missed over nine thousand shots in my career. I've lost over three hundred games. Twenty-six times I have been trusted to take the game-winning shot and missed. I've failed in my life over and over; that's why I succeed." Learning to live again is about using the experience from painful memories to build a launch pad for future successes.

The Old Testament character Joseph is a great biblical example of a comeback story. DreamWorks spent millions of dollars and glamorized it as a movie for all to see, although it never appeared on the big screen. The full-length movie *Joseph: King of Dreams* was prepared for VHS and DVD formats, and its theme song "Better Than I" appears on the shelves of music stores all over the country. Imagine that you were Joseph: Would you have envisioned someone taking your painful life and turning it into a film that could be viewed all over the world? Never! Not in a million years. But Hollywood understands the redemptive value in the pain of yesterday.

Live Again By Serving Others

Trials and hurts do not have the power to kill your life's purpose when you decide to live *during* and *after* painful experiences. Remember, your life's purpose ultimately stems from God. Therefore, your purpose is bigger than your pain: your purpose will outlive your pain.

Joseph demonstrated this reality through his choice to live again. He equated his drive to live with the drive to serve God. He determined that serving God was a worthwhile purpose that should continue, despite his present calamity. In fact, serving God *was* his purpose. The Bible testifies to this fact when it states,

> *While Joseph was there in the prison, the LORD was with him; he showed him kindness and granted him favor in the eyes of the prison warden. So the warden put Joseph in charge of all those held in the prison, and he was made responsible for all that was done there. The warden paid no attention to anything under Joseph's care, because the LORD was with Joseph and gave him success in whatever he did.*
> (Gen. 39:20–23)

The choice to live again starts from acknowledging that your life is a gift from God. The best way this gift can benefit you or the world is by offering it back to God, serving Him and the people in your midst. For Joseph, the people in his midst were prisoners. He did not balk at that. He served them in a stellar way, which earned the attention and favor of the warden. God used this worldly man, who had no concept of His existence, to bless Joseph. When you are in situations where you lack the power to do what you really want to do, or lack the freedom to go where you really want to go, learn to live by finding purpose in serving others.

Joseph had an incredible administrative and organizational gift that provided leadership to people in responsible positions. While in Potiphar's household, he climbed the management ladder among the slaves to be chief of staff (Gen. 39:6). Although Joseph was a slave, he continued to demonstrate a willingness to serve God by walking with Him (Gen. 39:2) and by assisting his Egyptian owner in the management of his business and household affairs. This perspective reflects a drive to keep living through the joy of serving. Joseph was committed to serving God and those around him despite his painful circumstances. Are you committed to serve in that manner? A Haitian pastor illustrates true commitment through the use of a parable:

> A certain man wanted to sell his house for $2,000. Another man wanted very badly to buy it, but because he was poor, he couldn't afford the full price. After much bargaining, the owner agreed to sell the house for half the original price with just one stipulation: he would retain ownership of one small nail protruding from just over the door.
>
> After several years, the original owner wanted the house back, but the new owner was unwilling to sell. So the first owner went out, found the carcass of a dead dog, and hung it from the single nail he still owned. Soon the house became unlivable, and the family was forced to sell the house to the owner of the nail. The Haitian pastor's conclusion: "If we leave the Devil with even one small peg in our life, he will return to hang his rotting garbage on it, making it unfit for Christ's habitation."[1]

Either God owns your life completely, or He does not. If He does, then using your strength to serve Him and your gifts in serving others, even when your life's circumstances are not the most ideal, should be easy. Serve God wholeheartedly, and don't give the devil ownership of anything, not even one small nail.

Live Again By Changing Your Attitude

People who are defeated are first defeated in their attitude. Show me someone who says he cannot live again, and I will show you someone with a deflated attitude. Psychiatrist Victor Frankl knew from experience how desperate you feel when painful circumstances take over your life. During World War II he was arrested and placed in a German concentration camp. His wife was taken away, all of his possessions were seized, and he was discarded in a cell. In the process of enduring the horrors of the death camp, he developed an approach to life that has helped many people who struggle to live again because of past tragedies.

After the war, Frankl wrote a book called *Man's Search for Meaning*. He told the story of an elderly man who had struggled with severe depression since the death of his wife. He loved her above all else and missed her terribly. Frankl said to the man, "What would have happened if you had died first, and your wife would have had to survive you?" The man said, "Oh, for her, this would have been terrible; how she would have suffered!" Frankl then said, "Such suffering has been spared her, and it was you who spared her this suffering—at the price that you now have to mourn her death." The man left Frankl's office that day changed. His situation wasn't changed—he was still alone and his wife was still gone—but his attitude toward his situation had changed.

Your attitude is a prized weapon against discouragement. There may be times when it is the only resource you have. It can help you through anything life sends your way. Whatever you may have gone through, decide right now to change your attitude. Making this decision will continue to feed the engine of your purpose.

Make the Decision to Live Again

The best time to decide to live again is during the trial. The winner of the 1970 Nobel Prize in Literature, Aleksandr Solzhenitsyn, writes: "It was only when I lay there on rotting prison straw that I sensed within myself the first stirrings of good. Gradually, it was disclosed to me that the line separating good and evil passes not through states, nor between classes, nor between political parties either—but right through every human heart—and through human hearts . . . I nourished my soul there, and I say without hesitation: Bless you, prison, for having been in my life."[2] Solzhenitsyn became a world-renowned encourager for those who have faced severe difficulties in their lives. This dimension of his purpose came as a result of making the decision while in prison to live again.

The death and subsequent 40-day embalming of Jacob publicly communicated his earlier choice to live again. When Joseph directed the physicians in his service "to embalm his father Israel [also known as Jacob]" (Gen. 50:2) for 40 days, this action had several meanings. To the Egyptian, embalming was done with the belief that a future reunion of the soul with the body would occur.[3] By making the request for this Egyptian custom to be carried out, Joseph too acknowledged, perhaps not with the same religious symbolism, the general belief that there is a life that is to come where a reunion would occur. In the mind of a Hebrew, the number 40 represents completion and fulfillment. The 40 days of embalming conveyed to all the completion and fulfillment of Jacob's life. This embalming also communicated that Jacob's purpose was being preserved.

Joseph concluded that one reason to live again was to complete the unfulfilled purpose of Jacob's life. A nation had to be formed and moved to Canaan—the Promised Land that God had spoken of several generations ago. This passion for life and for life's purpose was also evident years later at Joseph's death when he urged his brothers to "carry my bones up from this place [Egypt]" to the Promised Land (Gen. 50:22–26). Before they could carry his bones up to the Promised Land, Joseph had to be embalmed. His purpose was being preserved since he did not complete the goal of having the Israelites return to Canaan as a mighty nation during his life. Embalm your life's purpose by making the decision to live again.

DAY 24 Points to Reflect Upon

How was Joseph able to bounce back from the thirteen years of traumatic ordeals in his life? The secret lay in his ability to recognize that one cannot abandon living. Life is a gift of God, and we must live it. You can learn to live again by

1. adopting the perspective that serving God and serving people are worthwhile and personally therapeutic.

2. changing your attitude—the one thing you really have control over when your life is steeped in debilitating circumstances.

3. acknowledging that your purpose must live on. Embalm it.

Step #7

Win the War Against Discouragement

The harder the conflict, the more glorious the triumph. What we obtain too cheap, we esteem too lightly: it is dearness only that gives everything its value. I love the man that can smile in trouble, that can gather strength from distress and grow brave by reflection. 'Tis the business of little minds to shrink; but he whose heart is firm, and whose conscience approves his conduct, will pursue his principles unto death.

Thomas Paine

DAY **25**

Overcome Discouragement

O ne of life's paradoxes is that a great victory or personal accomplishment is often followed by a bout with discouragement. The English word *discouragement* is borrowed from Old French, which is a combination of two words: *des* meaning "away" and *corage*, which is "courage." Together *discouragement* means "courage that has left" or "courage that has gone away." Discouragement does not discriminate when choosing its victims. It strikes everyone at one point or another.

Like an uncontrolled virus, discouragement attacks your emotional immune system—the heart of your life's purpose. Discouragement challenges your belief in God's promises. It works at disabling your ability to hope for a better tomorrow, to dream for a perfected purpose, or to lay hold of God's answers for your dilemma. Fortunately, there are powerful antidotes for this dreaded virus. In the life of Israel's prophet Elijah, four powerful principles helped him defeat discouragement during a 40-day Transforming Interval. These principles can successfully combat the onslaught of discouragement in the immune system of your purpose.

Over the next four days these four principles will be expounded in the hope that you will experience (1) a renewed outlook regarding discouragement and your life's purpose; (2) acceptance of God's correction; (3) a secured hope by mentoring the next generation; and (4) a lifetime habit of helping others discover their purpose. Let's begin our journey.

Getting a Full Perspective of Elijah

Imagine interviewing Elijah the way a television reporter would. To best understand and appreciate his victory over discouragement en route to perfecting his purpose, you would have to dig into his past. There, you would learn how he intentionally adopted a renewed outlook toward his life's purpose, which proved to be a prescription against the poison of discouragement. His story begins with these experiences:

- Queen Jezebel was still killing off the Lord's prophets (1 Kings 18:4) because of Elijah's prophetic decree that no rain would occur in Samaria (1 Kings 17:1). Since she could not harm God, she decided to harm His messengers, the prophets.

- Elijah called for a showdown against the false prophets who counseled King Ahab and Queen Jezebel—450 prophets of Baal and 400 prophets of Asherah. The false prophets were instrumental in turning the entire nation away from God.

- After publicly humiliating the false prophets because their god could not respond to their pleas, Elijah prayed to the one and true God, who answered him openly. The people of Israel immediately saw that God is true and all other idolatrous practices are false. Elijah ordered the slaughtering of all 850 false prophets, which occurred in the Kishon Valley (1 Kings 18:40).

- Having facilitated this miracle of inviting God to demonstrate His power publicly and nationally, Elijah prayed for God to send rain. In moments, "the sky grew black with clouds, the wind rose, a heavy rain came," and all Israel learned that Elijah was God's prophet and God wanted His people to return to Him with their hearts (1 Kings 18:45).

- When Queen Jezebel heard of Elijah's authorizing the slaying of her 850 prophets, she issued a death threat against him. Her murderous threats led to Elijah's deep fear, depression, and discouragement. Deathly afraid and suicidal, he ran for his life (1 Kings 19:1–4).

- Elijah ditched his servant and ran to Horeb, the mountain of God. As he ran, he instituted a 40-day fast, which proved to be a Transforming Interval in his life.

Elijah's Look into the Mirror of His Life

Can you imagine this "man of God" publicly moving mind-boggling levels of faith to initiate the slaying of 850 false prophets? Yet at the word of one wicked woman, he succumbed to deep discouragement that rendered him suicidal? He truly was "a man just like us," as noted in James 5:17.

Have you ever noticed that you can spot something brewing in the lives of others but cannot see the glaring hole you're about to fall into? A word picture that captures this truism is about two prophets. As you are aware, prophets have an uncanny ability from God to discern what is going on in the lives of others. They are like x-ray machines that see our plight and can tell us what God is about to do in response to the situation. Well, the two prophets meet on the road, and one says to the other, as he discerns his state: "You're doing well! Now tell me how I'm doing." In other words, you can see someone else's condition, but you don't have a clue about your own state.

Elijah did not know how susceptible he was to discouragement, even though God used him mightily on a national level. Likewise, if you find yourself in a pit, you may not understand how you got there, especially when you seemed to have been doing so well. Now, all of a sudden you are discouraged about your purpose, your life's direction, and you find yourself trying to claw your way out. Elijah discovered how to gain a renewed perspective on life as he sat in the cave hewn out of the mountain of God. The prophet was postured to hear a word from the Lord:

> *When Elijah heard it, he pulled his cloak over his face and went out and stood at the mouth of the cave.*
> *Then a voice said to him, "What are you doing here, Elijah?"*

He replied, "I have been very zealous for the LORD God Almighty. The Israelites have rejected your covenant, broken down your altars, and put your prophets to death with the sword. I am the only one left, and now they are trying to kill me too."

The LORD said to him, "Go back the way you came, and go to the Desert of Damascus. When you get there, anoint Hazael king over Aram. Also, anoint Jehu son of Nimshi king over Israel, and anoint Elisha son of Shaphat from Abel Meholah to succeed you as prophet. Jehu will put to death any who escape the sword of Hazael, and Elisha will put to death any who escape the sword of Jehu. Yet I reserve seven thousand in Israel—all whose knees have not bowed down to Baal and all whose mouths have not kissed him."

(1 Kings 19:13–18)

Elijah Gains a Renewed Outlook

God's answer to the prophet's discouragement can be summed up in a few words: "Living selflessly is the antidote to the poison of discouragement." In other words, God told Elijah to go and anoint three men—Hazael, Jehu, and Elisha—for specific life tasks. *To anoint* means "to set apart for a specific function." God recognized that Elijah needed a new perspective—and one not based in selfishness, as in the case of so many of us. We are discouraged because our lives are not going the way we think they should, our families are not acting the way we would like, our jobs do not pay us the money we feel we deserve. And our God is not moving at the speed we believe He should be moving in our lives. *Our, our, our!* That's the problem, and it is the root of much discouragement. God stopped the prophet's complaining by sending him on a mission, a life purpose—"Go and anoint Hazael, Jehu, and Elisha." God's solution to Elijah's discouragement was to engage the prophet in an unselfish mission, a life's purpose that involved selflessly helping others.

A few years after my wife and I planted Christ Church in 1986, the congregation still included fewer than one hundred people. I became very discouraged because I felt the strength of the leadership I had around me was inadequate to complete my grand vision for the fledgling church. I used to complain daily to Marlinda, saying, "I wish I had a stronger leadership team, a more capable group of leaders to help me carry out the work of ministry." One day she became fed up with my complaining and said, "David, stop complaining about the level of leaders around you, and do something to change them!" I became angry with her response because the truth was too painfully honest. And it put the responsibility back on me.

After I calmed down, I realized that she was right. I started to create leadership training and mentoring curricula to develop our men and women into effective leaders. Amazingly, I noticed fantastic growth in their lives as I unselfishly gave myself to their betterment. Within a few years, I was receiving invitations from all over the world to host leadership training seminars. If my wife had not shocked me with the truth that was underlying my discouragement—my selfishness—our church would not have grown to its present size of more than five thousand people. Unselfishness breaks the back of discouragement so that your life's purpose does not die before it is birthed.

DAY 25 Points to Reflect Upon

How could a great prophet like Elijah succumb to the clutches of discouragement? The answer: he was an ordinary person like you and me. Discouragement is not selective in its victims. You combat this satanic weapon by renewing your perspective of your purpose.

1. Ask yourself: Is my complaint masking a selfish perspective? If so, adopt an unselfish view of your life.

2. Change your attitude toward others. Live an unselfish life by seeking to assist others in the fulfillment of God's purpose for their lives.

3. List three people in your life who could use your input in launching their life's purpose. Now help them perfect their purpose.

DAY **26**

Accept God's Correction

One timeless principle that unfolds from Elijah's Transforming Interval is that godly correction ensures the attainment of your purpose. His life's purpose became cloudy because of Queen Jezebel's death threat (1 Kings 19:1–2), because of his suicidal thoughts (1 Kings 19:4), and because of his false idea that he was the only prophet of God still alive in Israel (1 Kings 18:22; 19:14). The emotions surrounding these circumstances led Elijah into depression. In Day 25 we learned that God renewed the prophet's perspective of his life's purpose by instructing him to become unselfish. But God offered another solution to Elijah's emotional dilemma. He offered him a strong word of correction.

> The word of the LORD came to him: "What are you doing here, Elijah?" . . .
> He replied, "I have been very zealous for the LORD God Almighty. The Israelites have rejected your covenant, broken down your altars, and put your prophets to death with the sword. I am the only one left, and now they are trying to kill me too." The LORD said to him, "Go back the way you came, and go to the Desert of Damascus. When you get there, anoint Hazael king over Aram. Also, anoint Jehu son of Nimshi king over Israel, and anoint Elisha son of Shaphat from Abel Meholah to succeed you as prophet. Jehu will put to death any who escape the sword of Hazael, and Elisha will put to death any who escape the sword of Jehu. Yet I reserve seven thousand in Israel—all whose knees have not bowed down to Baal and all whose mouths have not kissed him."
>
> (1 Kings 19:9, 14–18)

178

The Lord graciously listened to the prophet's complaint about the moral decadence of the nation, its murderous vehemence toward God's messengers, and his isolation from the world because of his unwillingness to live a life of compromise. One would think that Elijah's plea would receive a sympathetic response from God, followed by an all-expense-paid vacation to the Prophet's Retreat Center in Jerusalem. But, no! Instead God gave him a threefold assignment, prefaced by these rebuking words: "Go back the way you came, and go to the Desert of Damascus" (1 Kings 19:15). Commentator Frank Gaebelein says that "God again dealt graciously with his prophet. He was to go back to the northern kingdom (v. 15), the place where he had veered off the track with God in his spiritual life."[1] Although God's words were firm, His tone was not harsh or unkind to the discouraged prophet. Correction that leads to positive change cannot be delivered in an unkind manner.

Years ago, I was in prayer about a friendship that was disturbing me. After some time, I felt that the Lord spoke something to my heart that would be a corrective message to a dear brother. When I shared the word of correction with him, he said, "Yes, you heard from God, but did the Lord tell you to tell me that way?" Isn't that like God? I was giving correction, but in the same instance I was being corrected for the *way* I had corrected. I quickly learned that correction does not have to be mean-spirited, unkind, or harsh. It must be firm but loving and gentle. That was what the apostle Paul instructed the Galatian Christians to do: "Brothers, if someone is caught in a sin, you who are spiritual should restore him *gently*. But watch yourself, or you also may be tempted" (Gal. 6:1, italics mine).

Three Benefits of Correction

The word *correction* means "a rebuke, punishment, a bringing into conformity with a standard."[2] The Bible speaks often on this theme. It warns that if we do not heed correction, we will not perfect our purpose. Like it or not, you have to learn how to receive correction if you are going to fulfill God's aim for your life. The book of Proverbs includes passages where the word *correction* or *rebuke* is used by Solomon, its author.

> *My son, do not despise the LORD's discipline*
> *and do not resent his rebuke,*
> *because the LORD disciplines those he loves,*
> *as a father the son he delights in.*

(Prov. 3:11–12)

> *To learn, you must love discipline; it is stupid to hate* correction.

(Prov. 12:1, NLT)

> *A fool spurns his father's discipline,*
> *but whoever heeds* correction *shows prudence.*

(Prov. 15:5)

> *Stern discipline awaits him who leaves the path;*
> *he who hates* correction *will die.*
> *Death and Destruction lie open before the LORD—*
> *how much more the hearts of men!*
> *A mocker resents correction;*
> *he will not consult the wise.*

(Prov. 15:10–12)

> *He who ignores discipline despises himself,*
> *but whoever heeds* correction *gains understanding.*

(Prov. 15:32)

If we heed Solomon's advice, we will not fall en route to our purpose. Receiving correction shows that we embrace the Lord's discipline, we are prudent, we enjoy life, and we are willing to gain understanding. Three significant benefits of correction are (1) correction changes your behavior; (2) correction changes your perspective; and (3) correction brings you closer to your purpose.

1. Benefit #1: Correction Changes Your Behavior

Elijah's behavior received a sudden adjustment at God's corrective words. The latter portion of God's rebuke to Elijah was: "Yet I reserve seven thousand in Israel—all whose knees have not bowed down to Baal and all whose mouths have not kissed him" (1 Kings 19:18). And Elijah heeded the assignment to anoint Hazael, Jehu, and Elisha. Elisha was the first person Elijah met, and Elijah soon fostered a mentoring relationship with him. Can you see how a young, inexperienced prophet tagging alongside an older, seasoned prophet removed the isolationist perspective that Elijah formerly held (1 Kings 19:19–21)? Correction changed his behavior.

When I first started in the pastorate, I preached for sixty to seventy-five minutes, thinking that the longer I preached, the more anointed I was. I recorded these long-winded sermons on cassette tapes. When I went to pick up a box of ninety-minute tapes, the owner—who was an elderly Christian man—asked me why I needed them. I proudly responded that I sometimes spoke as long as seventy-five minutes. I'll never forget his words of correction. "David," he said, "the more you study, the less time you need to speak because you will know what you're talking about. The longer you speak shows that you don't know what you're talking about, and you're figuring it out as you go along."

Wow! I instantly changed my behavior. I started studying longer and more effectively. I soon found out that my ability to express and explain the truths of the Bible took significantly shorter periods of time. And the people did not feel cheated by the sermon length. Now, my thirty-five-minute sermons are more precise and power-packed than the previous seventy-five-minute ones.

2. Benefit #2: Correction Changes Your Perspective

Perspective is our mental point of view of how we should feel and think about the road ahead. Emotional intelligence and emotional competency are critical to the perspective we form about ourselves and to the plans we make based on our circumstances. Daniel Goleman, who authored the book *Working with Emotional Intelligence*, indicates that our emotional competence is determined by our emotional awareness, accurate self-assessment, and self-confidence.[3] The prophet was emotionally incompetent at the moment, not knowing how to properly manage himself or formulate an accurate perspective.

Elijah's perspective on his situation was totally out of sync with God's, which automatically made it the wrong perspective. Elijah was living with a debilitating fear because of what one wicked queen said she would do to him. The Bible shows no record of Elijah seeking God's guidance about how to combat her threat. He ran without researching the situation on a spiritual level. The prophet ran from Mount Carmel to Beersheba and then to Horeb, the mountain of God. God's rebuke pointed him north to the desert of Damascus.

Once the heavenly perspective was offered through God's correction, Elijah's overwhelming fear dissipated. He was no longer suicidal. He no longer had a martyr complex. He was assured that another seven thousand prophets of God were dwelling in Israel. God's correction shed light on his actions and dilemma. He was no longer walking around in a fog. He had clear direction. He was to go and anoint three men to fulfill their divine purposes. Elijah was to mentor one of them, namely, Elisha, who was destined to "succeed" him as a prophet (1 Kings 19:16).

3. Benefit #3: Correction Brings You Closer to Your Purpose

One of Elijah's life purposes was to train young men in prophetic ministry. Even prior to his Transforming Interval, the Scripture shows us a glimpse of this aspect of Elijah's purpose in that he had a servant (1 Kings 19:3), who most scholars agree was a protégé to his prophetic ministry. The unique office of a prophet requires a deep firsthand knowledge of the temperament of God, the voice of God, and ways to prophesy on a geopolitical level in order to foster societal change. Rabbi Abraham Heschel says that "the prophet is not only a prophet. He is also poet, preacher, patriot, statesman, social critic, moralist."[4]

After God corrected Elijah's faulty perspective that he was the only prophet left in Israel, Elijah started to mentor Elisha in response to the word of the Lord. The mentoring program did not end with that emerging prophet. A school of the prophets was launched in Bethel, Jericho, and Jordan (2 Kings 2:1–6). It is not clear that Elijah was the founder of these three schools, but from the biblical narrative it is definite that he had a strong mentoring role in the developmental process of the students. God's correction brought him closer to his purpose.

An old joke among Christians is a play on words referring to seminary as a cemetery. It conveys the idea that if you attend seminary to grow in the knowledge of the Bible, you will end up spiritually dead in your passion for Christ. Although some seminaries have that effect, many more are thriving places where true biblical scholarship takes place with the aim to train men and women to fulfill the Great Commission of evangelizing the world. My church background was one where this joke was often repeated from the pulpit. Everyone laughed; I laughed. Unbeknownst to me, I had unconsciously built up a prejudice against seminaries.

During the early days of my pastoral experience, I called churches, schools, and catering halls to find a space to rent for our young congregation. After several polite rejections, I happened upon a pastor who, though he could not accommodate my request, asked me if I had attended seminary. "No," I quickly responded. I had earned a master's degree in civil engineering, and more schooling—especially cemetery, oops I mean seminary—was not in my plans. He gently apprised me of the benefit of a good seminary education, pointing out that I would have a greater confidence when teaching the Bible and that my congregation would feel intellectually safe when I dealt with controversial topics.

I hung up the telephone and announced to Marlinda that I was going to seminary. Her eyes flew open because her perspective, too, had been marred by that silly joke. Thankfully, God saw fit to use that dear man to correct me. A few weeks afterward, I enrolled in seminary at Alliance Theological Seminary, and several years later I completed a graduate degree in divinity. I now serve on the board of trustees for the seminary, and I am fulfilling part of my life's purpose: to equip others to serve their generation with biblical truths. Correction brings you closer to your purpose.

DAY 26 Points to Reflect Upon

Numerous benefits stem from correction. To enjoy them, you must be open to receiving godly rebukes and sometimes not-so-godly rebukes.

1. What kind of attitude did you display the last time you were

corrected? If it was poor, what are you going to do to correct your response?

2. Recall three benefits of correction: (*a*) correction changes your behavior; (*b*) correction changes your perspective; and (*c*) correction brings you closer to your purpose.

3. Have you been avoiding some people because they need correction? According to Proverbs 15:32, what will they miss because you withhold correction?

Impact the Next Generation

A godly purpose lives beyond one generation. Elijah struggled through depression, discouragement, and isolation to secure victory in his purpose of impacting emerging leaders through his office of prophet. At the end of his 40 days of fasting (1 Kings 19:8), he received this transformational word from God:

> *The LORD said to him, "Go back the way you came, and go to the Desert of Damascus. When you get there, anoint Hazael king over Aram. Also, anoint Jehu son of Nimshi king over Israel, and anoint Elisha son of Shaphat from Abel Meholah to succeed you as prophet. Jehu will put to death any who escape the sword of Hazael, and Elisha will put to death any who escape the sword of Jehu. Yet I reserve seven thousand in Israel—all whose knees have not bowed down to Baal and all whose mouths have not kissed him."*
>
> (1 Kings 19:15–18)

Concern for the next generation was in God's heart. The solution to Elijah's discouragement was his assignment to anoint Hazael, Jehu, and Elisha. Hazael was to become the future king of Aram—the actual timing of the fulfillment of this prophetic commandment is not specifically identified in the biblical narrative. Jehu was to be set apart as the future king of Israel. Interestingly enough, Elijah did not anoint Jehu to be king prior to his supernatural translation to heaven. Elisha performed this function many years later, which showed that Elijah passed on the unfulfilled directives given him by God (2 Kings 9:1–10). The third person to be anointed by

Elijah was Elisha, who was to become Elijah's replacement in his prophetic ministry to Israel.

This directive, to anoint three men responsible for both political and prophetic arenas, shows Elijah's purpose clearly would extend beyond his lifetime. God's transgenerational perspective regarding the perfecting of Elijah's purpose helps us to see that our purpose should also extend beyond our own generation. When you consider God's remedy for the prophet's depression, the mentoring of a younger generation, you cannot ignore God's ingenuity. In essence, God offered to exchange Elijah's depression for the prophet's ability to impact future generations of leaders. Elijah quickly made the trade. His depression broke; his purpose lived on.

What made this prophet accept God's call to serve a subsequent generation? I offer three answers: (1) he saw the need; (2) he experienced God's stubborn love; and (3) he had a spiritual reality that was perpetually relevant.

1. The Next Generation's Need

In 1940, schoolteachers were asked to describe the top seven disciplinary problems they faced in the classroom. They listed:

- talking
- chewing gum
- making noise
- running in the halls
- getting out of turn in lines
- wearing improper clothing
- not putting waste paper in the waste paper basket

In 1990, college researchers asked educators the same question. Here are the disciplinary problems of modern-day teachers:[1]

- rape
- robbery

- assault

- burglary

- arson

- bombing

- murder

The disciplinary problems of contemporary educators are frightening compared with those of an earlier generation. If that comparison was not enough, let me share statistical information about the need before us.[2] Every day in America the following occurs:

- 1,000 unwed teenage girls become mothers.

- 1,106 teenage girls get abortions.

- 4,219 teenagers contract sexually transmitted diseases.

- 500 adolescents begin using drugs.

- 1,000 adolescents begin drinking alcohol.

- 135,000 kids bring guns or other weapons to school.

- 3,610 teens are assaulted; 80 are raped.

- 2,200 teens drop out of high school.

- 6 teens commit suicide.

The bottom line is that future generations need the help of their predecessors, who have virtuous skills to pass on. Just as a great need exists for us to impart truths to the following generation, Elijah was moved by the need to train emerging prophets for the betterment of the ministry and his nation.

2. God's Stubborn Love

Elijah learned firsthand that God did not give up on him when he was down. He was battling fear, depression, and a martyrdom complex. He thought that he was the only prophet still alive who was not comprising his faith (1 Kings 19:3–4, 14). Despite those complications, God affirmed Elijah by showing concern for him and by giving him an extended mission (1 Kings 19:15–18). God's stubborn love was at work in the life of Elijah. Experiencing God's love is certainly different from reading about it or studying it on a devotional level. The validation of its reality must come from firsthand experience. The next generation needs an oral history of our experience with the stubborn love of God. Share your testimony with others—younger people who may have no firsthand knowledge of God's acceptance or forgiveness.

Your testimony will pave the way for them to desire their own experiences with God's love. Children want proof of God's stubborn love. You are the proof! And your testimony will show how your experience has transformed you into someone who can stubbornly love them.

In 1975, Lynette "Squeaky" Fromme exploded onto every front page in America. The young woman had pushed her way through a crowd in an attempt to kill the president of the United States. Investigators found that she was a proud follower of Charles Manson. The world knows Manson as a crazed killer who worked through his small, dedicated band of fanatical disciples. News magazines dug into the background of this tragic young woman and discovered that Squeaky had felt like a misfit in her town. She had wandered to Venice Beach after her father removed her from his Redondo Beach home in the suburbs of Los Angeles. There, Charles Manson met her and promised to take care of her. She went with him and was willing to kill and die for him.

Reporters wanted to know, "Why would you give your life to a man like Manson?" The answer was unforgettable. Squeaky explained that she had decided early in her teenage years that "whoever loves me first can have my life."[3]

How many young people like Squeaky are in your life? Have you failed to see their need because they are in a younger generation? Elijah answered the call to extend God's stubborn love to the emerging generations by mentoring Elisha and by training the prophets at the Bethel, Jericho, and Jordan schools (2 Kings 2:1–6).

3. A Spiritual Reality

Every generation needs a spiritual reality. But our generation cannot pass on such a reality unless we have it working in our midst. By spiritual reality, I mean that you are keenly aware of who you are, who God is, and your need to respond to God's love by serving His Son, Jesus Christ, on a daily basis.

The majority of Christian parents surveyed in a Barna Research Group project said that church and the Bible do not influence the way they parent their children. Only 33 percent of born-again parents surveyed said their church or faith has been a dominant influence in the way they parent; and only half of born-again parents mentioned anything related to faith (including the Bible, church, or religion) as significantly influencing the way they raise their children. The main influences listed by parents included their upbringing (45 percent); friends, relatives, and spouses (35 percent); and books, magazines, and articles on parenting (34 percent).

Nearly 63 percent said they expect the church to take a more active role in assisting parents. And 80 percent said the church should do more to help people become better parents. "Family ministry will be one of the hot issues facing the church over the next few years," said George Barna, president of Barna Research Group. "The challenge facing churches is to know what types of support parents and family members need to become productive Christians and citizens and to provide that support in useful ways."[4]

I want to invite you to find a quiet place and pray for the state of affairs with the next generation. There is a great need, and we have the assignment of allowing our purpose to positively impact future lives. Join me in answering the call of God to touch the next generation.

DAY 27 Points to Reflect Upon

One visible sign of a godly purpose is touching the next generation by executing your assignment.

1. The next generation has a big need.

2. God's love is stubborn—it never gives up on us. Think of two experiences in which God could have easily turned His back on you, but instead chose to display His love for you.

3. How are you passing on a spiritual reality to the next generation?

DAY 28

Leave a Spiritual Legacy

Elijah was one of those rare men who made the pursuit of God a lifestyle. Facing a death threat and severe discouragement, and battling thoughts of suicide, the prophet still had a penchant for keeping covenant with God. After he completed a 40-day period of fasting, a Transforming Interval occurred as God asked him this penetrating question: "What are you doing here, Elijah?" (1 Kings 19:13). He replied,

> "I have been very zealous for the LORD God Almighty. The Israelites have rejected your covenant, broken down your altars, and put your prophets to death with the sword. I am the only one left, and now they are trying to kill me too."
>
> The LORD said to him, "Go back the way you came, and go to the Desert of Damascus. When you get there, anoint Hazael king over Aram. Also, anoint Jehu son of Nimshi king over Israel, and anoint Elisha son of Shaphat from Abel Meholah to succeed you as prophet. Jehu will put to death any who escape the sword of Hazael, and Elisha will put to death any who escape the sword of Jehu. Yet I reserve seven thousand in Israel—all whose knees have not bowed down to Baal and all whose mouths have not kissed him."
>
> (1 Kings 19:14–18)

The dialogue between God and Elijah ended when God pointed Elijah to the reality that his commitment to walk in covenant with Him must ultimately translate into leaving a spiritual legacy. The prophet's spiritual strength and unswerving commitment to honor

God, even in trying times, were a wonderful heritage that God wanted passed down to future generations.

Establishing a Spiritual Will

Most often, we sit with our attorneys and craft our wills—legal documents that dictate what portion of our property will go to whom. Consider establishing a spiritual will—a document that intentionally outlines the enduring spiritual legacy you want passed on to your heirs. When my attorney drew up my will, I had to pay particular attention to three questions. First, who do I want in charge of my estate upon my demise? Second, what belongings (i.e., property, jewelry, possessions, etc.) do I want to assign to the heirs of my estate? Third, when do I want these heirs to get the property? This third question points to the matter of age, especially heirs under the age of eighteen.

Why not construct a document, whether in writing or in your mind, that answers those three questions?

1. Who Is in Charge of My Spiritual Estate?

Who do I want in charge of my spiritual estate upon my transition to heaven? According to our nation's legal system, if you have no legal heirs upon your demise, your property will not be apportioned to any family member until the legal case is completed in probate court. Your in-laws and out-laws will fight until the person who has the greatest legal burden wins the right to get your stuff, whether you wanted him to have it or not. In the case of a spiritual estate, if there is no heir, the knowledge (or possessions) that you have gained all these years fighting the devil, trusting in God's promises, pursuing your purpose, and engaging your faith to grow spiritually, will be for naught. If you have no heir, you have no one to whom to pass your spiritual property.

God gave Elijah an heir. Elisha was named as the prophet who would take his place or get his spiritual possessions after he departed to heaven (1 Kings 19:16). Recently, I sat with a dear pastor who was in his early seventies. He had a significant request that I felt privileged to entertain. He wanted me to recommend a couple who would be able to assume the pastorate of the congregation he had served for approximately forty years. He did not have an heir. I learned that the couple I had in mind for the role would not do after I interviewed them because their marriage was too weak. I dreaded my response to the senior minister because I had no one else to suggest. The lesson I learned was to choose heirs early in life so that when I approach my latter years, I can successfully pass on my legacy.

Elisha knew his purpose. He was called to fill Elijah's vacant post upon his ascension to glory. When the time came, the event was glorious. Elijah's spiritual estate was passed on.

> When they had crossed, Elijah said to Elisha, "Tell me, what can I do for you before I am taken from you?"
>
> "Let me inherit a double portion of your spirit," Elisha replied.
>
> "You have asked a difficult thing," Elijah said, "yet if you see me when I am taken from you, it will be yours—otherwise not."
>
> As they were walking along and talking together, suddenly a chariot of fire and horses of fire appeared and separated the two of them, and Elijah went up to heaven in a whirlwind. Elisha saw this and cried out, "My father! My father! The chariots and horsemen of Israel!" And Elisha saw him no more. Then he took hold of his own clothes and tore them apart.
>
> He picked up the cloak that had fallen from Elijah and went back and stood on the bank of the Jordan. Then he took the cloak that had fallen from him and struck the water with it. "Where now is the LORD, the God of Elijah?" he asked. When he struck the water, it divided to the right and to the left, and he crossed over.
>
> The company of the prophets from Jericho, who were watching, said, "The spirit of Elijah is resting on Elisha." And they went to meet him and bowed to the ground before him.
>
> (2 Kings 2:9–15)

Immediately after Elijah's transition to heaven, the community of prophets knew that Elisha was his heir—God began to work similarly in his life. Who is your heir? Look for people who want to be mentored. Look for people who are worthy to receive the wealth of the knowledge of God you possess. Don't belittle yourself in this area or devalue your spiritual strength. You have climbed the spiritual ladder farther than most people in the world. Just reading this book shows that you desire to enrich your spiritual life. Go for it! Find an heir! Pass on your spiritual estate to someone who will benefit from your hard-earned spiritual possessions.

2. What Belongings Do I Want to Assign My Heirs?

In the natural world, I want to bequeath to my children money, property, and other tangible valuables. In the spiritual world, I want to leave them and my other heirs, people whom I mentor whether in person or through books, the ability to walk effectively with God. I have created a number of mentoring programs to develop Christians into strong leaders who can successfully serve society and the church. The spiritual component of these programs consists of teaching the protégé how to pray, how to fast, how to hear the voice of God. It continues into areas such as how to live a life of discipline, how to submit to the leadership of the Holy Spirit, how to discover your purpose, and how to perfect it.

The spiritual legacies I want to pass on contain gems that cannot be found easily in textbooks. Certainly, you can read about the Christian disciplines, but you cannot see them fleshed out by looking at a black-and-white printed page. Discipleship is taught and caught. Jesus used the latter style when He passed on spiritual riches to the world through His disciples—His spiritual heirs. The Scriptures declare, "He appointed twelve, whom he also named apostles, *to be with him*, and to be sent out to proclaim the message" (Mark 3:14, NRSV, italics mine). Reading about Jesus, singing about Jesus, and even preaching about Jesus are not the best ways to become a spiritual heir. You must be *with* Jesus. That is why the Bible says of Elisha, "He set out to *follow* Elijah and became his attendant" (1 Kings 19:21, italics mine).

The belongings you want to assign your heirs can be passed on only when they are *with* you. In other words, people you impact are up close while others you impress are at a distance. Do you want to impact or impress people? The choice is yours. You leave a spiritual legacy by impacting people; you bequeath a nice dinner conversation when you try to impress people.

Unlike other major evangelists such as Charles Finney, Dwight L. Moody, and Billy Graham, the fiery preacher Billy Sunday preached only in North America and left no institutions to carry on his work. However, his legacy was in the lives of an estimated one million who walked "the sawdust trail" at his invitation to make a decision to serve Christ. By leading people to Christ and having them pass the torch of that relationship to others you can make a real and permanent impact.

The world-renowned neurosurgeon Dr. Benjamin Carson rose from humble origins to become the director of pediatric neurosurgery of the prestigious Johns Hopkins Hospital in Baltimore, Maryland. It all began when his mother, Sonya—who had faced tremendous challenges in her youth, transferring in and out of foster homes, receiving only a third grade education, being married at thirteen, and having heart problems—sought God's wisdom for her two troubled sons. In prayer she received the wisdom to limit the boys' television watching to only two preselected programs per week and have them read two books per week and complete a written report on them. Years later Carson received a scholarship to Yale University, and the rest is history.[1] It is amazing what can happen when a woman with humble means turns to God for His wisdom concerning her son.

3. When Do I Want My Heirs to Receive My Spiritual Property?

The time to hand over your spiritual property to your heirs depends on when they can handle the responsibility. Most scholars agree that Elijah mentored Elisha for a ten-year period before being translated to heaven. I think that we would agree that there must be a testing period. There is a need to safeguard the wealth by staging the timing for an adult child to gain access to the valuables. Some percentage will come at age eighteen, while another portion may be accessed at age twenty-five, and then the final percentage may be available at age thirty or thirty-five. Using this staging ensures that your adult child will make wise decisions with your hard-earned money and that the newfound wealth will not fall into immature hands.

An Enduring Legacy

Do not limit perfecting your purpose to cold vocational tasks or personal accomplishments. These activities are impotent to impacting your family or society spiritually. Your purpose must include spiritual power, a solid walk with God that others want to emulate because your life sends the message loud and clear: follow me as I follow Christ.

Anyone can leave a spiritual legacy. Whether you are a famed evangelist or you have a job out of the spotlight, you can add a dimension of spiritual strength to the world after your departure. The story is told of a bus driver and a minister who died around the same time. Immediately, they found themselves standing in the line to enter heaven through the pearly gates. Saint Peter was at the gate checking everyone's legacy on earth. The bus driver went first. Peter greeted him politely and said, "Frank, welcome to heaven. Do you see that great big mansion on top of the rolling hill to your right? That's yours! Enter into the joy of the Lord."

The minister moved up. Peter gave his customary greeting and began to dole out the reward. He said, "Reverend, do you see that little wooden shack in the valley down on your left? That's your reward. Enter into the joy of the Lord." The minister seethed with anger when he saw his shack in contrast to the bus driver's mansion. He could not control himself, so he blurted out to Saint Peter: "This is unfair! I protest! Why would God give this mere bus driver a palatial mansion while to me—a preacher of the gospel—a beat-up wooden shack? I insist that you check the records again." Peter complied. He walked over to the computer, pulled up the database, and found the reverend's name and that of the bus driver. He returned to the minister and said, "Yep, our records are right. They show that every time you preached, people fell asleep. But every time the bus driver drove, people prayed."

DAY 28 Points to Reflect Upon

Perfecting your purpose must include leaving a spiritual legacy for the people your life has touched. Remember to answer these three questions when you establish a spiritual will:

1. Who is in charge of my spiritual estate upon my demise?

2. What belongings do I want to assign my heirs?

3. When do I want my heirs to receive my spiritual property?

Step #8

Overcome Fear

Courage is resistance to fear, mastery of fear, not absence of fear.
Mark Twain

DAY 29

Gain Strength from Past Experiences

One of the most famous Bible stories is that of David defeating Goliath—the nine-foot-plus giant of a man. Goliath filled the army of Israel with fear for exactly 40 days by daily issuing a challenge for any of their warriors to fight him one-on-one. Fear of him rendered the entire army of Israel impotent. This fear came to a screeching halt when David—a teenager with boundless courage—slew Goliath with a slingshot. David's boldness and ability to overpower fear stemmed from practicing four habits that we will discuss over the next four days: (1) he drew strength from his past experience; (2) he saw value in making a faith confession; (3) he developed his own style of fighting; and (4) he held the perspective that God was almighty. Once he killed the object of fear, David eventually sat on the throne as king over the nation. If you practice the lifetime habit of overcoming fear, you will eventually occupy your seat of purpose, authority, and success in life.

Over my twenty-plus years of walking with Jesus, I have learned by Scripture and by experience that we must defeat fear if we are to fulfill our purpose. Hence, I pose this question to you: What would you do if you weren't afraid? Fear stands in the pathway daring you to try, daring you to use your faith, daring you to take a risk, daring you to advance into your purpose. Like Goliath, fear screams at you with threats to embarrass you, render you impotent, convince you to retreat, quit the project. Thankfully, we learn from David, past experiences have power to combat fear. Use them.

Draw strength from them. Don't ignore them. Realize that when you serve God, nothing goes to waste. The Lord uses all of your experiences—the ones in your preconverted past as well as the ones from your postconverted life. Rest assured when you give your life to Jesus, He will work to perform His purpose in you and through you, using every one of your experiences as an ingredient in your success.

To practice the principles David employed in overcoming fear, you need to understand that Transforming Intervals can come at any time. In the earlier episodes presented in this book, we learned that significant change occurred for people like Moses, Elijah, and Jesus in response to engaging in a 40-day practice. In this episode, however, we learn that David's Transforming Interval occurred following the 40 days that Goliath shouted threats to frighten the army of Israel (1 Sam. 17:16). It seems that the 40-day period was independent of David. But God was counting the days. The 40 days captured a fullness of time or behavior that released a response from God. God chose to use this episode as a Transforming Interval for David.

God accomplished two objectives with one incident. I call it killing two birds with one stone: (1) David was the agent God used to bring about His desires against the Philistines; and (2) the 40 days launched David into the national limelight as preparation for his future position as king over the nation of Israel.

Care Summons Courage

Every now and then we get a chance to glimpse the hero in our souls. Without any notice, words of courage spew out of our mouths, and we spring into action, showing the world around that we care. Moreover, we care so much that we are willing to risk our reputations, our money, our names, and possibly our lives to stand for what we believe. An older issue of *Guideposts* magazine featured an article entitled "The Rewards of Caring," in which a young boy witnessed a near tragedy. He was at the beach when a young woman stepped off a sandbar into deep water. There were at least twenty adults in swimming suits watching—apparently too afraid to try to help. Finally, a young man plunged into the water fully clothed and dragged the woman to safety. Arthur Gordon admired the young man's bravery, and he despised the onlookers' cowardice. His father said to him, "Don't judge them too harshly. It takes great courage to care greatly."[1]

I couldn't have said it better. The nation of Israel saw such courage in David that day in the Valley of Elah (1 Sam. 17:2). Each morning Goliath made his threats against the army of Israel. To motivate the men, or perhaps just one man, to accept Goliath's challenge, Saul offered a reward. No one stood up to the challenge—the soldiers were too afraid to act. The Scriptures declare:

> *The Israelites had been saying, "Do you see how this man keeps coming out? He comes out to defy Israel. The king will give great wealth to the man who kills him. He will also give him his daughter in marriage and will exempt his father's family from taxes in Israel."*
>
> *David asked the men standing near him, "What will be done for the man who kills this Philistine and removes this disgrace from Israel? Who is this uncircumcised Philistine that he should defy the armies of the living God?"*
>
> *They repeated to him what they had been saying and told him, "This is what will be done for the man who kills him."*
>
> (1 Sam. 17:25–27)

Like the rescuer in the story of a near drowning, David readied himself for action because he cared about the army's reputation. He cared about how ungodly people viewed God. He cared about the state of affairs in the nation. He cared about marrying a king's daughter. He cared about making his father's family tax-free. David cared (1 Sam. 17:26). He cared too much to be afraid. His care precipitated the courage to act. It was Mark Twain who said, "Courage is resistance to fear, mastery of fear—not absence of fear."[2]

David's care drove him to say to King Saul:

> *"Let no one lose heart on account of this Philistine; your servant will go and fight him."*
>
> *Saul replied, "You are not able to go out against this Philistine*

and fight him; you are only a boy, and he has been a fighting man from his youth."

But David said to Saul, "Your servant has been keeping his fa-ther's sheep. When a lion or a bear came and carried off a sheep from the flock, I went after it, struck it and rescued the sheep from its mouth. When it turned on me, I seized it by its hair, struck it and killed it. Your servant has killed both the lion and the bear; this un-circumcised Philistine will be like one of them, because he has defied the armies of the living God. The LORD who delivered me from the paw of the lion and the paw of the bear will deliver me from the hand of this Philistine."

Saul said to David, "Go, and the LORD be with you."

(1 Sam. 17:32–37)

Drawing Strength from Yesterday

David highlighted two incidents that he felt had qualified him to go against a giant. He had defeated a lion and a bear because they attempted to take what was his, the family sheep. Sometimes we in-wardly retreat, thinking that our past lacks the breadth of experi-ence needed to handle the future scope of our purpose. Not David. He was too busy thinking about defeating Goliath to consider that he had never fought in a war, had never tangled with a giant, had never been on the national scene. David was in "the zone." Fear was under his feet. When he considered his humble past, he saw traces of a similar experience to giant slaying—lion slaying and bear slay-ing. Others saw a little shepherd boy taking care of a few sheep (1 Sam. 17:28). He saw himself differently. He saw a threat against God's army, and he would not allow it on his watch.

Don't let your actions be based on others' interpretation of your past successes or experiences. You must look at your past and glean treasures where others may see junk. You know what happened in-side your heart when you won victories in the past. You know how you labored in prayer and how God wrought a victory through you. You know how you dared to believe God against all odds to get where you are today. Arm yourself with that truth, and move to the next rung on your ladder of purpose by drawing strength from your past.

David declared, "When a lion or a bear came and carried off a sheep from the flock, I went after it, struck it and rescued the sheep from its mouth. When it turned on me, I seized it by its hair, struck it and killed it" (1 Sam. 17:34–35). David never knew that tending to a few sheep was preparation for killing a giant in the national limelight. God knew.

Remember, nothing goes to waste with God. He uses *all* your experiences for His purpose. Your job is not to be afraid when God recalls one of your past experiences to serve as a foundation for perfecting your purpose.

When David met the Philistine giant on the battlefield, this is what happened:

> *David triumphed over the Philistine with a sling and a stone; without a sword in his hand he struck down the Philistine and killed him.*
>
> *David ran and stood over him. He took hold of the Philistine's sword and drew it from the scabbard. After he killed him, he cut off his head with the sword.*
>
> *When the Philistines saw that their hero was dead, they turned and ran.*
>
> (1 Sam. 17:50–51)

David learned from experience that killing the nine-foot giant was a natural progression from slaying the lion and the bear. Although lions tend to stalk their prey while bears are inclined to openly overpower their victims, David gleaned tactics that enabled him to take back what rightfully belonged to him. David took back national dignity from Goliath. He took back the soldiers' courage. And he won the heart of the nation. The army moved with the courage sparked by David's victory and defeated the Philistines.

Fear stops you dead in your tracks from continuing the climb toward your purpose. Fear affects your perspective of God, your perspective of your gifts, and even your judgment. How many Israelite soldiers had similar accounts of killing lions and bears as they shepherded their fathers' sheep? It is unreasonable to think that none of the thousands of warriors had a similarly powerful experience where their bravado was called to the fore. The big difference between them and David was that David responded. They stood by watching like the twenty adults in Arthur Gordon's story.

It's your turn now. What's stopping you? You must answer the question I posed earlier: What would I do if I wasn't afraid?

DAY 29 Points to Reflect Upon

Drawing strength from past experiences is about seeing how the Spirit of God was at work in helping you overcome previous obstacles. In the same way, you can forge a path toward your purpose by overcoming the present attack of fear.

1. Make a mental list of three experiences where others saw the hero in your soul.

2. Read the story of David and Goliath found in 1 Samuel 17.

3. Answer the question: What would I do if I wasn't afraid?

DAY 30

Make a Faith Confession

Lawyer jokes invite a lot of laughter. But whenever I share one during a sermon, I usually preface it by saying: "If you're an attorney, don't sue me for what I'm about to say." Well, here is the joke: A California university research scientist brings three professionals—an engineer, a medical doctor, and an attorney—in a room to find out their answers to the question: What does two plus two equal? The engineer answers, "It depends on what you mean, relative two or absolute two. But in either case, the result is four." The medical doctor replies, "When I diagnose the complication carefully, my prognosis of the mathematical situation is four." The attorney lowers his voice to a whisper and says, "Close the door. What would you like it to be?"

In other words, when faced with a dilemma, solve it in a creative way. Bend the answer so that it fits the contour of the problem like a perfect match. That was the thinking behind David's combat against fear. In a 40-day period a nine-foot-tall giant, a Philistine named Goliath, taunted the entire army of Israel:

> *"Why do you come out and line up for battle? Am I not a Philistine, and are you not the servants of Saul? Choose a man and have him come down to me. If he is able to fight and kill me, we will become your subjects; but if I overcome him and kill him, you will become our subjects and serve us." Then the Philistine said, "This day I defy the ranks of Israel! Give me a man and let us fight each other." On hearing the Philistine's words, Saul and all the Israelites were dismayed and terrified.*

(1 Sam. 17:8–11)

The threat sent a fearful chill throughout the army of Israel. David, who wasn't even a member of the army, rose to combat the crisis. His perspective of the crisis was different from everyone else's. He saw it as an opportunity while the others saw it as an obstacle. David had successfully dealt with fear numerous times as he slew a lion and a bear that attacked his father's sheep (1 Sam. 17:34–35). He now saw fear as a motivator toward his purpose. In the Chinese language the word *crisis* is made up of two characters, *way gee*. Each of these is half a word, the first meaning "danger" and the second, "opportunity." Hence a *crisis* is literally a "dangerous opportunity."[1]

Since David saw Goliath's threat as an opportunity, he made a faith confession to ward off fear and moved in for the kill. His confession was: "Who is this uncircumcised Philistine that he should defy the armies of the living God?" David said to Saul, "Let no one lose heart on account of this Philistine; your servant will go and fight him" (1 Sam. 17:26, 32). The four steps in David's faith confession are (1) get in sync with God; (2) visualize the object of your faith; (3) don't listen to cowards; and (4) stake your claim against the devil.

1. Get in Sync with God

A faith-based confession is steeped in biblical authority. When we confess, we say what God says. Some groups within the Christian community have entered into error because of a misunderstanding of the confessional dimension of faith. My book *Why Drown When You Can Walk on Water?* corrects this error and provides biblical guidelines on how to apply faith in order to lay hold of God's promises for your life.[2] When I use the term *faith confession*, I am not talking about parroting words that you've read in the Bible or reciting what you believe to be true. The word *confess* means "to declare faith in or adherence to; to profess." It is best understood from Paul's advice to the Roman Christians: "If you confess with your mouth, 'Jesus is Lord,' and believe in your heart that God raised him from the dead, you will be saved. For it is with your heart that you believe and are justified, and it is with your mouth that you confess and are saved" (Rom. 10:9–10).

When you declare what God has already declared, a true faith confession is at work. A verbal confession flows from a heart that has discerned the will of God and submits completely to that plan. Your heart and your verbal confession must be aligned so that you may experience harmony with God's will. If someone who is unable to speak desires to make a faith confession, his thoughts must line up with his heart and with God's will.

When David declared, "What will be done for the man who kills this Philistine and removes the disgrace from Israel? Who is this uncircumcised Philistine that he should defy the armies of the living God?" (1 Sam. 17:26), he was harmonizing with God's will. David's confession was in sync with God's desires (1 Sam. 14:20–23). Fear could not stand in the way of his faith confession.

2. Visualize the Object of Your Faith

You need to visualize the object of your faith. This principle does not contradict Paul's statement to the Corinthian church: "We walk by faith, not by sight" (2 Cor. 5:7, KJV). Paul had been discussing the Christian's ability to live victoriously on this earth although physically separated from our Lord. I use the term *visualize* to refer to formulating a mental picture that helps you lock in on God's promise or your anticipated outcome.

At a weak point in Abraham's faith, God invited him out of his tent to get a mental picture of his destiny to become a father of nations even though he was still childless. God spoke to the patriarch: " 'Look up at the heavens and count the stars—if indeed you can count them.' Then he said to him, 'So shall your offspring be.' Abram believed the LORD, and he credited it to him as righteousness" (Gen. 15:5–6). Visualization is biblical, since its origin begins with God.

David's visualization of the object of his faith was far easier than Abraham's experience. David saw and heard the giant shout his threats to the army of Israel. "Why do you come out and line up for battle?" Goliath said. "Am I not a Philistine, and are you not the servants of Saul? Choose a man and have him come down to me. If he is able to fight and kill me, we will become your subjects; but if I overcome him and kill him, you will become our subjects and serve us" (1 Sam. 17:8–9).

You cannot make a faith confession without understanding what promises or items you believe God will provide for you. What is the object of your faith? Get something to symbolize that item or promise, and thank God for fulfilling your heart's desire, which is also His will for your life.

3. Don't Listen to Cowards

In Clint Eastwood's movie *The Pale Rider*, one of the fearful cowboys was asked by a friend who was seeking to rally the troops against a town bully: Are you going to join forces with us? His reply: "I'm not a brave man, but I ain't no coward neither." I was confused because the cowboy was mixed up about his own identity. He was essentially saying, "I am a coward; don't count on my help when the fight starts."

To win victories, make a habit of not following the advice of cowards. They never see confrontation as positive. They seldom know that there is a time for war and a time for peace. Although our war should not be against flesh and blood, but against the powers of darkness (Eph. 6:12), we have to muster up courage if we are to secure and perfect our purposes. Daily, Goliath kept making threats (1 Sam. 17:16). With the exception of David—a nonenlisted youth who was at the site of the battle by chance—the Israelite army was terrified (1 Sam. 17:11).

When David inquired about what was going on, his oldest brother tried to shame him. Here's the fiery exchange:

When Eliab, David's oldest brother, heard him speaking with the men, he burned with anger at him and asked, "Why have you come down here? And with whom did you leave those few sheep in the desert? I know how conceited you are and how wicked your heart is; you came down only to watch the battle."

"Now what have I done?" said David. "Can't I even speak?" He
then turned away to someone else and brought up the same matter,
and the men answered him as before. What David said was overheard
and reported to Saul, and Saul sent for him.

(1 Sam. 17:28–31)

Eliab, like the other soldiers, exhibited true cowardice. He intended for his words—"few sheep" and "I know how conceited
you are" and "how wicked your heart is"—to scold David and
chase him to the proverbial corner of the room. But David was un-
moved by what cowards thought, particularly when the setting was
a perfect opportunity for God to display His power.

Are cowards trying to stop your expression of faith? Are they
using words meant to hurt you or shame you? Perhaps they are more
sophisticated in spewing their cowardice. Maybe they use a more ra-
tional approach, or a politically correct route, one that cautions: don't
take sides; stay neutral.

In 1986 the Nobel Peace Prize winner was Elie Wiesel. This Jewish author has taken on the commitment to never let the world forget the Holocaust, in which six million Jews were murdered during
Hitler's reign in Germany. Wiesel warned against neutrality on clear
right and wrong issues when he said, "Take sides! Neutrality helps
the oppressor, never the victim. Silence encourages the tormentor,
never the tormented. . . . We too must be willing to take a stance."[3]
Cowards are known for their logic and rationale, surmising that neutrality is the preferred stance. That wasn't David's position. He was
no coward, and he certainly did not listen to them. He chose to believe God for His promises to be seized that day in battle.

4. Stake Your Claim Against the Devil

On a recent vacation, Marlinda and I went to Antigua, one of the
Caribbean Islands. Early one morning while jogging around the resort, I noticed that vacationers were coming out of their villas with
beach towels in hand. The sun was just rising. It was too early to lie
on the beach. The water was cold. No heat, no tanning. So, I won-
dered, why the flurry of activity? Then I realized that they were

staking out the good spots for later that day. They wanted no one else to get the sweet spot on the beach. As soon as they placed their towels and other beach items on specially positioned lounge chairs, they went back to their hotel rooms to pick up where they had left off with their sleep. They could rest easily since they had staked their claim on the beach.

The final stage in making a faith confession is staking your claim against the devil's fear tactics. Draw a line in the sand and confess: "I'm not backing down in the name of Jesus." David staked his claim this way: "Let no one lose heart on account of this Philistine; your servant will go and fight him" (1 Sam. 17:32). The rest is history. David moved ahead after he made his faith confession. Goliath was defeated the moment David started saying what God wanted.

It's your turn now. Lay hold of an area of your purpose, and make a faith confession. Say what God has already declared He desires to complete on your behalf. And patiently wait on His timing for the victory to come to full manifestation.

DAY 30 Points to Reflect Upon

Making a faith confession is another way of overcoming the fear that may be attempting to hinder you from apprehending God's purpose for your life. While in sync with God you can make a faith confession when you

1. visualize the object of your faith.

2. don't listen to cowards.

3. stake your claim against the devil.

DAY **31**

Develop Your Own Style
of Fighting

Every now and again you meet a young adult who is secure enough to be his true self. David was such a young
man. Anointed by Samuel the prophet to be a king, David experienced the unveiling of God's purpose for his life at an early age.
Learning your purpose and walking in your purpose are usually
separated by time and trials. Time, because you need maturity; and
trials, because you need wisdom. You cannot walk securely in your
purpose without maturity and wisdom. Satan—the enemy of your
soul—does not want to see you serve God and, more particularly,
serve God's purpose for your life. He will fight you tooth and nail
to hinder you from forging ahead toward your destiny.

David was a skilled fighter. One of the things that made him exceptional at a young age in fighting was that he had his own style
and he was comfortable with that. How rare to find a young man
who is comfortable with himself! As chance would have it, David's
father, Jesse, asked him to take some food to his brothers, who were
camped out with the other soldiers to do battle against the
Philistines. The nine-foot giant, Goliath, a member of the opposing
army, made a threat against the army of Israel (1 Sam. 17:10–11),
causing the entire army to cower in fear. Not David. He sprang into
action, countering the threat with confidence. David said to Saul,
"Let no one lose heart on account of this Philistine; your servant
will go and fight him" (1 Sam. 17:32).

David was concerned about the men's morale. They were paralyzed by the giant's threats. David recognized that you cannot fight to get closer to your purpose if fear grips your heart. The goal of perfecting your purpose will die at the hands of fear. David exhibited two timeless lessons about combating fear: (1) be yourself; and (2) use your own style.

1. Be Yourself

This lesson stems from a quick conversation between King Saul and the courageous young man, David. The conversation went this way:

> *"The* LORD *who delivered me from the paw of the lion and the paw of the bear will deliver me from the hand of this Philistine."*
> *Saul said to David, "Go, and the* LORD *be with you."*
> *Then Saul dressed David in his own tunic. He put a coat of armor on him and a bronze helmet on his head. David fastened on his sword over the tunic and tried walking around, because he was not used to them.*
> *"I cannot go in these," he said to Saul, "because I am not used to them." So he took them off. Then he took his staff in his hand, chose five smooth stones from the stream, put them in the pouch of his shepherd's bag and, with his sling in his hand, approached the Philistine.*
> (1 Sam. 17:37–40)

Saul was "a head taller than any of the others [men in Israel]" (1 Sam. 9:2). His battle attire would not fit David. Furthermore, David was not used to wearing regal apparel and fighting gear. After all, he was only a shepherd boy and a musician. If he was to defeat Goliath, he would have to be himself when he went into battle. Someone else's stuff would not do; it would seem awkward and cumbersome. Being yourself is the easiest approach when you are fighting for your purpose. David knew this. He put Saul's gear down and picked up the familiar shepherd's staff and slingshot. He was ready for battle. He was satisfied with his preparation. He was being himself.

The most powerful advice I've ever heard is: David Ireland, be yourself! Be yourself! I heard this wise counsel during the formative stages of my purpose. Hearing this tidbit of wisdom and *doing it* are two completely different things, however. The advice sounds simple, but the execution is often painstaking because you don't always know when you are not being yourself. Put another way: you may be trying to be something or someone that you are not, and you don't realize it. Identity theft is not just when some unsavory character steals your credit card number and racks up a pile of bills using your name. Identity theft also occurs when you take on the persona of someone else for any reason. Perhaps you like the effectiveness of the person's style. Or maybe you prefer someone else's personality over your own. Even if you like someone else's personality or style better than your own, you must stay true to yourself in order to succeed at the purpose God has carved out for you.

A crowd watched a peacock spread its tail and show a dazzling plumage one day in a park zoo. The bird drew oohs and ahs from the people as it regally strutted about its pen. Then a dull-looking, brown-colored duck waddled between the peacock and the crowd. The peacock became angry and chased the duck back into a nearby pond. In its rage, the peacock's tail closed like a fan, and it suddenly seemed ugly. The duck began swimming and diving gracefully in the pond and no longer seemed unattractive. Those who had been singing the praises of the peacock now loved the duck.

Be yourself! You will feel better about life and the attainment of life's purposes.

2. Use Your Own Style

One of the world's famous martial arts experts was the late Bruce Lee. Bruce was known on and off the big screen for his physical prowess and confidence in defeating other martial arts professionals because he mastered his own technique of fighting called Jeet Kune Do. Bruce developed his own martial arts style because he saw the weaknesses in other styles. He decided to open a martial arts school and teach his technique. When challenged by a local kung fu man who thought Bruce's style could not hold its own, he found out in less than three minutes that he was wrong.[1]

David sought to put an end to the stalemate between the Philistines and Israel. He was going to finish off Goliath once and for all. But he knew that he could not do so using Saul's style of fighting. In drawing from his past victories, successfully retrieving a sheep carried off from the flock by a lion and a bear, David used his faithful shepherd's club, a slingshot, and his bare hands to kill the wild animals (1 Sam. 17:34–37). He was going to use the same style to fight Goliath.

After choosing five smooth stones from the stream, David whirled the sling around and around and fired it at Goliath's head. Bull's-eye; Goliath went down. David, using his own style, killed the Philistine giant. The Israelite army went wild. The Philistine soldiers ran for safe cover, but to no avail. That day in Judah, a new chapter was opened in the life of David. He was to go down in history as a man who fought against fear by staying true to his own style of fighting. That day, his decision and brave action moved him several steps closer to his purpose of becoming God's man—someone who would one day sit on the throne of Israel.

Do not pour the clay of your purpose into a mold that you feel compelled to emulate. If your purpose involves sales, your sales pitch must fit your personality. If you're an educator, your teaching style must be true to you. If you are a business professional, your execution of business practices must be in keeping with your personality and style. If you're called to be a preacher, do not try to preach like Billy Graham, T. D. Jakes, or Joyce Meyer. If you fail, and you will, you will look foolish. And if you succeed, you will succeed only in communicating to the world that you are not very comfortable with yourself. Instead seek to preach well and without self-consciousness. Then your unique style will emerge.

In the pioneer days of aviation, a pilot was making a flight around the world. After he had been gone for some two hours from his last landing field, he heard a noise in his plane, which he recognized as the gnawing of a rat. He realized that while his plane was on the ground, a rat had gotten in. For all he knew, the rat could be gnawing through a vital cable or fabric of the plane. It was a very serious situation. The pilot was concerned and anxious. At first he did not know what to do. It was two hours back to the landing field from which he had taken off and more than two hours to the next field ahead. Then he remembered that the rat is a rodent. It is not made for heights; it is made to live on the ground and under the ground.

Therefore, the pilot began to climb. He went up a thousand feet. The gnawing ceased. The rat was dead. It could not survive in the atmosphere of those heights. More than two hours later the pilot flew the plane safely to the next landing field and found the dead rat.

Worry is a rodent. It cannot live in the atmosphere of fearlessness. It cannot breathe in the atmosphere made vital by praying and walking in God's purpose for your life. Like fear, worry dies when you ascend to the Lord through prayer, passionate pursuit, and purposeful living.[2]

DAY 31 Points to Reflect Upon

To attain your purpose, you have to learn how to fight resistance and fear. David taught us key principles to overcoming fear:

1. Be yourself. Ask yourself, In what way am I *not* being true to myself? If this question opens a can of worms, don't close the can. Work through the issues.

2. Develop your own style of executing your plans.

3. Don't allow criticism to cause you to worry.

DAY 32

Recognize that God Is Almighty

The story is told of an Eskimo who walks into a village with his two big dogs, one white, the other black. Each Saturday he takes bets from the men of the village on which of his dogs would win if they fought each other. Invariably, he would win, taking the gamblers' money. The following Saturday he would return and go through the same solicitation. One Saturday he would choose the white dog over the other, and he would win. Next time, he would choose the black dog over the white, and sure enough the black dog would win. After taking the villagers' money several weeks in a row, a little boy asked, "Sir, how do you know which dog will win?" The man looked around making sure no one else heard his answer: "Son, that's easy. During the week, I feed one dog and starve the other." This story illustrates a key point: if you feed your faith, doubt and fear will starve to death. Fear must be replaced by faith.

David's 40-day Transforming Interval had to do with combating fear precipitated by Goliath's daily death threats against the army of Israel. Goliath was a nine-foot-tall giant who was the Philistines' fiercest warrior. David overcame fear in a number of ways, including having a healthy faith in God Almighty. Jesus said that we ought to "have faith in God" (Mark 11:22). The grammatical tense He used in this New Testament passage is the present continuous tense, which causes the text to mean: have faith and *keep on having faith* in God. Applying faith is not a one-time expression. David learned to use his faith in the past, and he continued having faith in God when he encountered new dilemmas. When he was faced with Goliath's challenge, he already had faith that God Almighty would help him gain victory.

Defeating Goliath proved to be a stepping-stone to David's purpose, solidifying national respect so that God's intention of making him Israel's next king was a surefire action. There are three ingredients in David's kind of faith: (1) a proper image of God; (2) a fear of the Lord; and (3) recognition that the battle belongs to the Lord.

1. Establish a Proper Image of God

Thinking dictates expectations. Your image of a situation or a relationship must be accurate if you are to receive the maximum benefits from it.

I have a great marriage, but it did not start that way. When Marlinda and I got married some twenty years ago, we were unconsciously trying to change each other. But to no avail; neither of us budged. Our personalities were different, our preferences were different, our timing was different, and we found that we liked our own styles. I remember the day when everything came to a head. We were in the kitchen of our one-bedroom apartment. The communication was tense, but we wanted to get through to each other without compromising our true feelings. When we paused from the intensity of the conversation to get a breather, the thought came to me: *Ask God to let me see Marlinda through His eyes and not my own.* I calmly shared with Marlinda the idea of our asking God to let us see each other through His eyes and not our own. She agreed. We held hands and prayed. From that moment, our perspectives of each other changed.

Remarkably, I started viewing Marlinda the way God saw her. Our differences were unimportant. In fact, our differences became strengths. I no longer sought to change her into another David Ireland. One was ample. She was free to be who God made her to be without my correction. My prayer helped me to establish an accurate image of Marlinda.

In a similar manner, to enjoy God, to walk with God, to benefit from God's power as David did, we must have an accurate image of

Him. David said, "You [Goliath] come against me with sword and spear and javelin, but I come against you in the name of the LORD Almighty, the God of the armies of Israel, whom you have defied" (1 Sam. 17:45).

Old Testament scholars Carl Keil and Franz Delitzsch say that this verse "does not mean 'God is for Israel,' but 'Israel hath a God,' so that *Elohim* [Hebrew word for 'Lord'] is used here in a pregnant sense. This *God* is Jehovah; war is His. In other words, He is the Lord of war, who has both war and its results in His power."[1] David saw God as the One who possessed absolute control in times of peace or in times of war. This accurate image of God was an element in his faith so that when he battled against Goliath, victory was imminent.

2. Cultivate Fear of the Lord

The Bible has much to say about the *fear of the Lord*. In fact, the phrase appears forty-eight times in the New Revised Standard Version of the Bible. The *fear of the Lord* speaks of reverence, honor, and esteem that God is to receive freely from His creation. *Fear* in this context does not suggest a cowering posture. A healthy fear of the Lord cherishes God's leadership, will, preferred lifestyle, and full oversight of our lives. I have italicized *fear of the Lord* in the following Bible passages to better convey its meaning:

- The *fear of the LORD* is the beginning of knowledge, but fools despise wisdom and discipline. (Prov. 1:7)

- To *fear the LORD* is to hate evil;
  I hate pride and arrogance,
  evil behavior and perverse speech. (Prov. 8:13)

- The *fear of the LORD* is the beginning of wisdom,
  and knowledge of the Holy One is understanding. (Prov. 9:10)

- The *fear of the LORD* adds length to life,
  but the years of the wicked are cut short. (Prov. 10:27)

- The *fear of the* LORD is a fountain of life,
  turning a man from the snares of death. (Prov. 14:27)

- Better a little with the *fear of the* LORD
  than great wealth with turmoil. (Prov. 15:16)

Someone who fears the Lord demonstrates a desire for knowledge, a hatred for evil, and an appreciation for wisdom. This person enjoys and gains long life and values God over money. David was such a person. His life reflected this valuing of God. That was why he became enraged when he heard Goliath touting prideful statements such as: "This day I defy the ranks of Israel!" (1 Sam. 17:10). These words reflected arrogance, a boastful attitude that disdained not only the Israelite army, but also God since the army represented His interests. David's ire rose, and out flew his verbal comeback:

> David said to the Philistine, "You come against me with sword and spear and javelin, but I come against you in the name of the LORD Almighty, the God of the armies of Israel, whom you have defied. This day the LORD will hand you over to me, and I'll strike you down and cut off your head. Today I will give the carcasses of the Philistine army to the birds of the air and the beasts of the earth, and the whole world will know that there is a God in Israel. All those gathered here will know that it is not by sword or spear that the LORD saves; for the battle is the LORD's, and he will give all of you into our hands."
>
> (1 Sam. 17: 45–47)

A young man and his fiancée sat in my office one afternoon trying to arrive at a decision regarding their future. I posed a searching question to him: "What would you do if God made it clear to you that it was not His will for you to marry Susan?" "I would still marry her," he replied defiantly. The session was over. Because of his statement, I knew that the young man was dangerous. He had no fear of the Lord. Whenever you are willing to run one hundred miles an hour toward *your* goals and *your* purpose without consulting the Lord or without being guided by His will, you have become a spiritual outlaw. The fear of the Lord helps you comport yourself within the parameters of the laws of God. If you choose, like Goliath, to be your own boss, you will get the same outcome as Goliath—no help from God in the time of trouble. Therefore, fear the Lord, and experience the fountain of life.

3. Recognize that the Battle Belongs to the Lord

Before he raced to meet Goliath at the battle line, David said, "All those gathered here will know that it is not by sword or spear that the LORD saves; for the battle is the LORD's, and he will give all of you into our hands" (1 Sam. 17:47). David demonstrated a true reliance upon God. He knew that victory would not occur if he depended solely upon physical weapons such as swords or spears. Behind the physical duel was a spiritual reality: God was not sitting on the sidelines watching to see what the outcome was going to be. He was in the battle. David claimed that the battle *belonged* to the Lord. Not just in the battle between him and Goliath, but in the entire clash between the two armies God was involved.

To have this assistance—God fighting for you, God fighting with you—you need pure motives in keeping with someone who fears the Lord. David was not interested in making a name for himself by fighting Goliath. He was consumed with the idea that God's army should not be humiliated since the soldiers represented Him. The battle was God's, not David's. This attitude ensured God's involvement.

Isn't it odd that faith needs a battle in order to reveal its presence? Without the presence of a need, faith sits quietly without calling attention to its presence. But when you stir it, watch out because you are about to see God's power in action. One of my professors—a soft-spoken petite woman—holds her doctorate in economics from MIT (Massachusetts Institute of Technology) and a law degree from the University of Connecticut. She often told us know-it-all Ph.D. students: "Don't mess with me. I may be small but I'm fierce." The first time we saw her intellectual prowess at work, we knew that her statement was true. We backed off from any intellectual debates with her.

Faith is the same way. Arouse it and you've got a mighty fight on your hands. If you've been wondering whether you have faith, enter a battle and you'll quickly find out. When Goliath "looked David over and saw that he was only a boy, ruddy and handsome, and he despised him" (1 Sam. 17:42), he made his biggest misjudgment of his opponent. Goliath did not understand the faith factor. He saw a little boy, but he did not see the little boy's gorilla-sized faith. David was small, but he was also fierce. Goliath roused David's faith, and it was all over. David pounced on him in the name of the Lord, and in a few moments, David was holding Goliath's decapitated head in his hand as a trophy of his faith.

James took faith out of the meek and docile do-nothing realm and said, "Show me your faith without deeds [works], and I will show you my faith by what I do" (James 2:18). Don't allow fear to render you powerless in advancing toward your purpose. Enter the battle for your destiny, and see how faith in God will release His power in your life. Since your purpose is steeped in God's will, the battle is not yours; it belongs to God.

DAY 32 Points to Reflect Upon

Combating fear requires clarity that God is almighty. In walking in this reality, remember what David demonstrated before the entire army of Israel:

1. He established a proper image of God.

2. He lived with knowledge of the fear of the Lord.

3. He declared that the battle belongs to the Lord.

Learn to Connect on a Deeper Level

If you want to see brotherhood in action, if you want to see sharing, helpfulness, cooperation, and togetherness, just watch a bunch of high-school kids taking a final examination. That is the time when there is no question of race, creed, or color. There is only one question: "Who's got the answer?"

Sam Levinson

Pass the Test

In his classic book *The Pursuit of God*, A. W. Tozer wrote, "Come near to the holy men and women of the past and you will soon feel the heat of their desire after God. They mourned for Him, they prayed and wrestled and sought for Him day and night, in season and out, and when they had found Him the finding was all the sweeter for the long seeking."[1] Those men and women left their marks on history because they allowed Transforming Intervals with God to become a lifetime habit.

If you had the opportunity to spend 40 days with Jesus Christ during His earthly ministry, what would be the outcome? Would the experience result in a changed life? There is no question in my mind that 40 days with the Master changed the apostles' lives. I often wonder *what* Jesus discussed with those men in an effort to shape their destinies, their life's purpose. What were the spiritual secrets He discussed during those 40 days that the rest of us might learn only in a lifetime? To set the tone for our search for answers, let me take you to the passage where the subject of "40 days" is mentioned:

> *After his suffering, he showed himself to these men and gave many convincing proofs that he was alive. He appeared to them over a period of forty days and spoke about the kingdom of God. On one occasion, while he was eating with them, he gave them this command: "Do not leave Jerusalem, but wait for the gift my Father promised, which you have heard me speak about. For John baptized with water, but in a few days you will be baptized with the Holy Spirit."*
>
> (Acts 1:3–5)

Following His resurrection, Jesus showed Himself to His disciples for a period of 40 days. He taught them a number of transformational lessons; we'll examine these over the next four days: (1) Jesus convinced His disciples that He had overcome suffering; (2) He saw the need for the disciples to have a personal, supernatural experience; (3) they learned firsthand of God's kingdom; and (4) Jesus invited His disciples to know Him on a deeper level. These lessons so transformed the apostles that they went on to transform their world. God's purpose is to give each of us a clear objective with which we are to positively affect the world around us. Let's begin our journey into a deeper relationship with Jesus.

The Call to Maturity

Have you ever felt that God pulled a fast one when He called you into relationship with Him? I have. I have always wished—not in a negative way, but in a philosophical way—that I could have known what it meant to walk with Jesus *before* I started walking with Him. I knew about the joy and peace of salvation. And accepting God's ability to do exceedingly, abundantly, above all that I could ask or think was a no-brainer. I even knew that He totally forgave my sins. But I didn't know about carrying my cross daily. I wasn't told about the need to love those who curse you or to do unto others what you would like them to do unto you.

I grew up in New York City so my thinking was *do unto others* before *they do unto you.* I was never told that those who *reign* with Christ must also *suffer* with Him. I wanted only the reigning part, not the suffering part. Now that I'm a Christian and have read the fine print of the salvation contract, I am brutally aware of the personal need to grow in my relationship with Christ. And I have learned that gaining victory over suffering is one of the steppingstones to a more intimate life with the Master.

About six months after I invited Jesus Christ into my life to be my Savior, I came face-to-face with a trial. I was months away from completing my master's degree in civil engineering when I prayed for the Lord to give me a job in my field. None came. I didn't sweat it because with my academic qualifications, I thought it was just a matter of time. I began college at sixteen, had earned my bachelor's degree in mechanical engineering at age twenty, and was walking down the platform armed with a graduate degree in engineering and a 3.6 grade point average some eighteen months later. I thought I was hot stuff, and God knew that I thought that about myself. He was going to send me to His school, where I had to make the Dean's List with good grades in humility, compassion, prayer, openness to the Holy Spirit, and that dreaded class: accepting the will of God over your own. I protested. I wanted nothing to do with God's classroom.

Since I had no job offers in my field one month before graduation, I thought I could sweeten the pot. I prayed, *God, if You would give me a job in my field, I will give You ten percent of my income.* Still, no job offers came. A week before graduation, my prayer reflected an even sweeter offer: *God, if You give me a job in my field, I will give fifteen percent of my income to you.* I didn't realize that I had been blackmailing God. In my spiritual naiveté, I was negotiating an engineering job with God. I now know that God was trying to grow me up spiritually and that He was teaching me that having a righteous character was more important than making lots of money. Back then, money was more important to me than submitting to God or having an honorable character. Fortunately, God knew how to get the junk out of me.

The only job I was able to find was working in a spaghetti factory. No, I was not the design engineer offering my scientific perspective on increasing the engineering efficiency of plant operations. I was an assembly line worker. I stood on a thirty-foot-high platform and put raw spaghetti in a chute so that it could be boxed at the other end. Imagine that. To outsiders, I was the hotshot engineer who graduated with a full academic scholarship from the prestigious Stevens Institute of Technology. But, to God, I was the son who had a problem with pride and needed to be adjusted, big time.

God's curriculum of discipline worked. He used the spaghetti factory job and other similar jobs over a six-month period to help me see myself and succumb to the maturity process He outlined. I would love to tell you that after twenty-two years of walking with

Jesus, I have fully arrived. If I did, I would be lying. He has other classroom experiences for me that I am not even aware I need. This is part of the process of spiritual maturity. God works through many awkward circumstances, some painful, some easy and joyous, to get us to the place where we can convey to others that Jesus is alive.

Adult Babies Are Not Cute

We cannot remain spiritual babies, even though the idea seems appealing. Growing up is part of life. Nowadays, teenagers fear growing up. They want to stay teenagers. I'll bet the limited responsibility, the limited expectations, the limited challenges, and the limited bills have a lot to do with it. When my older daughter turned eighteen, she was depressed for a few days. I said, "Sweetheart, what's wrong?" Danielle's response: "Dad, I don't want to grow up."

Following His victory over suffering, Jesus gave many convincing proofs that He was alive. His suffering was not due to spiritual immaturity or poor choices. Jesus' suffering was substitutionary. He suffered to pay the debt we owed God. Jesus suffered on the cross to vicariously pay for our sins. Thus, through His death, burial, and resurrection, we have been granted the right to access God's salvation and a new life. In His postresurrected state, He appeared to the apostles for 40 days to convince them that He was successful over death, sin, and suffering. This testimony is also an encouragement, declaring that we, too, can overcome suffering through His power.

Overcoming suffering is one factor in the spiritual growth equation. You cannot grow up unless you overcome something. In my spaghetti factory days, my stubbornness against growing spiritually caused God to turn up the fire of trials, which made me learn about the strict teacher of suffering. I do not believe that God calls us to suffering, but I do know that God can use the suffering we sometimes experience in this fallen world to produce the character qualities and overall life purpose He desires us to attain.

James writes:

> *Consider it pure joy, my brothers, whenever you face trials of many kinds, because you know that the testing of your faith develops perseverance. Perseverance must finish its work so that you may be mature and complete, not lacking anything.*
>
> (James 1:2–4)

James tells us that our attitude when facing trials—testing ordained of God—should be one of joy, especially since perseverance is going to be the fruit produced in our time of suffering. Then our perseverance will help bring about our maturity and completeness.

When you consider the pain that a grain of sand causes an oyster, you must focus on the fruit of the pain—a pearl. In a similar way, our pain caused by the suffering will produce a pearl in our lives. Take a trip down to the local jewelry store, and discover the cost of a nice cultured pearl. It will put a dent in your wallet. But in God's economy, He is making you the pearl.

Let's go back to the same passage in the book of James, but this time in the words of the modern translation by J. B. Phillips, the renowned New Testament Greek scholar:

> *When all kinds of trials and temptations crowd into your lives, my brothers, don't resent them as intruders, but welcome them as friends! Realize that they come to test your faith and to produce in you the quality of endurance. But let the process go on until that endurance is fully developed, and you will find you have become men of mature character, men of integrity with no weak spots.*[2]
>
> (James 1:2–4)

Phillips advises you to treat trials not as intruders but as friends. What a difference in perspective! An intruder is an unwanted guest, someone who has crashed the party of your life. This is one way to view trials and suffering. The flip side is for you to treat a trial as a friend, a wanted houseguest, someone who has an open invitation into your life. This perspective does not suggest that you seek a trial; that would make you a masochist. Welcoming trials as friends, however, tests your faith in order to produce the endurance needed to finish the spiritual race. God knows that you need endurance to perfect your life's purpose. This reality should make you say, "C'mon over, trials ... I mean friends ... I'm serving lobster tonight."

When Jesus appeared to the apostles after His victory over the suffering of the cross, He offered them proof that He had completed His course. He was successful over death and the grave through His bodily resurrection. The purpose of Christ to live a sin-free life, die a sinless death, and rise again from the dead was now complete. His victory over suffering armed the apostles with the needed testimony that Jesus died for our sins. We have been forgiven. All is well with God. Heaven will be our home. The way has been paved. Jesus died for their sins and was resurrected to seal their salvation. The good news was the hot story then and is still the hot story today.

DAY 33 Points to Reflect Upon

Oftentimes our purpose must emerge from the bed of suffering. Following Jesus' suffering of the cross, He gave many convincing proofs that He was alive after He was resurrected. How can your life benefit from the spiritual development produced by suffering?

1. In what areas of your life is God calling you to mature spiritually?

2. Are you afraid to grow up spiritually?

3. Why should you regard suffering as a friend instead of an intruder in your life?

DAY 34

Welcome Supernatural Experiences

D id you ever make excuses to avoid going to church when you were not a believer in Jesus? I had a whole list of excuses I could use whenever someone invited me to church. I was a cynical college student who took pride in my philosophical position as a scientific atheist. Little did I know that God was waiting to show me a few things.

When I was finally roped into attending church, I took my seat toward the rear. About three hundred people were in attendance. The moment worship began I thought: *This certainly is different from the little neighborhood church I attended while I was growing up.* Musicians played the clarinet, flute, congas, and saxophone, orchestrated with drums and piano. People sang loudly and joyously.

I was blown away. But then I started thinking it must certainly be a cult. I had no experience with a church where people actually believed that Jesus Christ changes lives and that He ought to be worshiped exuberantly. As the preacher mounted the platform to talk about God, I was still apprehensive. About fifteen minutes into his sermon I said to myself: *If I ever get saved* (from hanging around a few Christians on campus, I was aware of their language), *I would never go to this church. I would go to a church that is a bit more intellectual.* The moment I finished thinking that thought, the preacher stopped in the middle of his message, pointed in my direction, and said, "It doesn't matter what your educational level is! Here we preach the Word of God so that a baby can understand." I got scared. I said to myself: *I will never think in church again.*

Dr. Jack Deere, former associate professor of Old Testament at

Dallas Theological Seminary, calls this phenomenon being "surprised by God."[1] I agree. That Sunday, God surprised me by letting me know that He listens to my every thought. Although I did not give my life to Christ that day, I became acutely aware that supernatural things are natural and ordinary with God.

To help the apostles discover their purpose to be heralds of the good news, Jesus hung out with them and offered convincing proofs that He was alive. The text reads:

> *After his suffering, he showed himself to these men and gave many convincing proofs that he was alive. He appeared to them over a period of forty days and spoke about the kingdom of God. On one occasion, while he was eating with them, he gave them this command: "Do not leave Jerusalem, but wait for the gift my Father promised, which you have heard me speak about. For John baptized with water, but in a few days you will be baptized with the Holy Spirit."*
>
> (Acts 1:3–5)

The proofs He offered were invaluable to their ability to preach the message of salvation. Convincing them was another way of solidifying their perspective that God's plan of freeing humanity from the trap of sin through the atoning death of His Son was complete. The apostles were empowered by witnessing the greatest miracle of their lives following their own salvation—the resurrected Son of God speaking with them for 40 days. Exposing them to the supernatural was a part of God's plan to secure their purpose.

Convincing proofs are not limited to miraculous feats of healing; they extend to making persuasive arguments that address the probing questions people frequently ask about God. The apostles were being trained over the course of 40 days to provide solid answers to troubling philosophical and religious questions that often become sticking points to people seeking their way to God. That was why the preaching of Peter and John was so amazing to the religious scholars of their day: "When they saw the courage of Peter and John and realized that they were unschooled, ordinary men, they were astonished and they took note that these men had been with Jesus" (Acts 4:13).

Stabilizing the Foundation

A group of young college students from some of the top schools in the nation were able to land a summer job selling Bibles door to door. Among the Harvard, Yale, and Princeton students was a guy who seemed like a misfit because he was from a no-name junior college. After several weeks of training, the students were shipped out to different neighborhoods to sell Bibles. Weeks later, they returned to the company for an evaluation and assessment. The young man from the junior college had sold five times as many Bibles as all of his counterparts. They were angry because he was not as bright as they were, and on top of that, he stuttered. When the boss evaluated everyone's sales, he finally offered this advice. "Everybody," he said, "listen up. Since Fred has sold far more Bibles than all of you, I want Fred to tell you how to do it."

Fred had their undivided attention. "Well," he stammered, "when I go to a . . . a . . . house . . . I . . . I ring the . . . the . . . the doorbell. And I . . . I . . . ask them . . . if the . . . the . . . they want to buy a case of Bibles or they want me to . . . to . . . read one to them."

When the boss heard Fred's approach he knew it couldn't work for the rest of the group. They needed a more stable foundation for the world of sales. Likewise, to attain your purpose, you need a supernatural encounter with God that cements His direction for your life. A person with an argument is always at a disadvantage to a person with an experience. Peter and the other early apostles could not be discouraged from carrying out their purpose of preaching Christ to the world. They had witnessed too much. They had experienced the supernatural power of God, and they knew the sweetness of being with Jesus during private moments. How could they become discouraged by hardships, persecutions, money challenges, or rejection from people? A supernatural encounter with Jesus empowered them to carry out their mission.

The Power of Experience

When Jesus decided to allow a 40-day Transforming Interval to occur with His disciples, He was demonstrating the power of experience. The men were privileged to have a supernatural encounter with Christ after His suffering. Why those men? They had proven their willingness to have their lives disrupted, adjusted, changed, and rearranged for the primacy of doing God's will. They had given up their occupations and other important matters to walk with Jesus. And they were poised to carry out new marching orders. They were ready to go into all the earth as witnesses of God's supernatural love and forgiveness.

I believe that another reason why Jesus revealed Himself to them supernaturally is that the power of their ministries was directly related to the reality of Christ to them. Show me someone who is ambivalent about the reality of God, His love, His power, and His willingness to change lives, and I will show you someone who gets discouraged easily, changes his purpose every time a roadblock gets in his way, or cannot muster up enough faith to shoo a fly off a kitchen table. Such a person has never had a supernatural encounter with the living God.

I challenge you to supernaturally encounter Christ by spending time with Him so that He becomes more real to you than your own life. This can happen. This should happen. If a few misguided Middle Eastern Muslim clerics (contrary to the Koran or the wider body of Muslims) can convince young men that they will receive seventy virgins after death as a reward for strapping explosives to their bodies, detonating them, and taking as many people with them into eternity as possible as an honorable act to Allah, why aren't we Christians sold out to God? God does not ask us to do anything that is unrighteous, disrespectful of other people's right to life, or dishonoring of our bodies. He simply asks us to live in a way that reflects total commitment to His purpose for our lives.

One day a chicken and a pig got together in the barn to try to think of a way to honor their master. The farmer was so loving and kind toward them that they wanted to do something nice to show their appreciation. The chicken said, "Let's make him breakfast." The pig said, "Great idea. What do you have in mind?" The chicken thought for a moment and then suggested, "Let's make him bacon and eggs." The pig said, "For you this is a sacrifice, but for me it means total commitment."

In his bestselling book *The Purpose-Driven Life*, Rick Warren writes, "It's time to settle this issue. *Who* are you going to live for— yourself or God? You may hesitate, wondering whether you will have the strength to live for God. Don't worry. God will give you what you need if you will just make the choice to live for him."[2] The question is: Are you going to relax in your relationship with God and do nothing? Or are you going to get fired up for the purpose of Christ through supernatural experiences of intimacy with Him and accomplish His will for your life and the world around you? Go for it!

DAY 34 Points to Reflect Upon

To live a victorious life that honors God and aids in perfecting your purpose, you need to have supernatural experiences with Him. Jesus spent 40 days with His apostles, giving them many convincing proofs that He was alive.

1. Ask God to cement His supernatural presence in your life.

2. What experience do you have with Christ that refutes an unbeliever's argument against the love of God?

3. Read Psalm 23 and ask yourself: How well am I letting God shepherd me?

Seek the Kingdom of God

I have two teenage daughters, and given the nature of our broken society, Marlinda and I have prayed for their moral success and for God's leadership in selecting their future mates. To keep my sanity, I have developed three simple rules for dating my daughters. I offer this cautionary advice to young men:[1]

Rule #1: The following places are not appropriate for a date with my daughter: Places where there are beds, sofas, or anything softer than a wooden stool. Places where there are no parents, policemen, or nuns within eyesight. Places where there is darkness. Places where there is dancing, holding hands, or happiness. Places where the ambient temperature is warm enough to induce my daughter to wear shorts, tank tops, midriff T-shirts, or anything other than overalls, a sweater, and a goose down parka zipped up to her throat. Movies with a strong romantic or sexual theme are to be avoided; movies which feature chainsaws are okay. Hockey games are okay. Old folks homes are better.

Rule #2: Do not lie to me. I may appear to be a potbellied, balding, middle-aged, dimwitted has-been. But on issues relating to my daughter, I am the all-knowing, merciless god of your universe. If I ask you where you are going and with whom, you have one chance to tell me the truth, the whole truth, and nothing but the truth. I have a shotgun, a shovel, and five acres behind the house. Do not trifle with me.

Rule #3: Be afraid. Be very afraid. It takes very little for me to mistake the sound of your car in the driveway for a chopper coming in over a rice paddy near Hanoi. When my Agent Orange starts acting up, the voices in my head frequently tell me to clean the guns, as I wait for you to bring my daughter home. As soon as you pull into the driveway you should exit your car with both hands in plain sight. Speak the perimeter password, announce in a clear voice that you have brought my daughter home safely and early, then return to your car— there is no need for you to come inside. The camouflaged face at the window is mine.

My rules offer a little humor, but every father or mother feels the same way. The world in which we live needs people who have a deep conviction of how society is to function based on their relationship with Jesus Christ. Jesus instilled this conviction in His apostles during the 40 days following His resurrection when He spoke to them about the kingdom of God.

God has wired me in such a way that I often think about society and its values. The topics that consume my thoughts center on such questions as: How is Christianity influencing the world in which we live? Is God concerned about the culture of the day? Is today's culture concerned about God? These concerns involve shaping society and its values, and finding your place in the world in which we live.

Jesus inaugurated the message of God's kingdom. Over the course of 40 days, a Transforming Interval occurred for the apostles who were charged to become His witnesses to the world (Acts 1:8) *after* they understood the kingdom of God.

After his suffering, he showed himself to these men and gave many convincing proofs that he was alive. He appeared to them over a period of forty days and spoke about the kingdom of God. On one occasion, while he was eating with them, he gave them this command: "Do not leave Jerusalem, but wait for the gift my Father promised, which you have heard me speak about. For John baptized with water, but in a few days you will be baptized with the Holy Spirit."

(Acts 1:3–5)

What Is the Kingdom of God?

Private conversations are usually the ones that transform you. The importance of the kingdom of God was privately conveyed to these apostolic men. The *kingdom of God* refers to the sovereign rule of God in the lives of people and the society.

1. Jesus Inaugurated the Kingdom

Jesus' birth established clearly that He was the King over the kingdom that Isaiah and other Old Testament prophets foretold (Isa. 9:6–7). Jesus inaugurated this kingdom that the Bible refers to as the kingdom of God (Mark 4:30); the kingdom of heaven (Matt. 13:31), which is also named the kingdom of Christ (Eph. 5:5). The kingdom was launched when Jesus declared, "I must preach the kingdom of God to other cities also: for therefore am I sent" (Luke 4:43, KJV).

2. Entrance into the Kingdom Occurs Through an Experience

Entrance into the kingdom of God happens via the salvation experience called the new birth. As He was teaching, Jesus said to the crowd, "I tell you the truth, the tax collectors and the prostitutes are entering the kingdom of God ahead of you" (Matt. 21:31). Before the birth of Jesus and His subsequent declaration that the kingdom of God was at hand, the Jewish people thought that the kingdom of God belonged exclusively to them as a nation. They thought the coming Messiah would overthrow the Greek and Roman government, reestablish Israel's autonomy as a nation, and create a dominion internationally and continuously.

Jesus was teaching about a kingdom in which people with morally and ethically broken lives could be forgiven and restored to a place of value and the worship of God. The reformer John Calvin commented that "by the kingdom of God which he [Jesus] declared to be at hand, he meant forgiveness of sins, salvation, life, and every other blessing which we obtain in Christ."[2] That was why Jesus declared that being born again was the basis of *seeing* and *entering* into the kingdom of God (John 3:3–5).

Why Is the Kingdom of God So Important?

The kingdom of God is important because it provides a common platform where all kinds of people can find justice, fair treatment, common respect, and equal opportunity from the King of the kingdom. Whether you are poor, rich, old, young, male, female, black, or white, the kingdom of God welcomes you into all of its blessings and promises. The world cries for this model. However, through various political and government models such as capitalism, communism, socialism, or even a monarchial state, we are still unable to duplicate the equitable treatment of human beings, businesses, environment, and animal values that the new birth experience and obedience to the laws of the kingdom of God deliver.

1. The Kingdom of God Grows in Influence

The importance of the kingdom of God can be summed up best through Jesus' parable of the mustard seed.

> *He said, "What shall we say the kingdom of God is like, or what parable shall we use to describe it? It is like a mustard seed, which is the smallest seed you plant in the ground. Yet when planted, it grows and becomes the largest of all garden plants, with such big branches that the birds of the air can perch in its shade."*
>
> (Mark 4:30–32)

A parable is an earthly story with a heavenly meaning. To be more technical, it is a form of speech called *rhetoric*—a speech that's solely intended to persuade the listener. Politicians make this kind of speech when they are campaigning for office, and ministers use it when they are delivering their sermons. Politicians want votes while ministers want disciples for the Lord. Jesus indicated that even though the mustard seed is small when it is planted, it grows to become the largest of the garden plants. Its size and strength are such that birds of the air can perch comfortably on its branches and in its shade.

The metaphor of the mustard seed and the birds symbolizes the kingdom of God and people. The tree is full and strong; so is the kingdom of God. Just as birds perch on its branches and experience comfort from its shade, people can come into the kingdom of God through the new birth and find rest and peace for their lives. With this parable Jesus helped the apostles understand that the kingdom of God was to have a powerful influence upon the lives of the people who entered it and this influence must transform their society. Real transformation happens when the citizens of the kingdom of God allow its power to affect change in every sector of their society.

2. Purpose and the Kingdom of God

Jesus calls us to "seek first his kingdom and his righteousness, and all these things will be given to you as well" (Matt. 6:33). This command to seek first the kingdom and God's righteousness is about knowing the priority of personal salvation and the lifestyle this kingdom requires. When you adhere to this priority, God will give you the things you need in order to live successfully in the world—clothing, shelter, money, the discovery and perfecting of your purpose. The knowledge and pursuit of the King's business, along with championing the values and the goals of His kingdom, must become your first priority. The King will make note of that focus and reward you with all the personal things you secretly desire so that you will be thoroughly equipped to walk in His will.

I am sure that you are familiar with the wealth of the late John D. Rockefeller Sr. His testimony, however, brings a perspective to what it means to seek first the kingdom of God, at least its principle of tithing—giving 10 percent of your income to the Lord's work. Rockefeller said,

> "Yes, I tithe, and I would like to tell you how it all came about. I had to begin work as a small boy to help support my mother. My first wages amounted to $1.50 per week. The first week after I went to work, I took the $1.50 home to my mother and she held the money in her lap and explained to me that she would be happy if I would give a tenth of it to the Lord. I did, and from that week until this day I have tithed every dollar God has entrusted to me. And I want to say, if I had not tithed the first dollar I made I would not have tithed the first million dollars I made. Tell your readers to train the children to tithe, and they will grow up to be faithful stewards of the Lord."[3]

DAY 35 Points to Reflect Upon

Jesus taught the apostles about the kingdom of God. This subject was important enough to be one of His postresurrection topics with the key leaders who would later champion the message of God's love to the world.

1. The *kingdom of God* refers to the sovereign rule of God in the lives of people and the society and realm in which this rule occurs.

2. In what way can you extend the kingdom of God and/or its values to your life (this includes your job, family, church, school, etc.)?

3. Memorize this powerful verse that Jesus spoke: "Seek first his kingdom and his righteousness, and all these things will be given to you as well" (Matt. 6:33).

DAY **36**

Enjoy Intimacy with God

S ongs have a way of communicating our feelings when other modes of communication can't capture the bottled up emotions. When I first heard the song "Lord, I Want to Touch Your Heart" by the New Zealand group known as the Parachute Band, I instantly became addicted to hearing it. Even reading the words communicates volumes about the cry of a heart that is desperate to grow in a deeper relationship with Jesus Christ.

I wish I knew the story that led to the composing of this song. My wife is a recording artist who has composed many worship songs that usher the worshiper into the presence of God. It is not unusual to find her in her study with her face buried in the carpet. She weeps before the Lord in prayer as she aches to know Him more intimately. If I wasn't secure in my relationship with my wife and my walk with the Lord, I would be moved to jealousy at seeing Marlinda declaring her undying affection to Christ. Whenever I happen to enter her study unannounced and find her in that worshipful posture, I slowly back out of the room, embarrassed that I almost interrupted a sacred moment.

Many of Marlinda's songs were birthed out of such passionate moments. Something similar may have happened to the Parachute Band as the song "Lord, I Want to Touch Your Heart" was penned. When they came to our church for a concert, you can believe that was one of the songs I requested them to share.

When Jesus met with His disciples over a 40-day period, one of His concerns was ensuring that upon His departure to heaven, they would have the spiritual tools needed to dig a deeper relationship with Him.

> *After his suffering, he showed himself to these men and gave many convincing proofs that he was alive. He appeared to them over a period of forty days and spoke about the kingdom of God. On one occasion, while he was eating with them, he gave them this command: "Do not leave Jerusalem, but wait for the gift my Father promised, which you have heard me speak about. For John baptized with water, but in a few days you will be baptized with the Holy Spirit."*
>
> (Acts 1:3–5)

Witnesses of God's Love

Jesus recognized that the apostles would not fulfill their purpose to herald the good news without the power of the Holy Spirit. In fact, Jesus went on to say, "You will receive power when the Holy Spirit comes on you; and you will be my witnesses in Jerusalem, and in all Judea and Samaria, and to the ends of the earth" (Acts 1:8). Notwithstanding all the functions of the Holy Spirit, including confronting, teaching, leading, guiding, and convicting us of sin (John 14:15–19; 16:12–15), He is also the One who empowers us to execute our life's purpose of honoring God.

In Acts 1:8, Jesus used the word *power*, which is the Greek word *dunamis* from which stems the English word *dynamite*. *Dunamis* is also to be translated as "miraculous power and ability that is imparted by the Holy Spirit." The word *witness* used in the verse is the Greek word *martus*, and it means "one who has information or knowledge of something."[1] The word is also defined as "martyr," representing that their witness to Jesus became the cause of death.

Stephen became the first martyr of the church (Acts 7:54–8:1). He was later followed into eternity by other bold martyrs, such as William Tyndale. By 1526, Tyndale had translated the New Testament into English and published it and then began on the Old Testament, adding comments to each book. The bishop of London and other official church leaders opposed Tyndale, and his books were publicly burned. In the intriguing book *Foxe's Christian Martyrs of the World*, the author provides this account of Tyndale's final moments:

> *Tyndale was eventually captured by the emperor in Antwerp, his books were all seized, and he was imprisoned for a year and a half before being condemned under the emperor's decree of Augsburgh. He was tied to the stake, strangled, and burned in Vilvorden in 1536, dying with these words: "Lord! Open the King of England's eyes!"*[2]

Jesus was not telling His apostles to become martyrs; rather, He was indicating that their intimacy with and commitment to the power of the Holy Spirit would enable them to do so, should the need arise. We, too, need this power in our lives. Living in a society in which it is unpopular to be a practicing Christian, we need the ability to witness of God's love to others. And, we know how many of our coworkers, family members, and people in the general population of society need the salvation that Christ offers. If we are empowered to witness of God's love, there is a greater probability that people will listen to us and our witness will be compelling if the power of the Holy Spirit charges it.

To witness of God's love, befriend someone and casually interject what Jesus has done in your life. Don't preach. Tell him or her in a caring way why Jesus is so important to you. Answer unasked questions about how accepting Jesus is different from becoming religious, and how becoming born again is an experience versus a nice idea. Go for it! Tell someone about what Christ has done in you.

Witnesses of God's Spirit

Jesus told His disciples: "Do not leave Jerusalem, but wait for the gift my Father promised, which you have heard me speak about. For John baptized with water, but in a few days you will be baptized with the Holy Spirit" (Acts 1:4–5). Over the centuries, there have been many heated debates on the subject of the baptism of the Holy Spirit. Without getting into that controversy here, five items are quite clear on the subject based on Acts 1:8.

1. Jesus taught that we needed the baptism of the Holy Spirit to be effective in witnessing God's love to the world around us.

2. The baptism of the Holy Spirit is a subsequent experience to salvation. The apostles had already been born again. They needed the empowering of the Spirit to execute the desires of God.

3. The baptism of the Holy Spirit is a free gift available to every believer in Jesus.

4. Clear evidence that you have received the baptism of the Holy Spirit is that you are able to powerfully share/witness your faith.

5. We are to be witnesses of the activities of the Holy Spirit in each other's life and in the world around us.

Baptize means "to immerse"; thus, the baptism of the Holy Spirit is to be immersed into the Holy Spirit or to experience the *coming upon* by the Spirit. No matter what measure of spiritual success you have experienced to date, you need the baptism of the Holy Spirit. The key to receiving this gift is to do what the apostles were instructed to do: they waited in Jerusalem. This waiting speaks of the preparation of the heart through prayer (Acts 1:14). The baptism is a free gift, not given based on merit, longevity in the family of God, or personal interpretation of one's level of holiness. We can never earn this gift by our good works or good living. Nothing we have is sufficient or can deem us worthy of God's gifts, apart from Jesus Christ, the Author of our faith. God gives us gifts because doing so gives Him pleasure.

As the apostles and other disciples totaling 120 people waited on God in prayer, the Bible captures the outcome:

When the day of Pentecost came, they were all together in one place. Suddenly a sound like the blowing of a violent wind came from heaven and filled the whole house where they were sitting. They saw what seemed to be tongues of fire that separated and came to rest on

each of them. All of them were filled with the Holy Spirit and began
to speak in other tongues as the Spirit enabled them.

(Acts 2:1–4)

Quite obviously, the dynamics of the Holy Spirit baptism lack this fanfare in our day. But the same principle is true: an atmosphere of prayer is the best environment for receiving the baptism of the Holy Spirit. I would like you to get in a quiet place right now so that you can focus on prayer without any distractions. Then pray this prayer:

Dear Lord, I want to receive the gift of the baptism of the Holy Spirit.
I am eager to serve You with my all heart, and I want to be fully
equipped to advance Your will in the earth, in Jesus' name. Amen.

You may not hear the sound of a violent wind, but you can discern the coming of the Holy Spirit upon your life in a new way after you've prayed. Expect the Holy Spirit to come upon you in such a way that you will have greater boldness and conviction to witness of God's love to others.

DAY 36 Points to Reflect Upon

Jesus prepared the apostles to seek a deeper relationship with Him by witnessing His love to others and by experiencing the baptism of the Holy Spirit. You must do the same.

1. What worship song do you think of that encourages you to grow in a deeper way with the Lord?

2. Witness to God's love with a friend or a family member this week.

3. Invite the Holy Spirit to fill your life with His power by making you a bolder witness for God.

Shout from the Housetop

You're here to be light, bringing out the God-colors in the world. God is not a secret to be kept. We're going public with this, as public as a city on a hill. If I make you light-bearers, you don't think I'm going to hide you under a bucket, do you? I'm putting you on a light stand. Now that I've put you there on a hilltop, on a light stand—shine! Keep open house; be generous with your lives. By opening up to others, you'll prompt people to open up with God, this generous Father in heaven.

Matthew 5:14–17, The Message

DAY 37

Dig for Gold

Remember the Sunday school lesson we've all been taught about Jonah—the man who was swallowed alive by a big fish? Once redirected to his original mission, Jonah found himself proclaiming God's word to a sinful community, telling the people that they had only 40 days to repent or face destruction. Sharing God's message demonstrated the four habits that we will explore over the next four days: (1) helping people make lifelong adjustments; (2) caring for others with a sense of urgency; (3) helping others discover their hindrances to faith, success, and godly obedience; and (4) learning how to finish well.

Dig for Gold, Not for Dirt

Helping other people make lifelong adjustments by adopting key habits is one of the lessons we can learn from Jonah's 40-day Transforming Interval. The prophet Jonah struggled with helping people because he wanted God to punish them for their sinfulness. Jonah could not see that sharing his life with others enabled him to fulfill his purpose as a prophet. Prophets are God's messengers who encourage people to dig for the gold in their lives, not for dirt. Whenever you're mining for gold, there is always a lot of dirt. But the goal is not the dirt; the goal is the gold. To understand God's solution for correcting the many excuses of the misguided prophet, let's review the events surrounding Jonah's 40-day Transforming Interval.

- Instead of going to Nineveh, Jonah went in the opposite direction, some eight hundred miles away to Tarshish. The prophet disobeyed God's clear directive because he did not really want the Ninevites to repent. Nineveh was the capital city of Assyria, which was hostile toward Israel. The Ninevites were known for their blatant prostitution, murder, cruelty and plundering during war, and other acts of social wickedness.

- In rebellion against God, Jonah ended up on a ship headed to Tarshish. A storm arose in connection with the prophet's disobedience, and the men on the ship decided to throw him overboard. Once he was overboard, the storm ceased, and the ship sailed on in peace. After a large fish swallowed Jonah, he realized his error and repented to the Lord. In response, God allowed the fish to regurgitate the prophet onto dry land.

- Jonah went to Nineveh and proclaimed, "Forty more days and Nineveh will be overturned" (Jon. 3:4). The Ninevites believed God's word, and everyone—from the king to the peasants—repented with prayer and fasting. God changed His mind and suspended the destruction that He had scheduled against the more than 120,000 people living in Nineveh.

- Jonah became angry because of God's gracious response of forgiveness. God used the prophet's anger to teach him a lesson on how to care for people who were unaware that they needed spiritual care and attention.

The toughest thing to do is to help someone who does not see that he needs help. God knew how to get through to Jonah, who was blinded by his prejudice against the Ninevites. What kind of a prophet—spokesperson for God—would you be if you disliked sharing God's message with certain people? Or what if you liked sharing God's message with only *your kind* of people? Jonah wanted to speak with good sinners, polite agnostics, people who sinned discreetly and demonstrated good manners while doing it. He wanted no part of the moral dirt that was publicly displayed by the

Ninevites. God saw things differently, and He was going to teach His prophet how to find the moral gold in the Ninevites.

God's purpose was for Jonah to be a messenger who was not prejudiced in the discharge of his duties and purpose. Since the Ninevites were notorious for their prostitution, victimization, murders, and witchcraft (Nah. 3:1–4), the prophet wanted no part of helping them correct their lifestyles. But Jonah had to learn that helping people make positive changes is part of living a life guided by God's purpose.

Has God placed some people in your life so that you can show them the right way to live, the right way to perfect their purpose, or even the right way to relate to God? Could it be that the very ones who seem so objectionable to you are your assignment?

I remember my second engineering job following graduate school. For the first thirty days, my coworker Frank walked past my desk never saying hello or even noticing that I was the new environmental engineer. Although he was twenty years my senior and was a principal in the firm, his daily behavior angered me. I should not have taken it personally, since he gave everyone else the cold treatment, but I did. I also noticed that no one bothered Frank as he worked tirelessly day after day with his head buried in engineering drawings and project notebooks. At the end of thirty days, he walked over to my desk and tersely greeted me, asking me to join him in the conference room. There he gave me an assignment while speaking gruffly. His tone further annoyed me, but I said nothing.

After several such meetings over the next couple of weeks, I was too annoyed to keep biting my tongue. I decided to confront him from the perspective that I was a "man of God" and his style offended me. One morning I walked over to Frank's work area and said that I would like to speak with him privately about a matter. Without looking up from his desk he said to me, "Maybe this afternoon when I'm not too busy." I went back to my desk, convinced that we would not have a meeting.

But, sure enough, he approached me in the afternoon and said, "Let's go to the conference room and talk." There I mustered up the courage to respectfully explain to Frank that the way he spoke to me was offensive. I used the argument that as a man of God, I wanted to receive a different tone of communication from him. (I was young in my faith and young in my vocation; I knew no other language to use than "man of God.") To my surprise, Frank apologized and began to ask me questions about the Lord. We struck up a friendship, and he took me along on assignments with him. He also probed me in an effort to examine the Christian faith. No one else in the firm received this friendly treatment from Frank. Through that lesson, I learned that God may send people your way who may not act like *your* kind of person, but you must become skilled at digging for the gold while overlooking the dirt.

Submission Versus Obedience

Having encouragement from God—and after being swallowed by a big fish—Jonah decided to go to Ninevah and preach against the people's wickedness. Although Jonah was walking in obedience, he was not walking in submission. The prophet was obedient when he shared God's message of their impending destruction. But his sudden anger in response to their repentance and God's forgiveness revealed his problem with submission. Obedience and submission are two entirely different things. We need both to care for people the way God wants us to care for them. Let me illustrate the difference.

A mother goes shopping accompanied by her five-year-old son, Freddy. Freddy loves to be his own boss. After a few minutes, he begins to run around the store. His mother walks over to him and gently says, "Freddy, stop this. Please sit down." Yet Freddy ignores her and keeps touching things. She fires off a second request: "Freddy, sit down and stop touching things." Freddy remains standing and touches all the objects in his reach. Finally, the mom says, "Freddy, if you don't sit down, the moment we get home you're going to get a spanking." At that, Freddy sits down and mutters this reply: "Mom, I may be sitting down on the outside, but I'm standing up on the inside." Freddy sits in obedience, but he isn't sitting in submission.

Obedience has to do with external behavior, while submission has to do with the internal disposition of the heart. God is more concerned with our attitude, our inner disposition of the heart, than with our physical actions. The Bible states, "The LORD does not look at the things man looks at. Man looks at the outward appearance, but the LORD looks at the heart" (1 Sam. 16:7). The lesson God wanted to teach Jonah was that he worked for God. Jonah should have freely submitted to serving people the way God wanted him to serve, but Jonah wanted no part of it.

Excuses Are Common

When I don't want to do something, I can come up with a million excuses about why I shouldn't do it. Jonah was no different. But turning people from the error of their ways to serve Christ is an awesome goal for any of us. James says, "Remember this: Whoever turns a sinner from the error of his way will save him from death and cover over a multitude of sins" (5:20). Not only was Jonah to know the joy of seeing sinners repent and walk uprightly before God, but he was to function as a partner with God in sacred work—evangelism.

If you are going to perfect your life's purpose, your strategy should include turning people from a lifestyle of waywardness, sinfulness, or purposelessness to one of alignment with God's plan. Furthermore, it is God's desire for you to love your neighbor as you love yourself (Luke 10:27).

One of my life's purposes is helping people discover and hone their leadership abilities. Although I personally give money to combat AIDS, poverty, and other humanitarian ills in developing countries, I also host leadership training seminars in these countries. I recognize that giving money is usually an easy way for us to feel that we've done our good deed for the day. But it is far more of an effort and a transforming action to use our purpose to serve the needs of people within our span of care.

In his book *Companion to the Poor*, wealthy New Zealander Viv Grigg went to live among the poorest of the poor in the Philippines in pursuit of an answer to the question: Why did Jesus say, "Blessed are the poor" (Matt. 5:3)? There in Tatalon, Philippines, he prayed:

How do you bring a whole city to the light? How can you rescue three million squatters and slum dwellers?

As I prayed, a beautiful gold and white creature scurried along some smoke-blackened rafters of my new house. It was a well-fed rat, sleek and cunning. I watched him silently, intrigued and curious. My thoughts drifted to two pieces of wood used many centuries before. The cross of Christ was surely made of the same rough wood as this squatter home. Within the inner recesses of my spirit God seemed to be speaking—directly, personally:

"You'll save them by carrying my cross. It is an instrument of death. You must die to yourself in order to be a servant of this people."[1]

As Viv Grigg did, look for a question among the concerns of God, and pour out your life's purpose in finding an answer that positively affects society.

DAY 37 Points to Reflect Upon

Jonah struggled with helping a certain group of people because he focused on the dirt in their lives rather than the gold. How are you mining the gold in the people around you?

1. Are you digging for gold or dirt when the people in your family are mentioned?

2. Are you walking in outward obedience or inward submission to God's plan for your life?

3. Contemplate and conquer the excuses you may have been using to hinder full submission to God's plan for your life to help someone else embrace a positive lifelong habit.

DAY 38

Care for Others with a Sense of Urgency

Whenever I get urgent e-mails, I open them with a bit of skepticism. Although I know the person sending the e-mail, I can't shake the thought: *What is so urgent?* Ninety percent of the time, the message is no more urgent than any other. To mark something as urgent when it is not shows how simplistic we humans can be. Or perhaps this exaggerated sense of urgency is just part of twenty-first century American culture.

A false sense of urgency can quickly erode the need for the *true* urgency required for the care of the souls of spiritually lost people. During the period preceding Jonah's 40-day Transforming Interval, the prophet had to be reprimanded for his lack of urgency in calling the Ninevites to repentance. Thereafter the Scripture declared,

> *Jonah obeyed the word of the LORD and went to Nineveh. Now Nineveh was a very important city—a visit required three days. On the first day, Jonah started into the city. He proclaimed: "Forty more days and Nineveh will be overturned." The Ninevites believed God. They declared a fast, and all of them, from the greatest to the least, put on sackcloth.*
>
> (Jon. 3:3–5)

What's the Urgency?

The Ninevites were a spiritually bankrupt people who displayed their bankruptcy in wickedness (Jon. 1:2). Two realities created a sense of urgency for the message of repentance to be preached in Nineveh. First, God hated their wickedness, which precipitated His urgent message to Jonah, "Go to the great city of Nineveh and preach against it, because its wickedness has come up before me" (Jon. 1:2). If the people's wickedness persisted, God would have no other alternative but to destroy them. Second, God loved the Ninevites and did not want them to perish. He wanted them to turn from their evil ways (Jon. 3:10; 4:2). God's urgent plea for change caused Him to summon the prophet to go to Nineveh. When Jonah fled to Tarshish, the Lord again moved with urgency and sent a "great wind on the sea, and such a violent storm" (Jon. 1:4) in an effort to have the prophet turn around. God's urgency resulted in Jonah's being thrown overboard by the sailors who discerned that his disobedience had precipitated the hazardous weather.

God's continued expression of urgency in wanting to deliver the call to repentance caused a great fish to swallow the prophet and later vomit him onto dry land. Jonah finally realized God's urgency in either destroying or embracing the Ninevites. On his first day in Nineveh, he shouted the warning, "Forty more days and Nineveh will be overturned" (Jon. 3:4).

The urgency is that God does not want anyone to perish in a state of sinfulness. The prophet Ezekiel was charged to communicate to Israel:

> Son of man, say to the house of Israel, "This is what you are saying: 'Our offenses and sins weigh us down, and we are wasting away because of them. How then can we live?'" Say to them, "As surely as I live, declares the Sovereign LORD, I take no pleasure in the death of the wicked, but rather that they turn from their ways and live. Turn! Turn from your evil ways! Why will you die, O house of Israel?"
>
> (Ezek. 33:10–11)

God wants unchurched (lost) people, dechurched people (backslidden people who have rejected the church), atheists, and agnostics to turn to Him in repentance. He wants no one to die in sin.

We serve this God, and His desire to welcome home the lost sinner is always an urgent one.

God Wants You to Share His Urgency

When Marlinda was pregnant with our younger daughter, I can remember how I raced on the highway at eighty miles per hour to get her to the hospital. I was not going to be on the evening news because my wife gave birth to our child in the front seat of the car. Our older daughter, Danielle, then three and a half years old, was yelling from her car seat in the back: "Daddy, why are you driving so fast? Slow down, Daddy. Slow down!" I yelled back, "I can't, sweetheart. Your mom is going to have a baby. I have to get her to the hospital right now." Little Danielle was trying to comprehend our urgency, but her maturity was not quite there to feel what we felt.

At times we appear this way to God. God is in a hurry, but we are taking our sweet time getting around to matters that require urgent responses. There are two ingredients to capturing God's sense of urgency regarding the poor spiritual condition of lost people: (1) compassion; and (2) an accurate knowledge of the signs of the times.

1. Compassion

After experiencing personal brokenness resulting from his adultery with Bathsheba and the murder of her husband, David wept before God, saying: "Have mercy on me, O God, according to your unfailing love; according to your great compassion blot out my transgressions" (Ps. 51:1). There is a common understanding of God's compassion. When we use that same compassion in our interaction with and judgment of others, something transformational occurs within the hearts of lost people.

The Salvation Army is one of the largest religious agencies in the United States. This Christian agency began in 1865 (named Salvation Army in 1878) when compassion moved William and Catherine Booth to do something about the churchless slum-dwellers of London. Aware that unconventional methods could work in helping such people come to Christ, William Booth held open-air meetings that were accompanied by a live band. They visited bars, jails, and factories, and even preached in theaters in an effort to reach lost people. Booth's compassion made him adopt a principle: if you feed people, they can hear the gospel message more easily. So he raised money to win the lost by alleviating their physical hunger, joblessness, and need for shelter.[1]

Not everyone can be a William or Catherine Booth, but everyone is called to demonstrate compassion for lost people. Not everyone who is lost is penniless or physically needy, but everyone who is lost is spiritually poor. Show the compassion of Christ by laboring through your God-given purpose to point people to the Savior.

2. Signs of the Times

In his book *Storm Warning*, Dr. Billy Graham urges us to share our faith with lost people because

> *in America we see deepening poverty, racial division, homelessness, crime, physical and sexual abuse, and the disintegration of the traditional family. And these storms are further complicated by plagues of many kinds, including AIDS, tuberculosis, and sexually transmitted diseases. Alcoholism, drug addiction, pornography, and other dangerous behaviors are eating away at society. All of these are combined with earthquakes, physical storms, and natural disasters of many kinds all across the land. But Jesus said these are merely a warning of things yet to come. This is merely the beginning of sorrows.*[2]

Dr. Graham notes the prophetic signs that Jesus said would precede His second coming and the end of the age. He strictly foretold these things to His disciples when they questioned Him: " 'Tell us,' they said, 'when will this happen, and what will be the sign of your coming and of the end of the age?' " (Matt. 24:3).

> *Jesus answered: "Watch out that no one deceives you. For many will come in my name, claiming, 'I am the Christ,' and will deceive many. You will hear of wars and rumors of wars, but see to it that you are not alarmed. Such things must happen, but the end is still to come. Nation will rise against nation, and kingdom against kingdom. There*

will be famines and earthquakes in various places. All these are the
beginning of birth pains."

(Matt. 24:4–8)

These signs confirm the very things that are happening in our day. Ethnic cleansing is widespread in the Balkans; the United States, along with an array of countries, is at war in Iraq; Pakistan is still having border wars with India; and Israel is continuing its fight against the Palestinians. There is an AIDS pandemic in Africa; human slavery is occurring in many countries, including the Sudan; children are being trained to be sex objects in the Philippines and other developing countries; there are 33 percent more African-American men in prisons and jails than in universities and colleges; and approximately 1.5 million abortions are performed annually in the United States. Many of the great European cathedrals are being turned into condominiums; women are being kidnapped in China and forced into unwanted marriages; there is social and political chaos in South America; and an epidemic of terrorism is sweeping across the globe.

These present-day maladies should answer the question: Why should I share in God's urgency? The answer is simple. The world is in moral chaos. People are dying at an alarming rate due to sickness and other catastrophes. And God has vehemently conveyed that He has no pleasure in the death of the wicked. If you care about God's heart and you recognize the signs of the times, you will share in the urgency to "let your light shine before men, that they may see your good deeds and praise your Father in heaven" (Matt. 5:16). There is no time to waste. Share your faith with others, and use your purpose to help bring lost people back to a loving God.

DAY 38 Points to Reflect Upon

Jonah needed to be taught how to show compassion toward lost people. How about you?

1. God demonstrates a sense of urgency when dealing with the souls of lost people.

2. God wants you to share His sense of urgency.

3. Through compassion and an understanding of the pending future storm, respond to His sense of urgency.

DAY 39

Remove Sticking Points

Jonah's 40-day Transforming Interval was about the need to warn a wicked city of God's impending wrath. In the opening statement to the small book of Jonah we feel God's anger burning the pages when He issues an order to the prophet: "Go to the great city of Nineveh and preach against it, because its wickedness has come up before me" (Jon. 1:2). The interesting reality about the people of Nineveh was that they did not know they were in such a horrible state. Imagine that the God of all patience, love, and long-suffering had become so fed up with their immorality that He issued a final order of warning of total annihilation. God was the only One who could ultimately bring correction to the people of Nineveh.

Wanted: Messengers of Good News

God is the solution to correcting the immoral behavior of people. Nonetheless, based on biblical instruction, we human beings are God's messengers to warn sinful people of an impending doom. The apostle Paul puts it this way: "How, then, can they call on the one they have not believed in? And how can they believe in the one of whom they have not heard? And how can they hear without someone preaching to them? And how can they preach unless they are sent? As it is written, 'How beautiful are the feet of those who bring good news'" (Rom. 10:14–15)! If we are the messengers but we choose not to declare the message of salvation, as Jonah attempted to do by fleeing to Tarshish instead of Nineveh (Jon. 1:3), sinful people who desperately need God's salvation will not hear the good news. Obviously, they will not experience the transformation that occurs when people embrace the message of salvation. They will face only the wrath of God—sudden destruction.

The perfecting of your life's purpose must include sharing God's message with folks like the Ninevites. If you reject this aspect of your purpose, you will have a selfish perspective of God. You exist to help God with His mission of building a righteous family. The great American evangelist Charles Finney instructed younger ministers that every sinner is always hiding under a rock. The preacher's job is to remove the rock (or sticking point) so that each person may come to Christ.[1] We glean three important lessons from Jonah's story: (1) people can be blinded by their own sin; (2) godly witnesses are needed; and, (3) you must avoid getting lost in a subculture.

1. Help People Blinded By Sin

Radio personality Paul Harvey tells the story of how an Eskimo kills a wolf. The account is grisly, yet it offers insight into the reality of the blinding and then self-destructive nature of sin. First, the Eskimo coats his knife blade with animal blood and allows it to freeze. Then, he adds another layer of blood and another until the blade is completely concealed by frozen blood. Next, the hunter fixes his knife in the ground with the blade up.

When a wolf follows his sensitive nose to the source of the scent and discovers the bait, he licks it, tasting the fresh frozen blood. He begins to lick more and more vigorously, lapping the blade until the keen edge is bare. Harder and harder the wolf licks the blade in the Arctic night. So great becomes his craving for blood that the wolf does not notice the razor-sharp sting of the naked blade on his tongue, nor does he recognize the instant at which his insatiable thirst is being satisfied by his *own* warm blood. His carnivorous appetite just craves more—until the dawn finds him dead in the snow! It is a fearful thing that people can be "consumed by their own lusts." But when we care deeply about others' spiritual state and share the message of God's love with them, then perhaps their spiritual eyes will open, and they will break free from a godless life.[2]

Like the Arctic wolf, the Ninevites were blinded by their sin.

They had no knowledge of how wicked they were and how destruction was looming over their heads. God dispatched a messenger—a prophet who had God's heart on the matter—to warn them, thus inducing them to change. Likewise, the people in your sphere of care may not be aware of their bankrupt spiritual state. Instead of complaining about it or fleeing to Tarshish—the opposite direction from the problem—do something about it. Pray specifically for them. Ask God to soften their hearts toward spiritual things. Then look for opportunities to share your faith with them in love.

2. Be a Godly Witness

A friend was in front of me leaving church one Sunday, and the preacher was standing at the door to shake hands. He grabbed my friend by the hand and pulled him aside. The pastor said to him, "You need to join the army of the Lord!" My friend replied, "I'm already in the army of the Lord, Pastor." The pastor questioned, "Why don't I see you except at Christmas and Easter?" He whispered back, "I'm in the Secret Service."

This story is funny, but true. A lot of people who purport to know Christ are not true witnesses of Christ. My imagination causes me to consider how many true believers lived in Nineveh during the days of Jonah. Did the Ninevites have any genuine witnesses modeling what it means to be godly and live righteous lives? The Bible is silent on the subject. But I have come to realize that if godly people live in a community and they do not aggressively witness to their faith, the lost people within that community remain unchanged. They are not even cognizant that there is another way to live. Our witness cannot be silent.

On a recent trip to Oakland, California, where I was to speak at a church, the pastor told me that there was a large Chinese population in their community. A couple from mainland China had been renting space in his church as a new church plant geared toward reaching the Chinese population. The American Chinese, who were qualified to plant a church to reach their fellow Chinese, did not have a burden in their hearts for *their* people to come to Christ. It took a couple from thousands of miles away to get a burden for people who had little opportunity to escape the clutches of their own sin.

All of us are guilty of not showing deep compassion and care for the people living in our midst. This is why it often takes someone outside your family to have a burden for the people inside your family to come to Christ. We become overly familiar with people's lethargic spiritual state if they are in our midst. May God help us to become witnesses of the good news so that lost people see there is indeed another form of life—the godly life.

3. Avoid Getting Lost in Your Subculture

Our Christian subculture, like any other subculture, is both a haven and a hideout. We find peace and solace from the world's mayhem, but if we're not careful, we can turn it into a place of exile where we have minimal contact, if any, with outsiders. Helping lost people establish a relationship with Christ is the essence of our mission and purpose as believers in Jesus. When the haven turns into a place of exile, you discover that your library consists only of Christian books, your social activities are all church-based, and the only non–Christian entering your home is the gas man to check the meter.

This story is about a rather old-fashioned lady, who was planning a couple of weeks' vacation in Florida at a Christian campground. She also was quite delicate and elegant with her language. She wrote a letter to a particular campground and asked for reservations. She wanted to make sure the campground was fully equipped but didn't know quite how to ask about the "toilet" facilities. She just couldn't bring herself to write the word "toilet" in her letter. After much deliberation, she finally came up with the old-fashioned term "Bathroom Commode," but when she wrote that down, she still thought she was being too forward so she rewrote the entire letter and referred to the "Bathroom Commode" simply as the "B.C." In her letter, she asked whether the campground had its own "B.C."

The campground owner wasn't old fashioned at all, though he was steeped within the Christian community. When he received the letter, he couldn't figure out what the lady was talking about. The letters

"B.C." really stumped him. After worrying about it for several days, he showed the letter to other campers, but they couldn't figure out what the lady meant either. The campground owner finally came to the conclusion the lady must be asking about the location of the local Baptist Church. So he sat down and wrote the following reply:

Dear Madam: "I regret very much the delay in answering your letter, but I now take pleasure in informing you that the 'B.C.' is located nine miles north of the camp site and is capable of seating 250 people at one time. I admit it is quite a distance away if you are in the habit of going regularly, but no doubt you will be pleased to know that a great number of people take their lunches along, and make a day of it. They usually arrive early and stay late. The last time my wife and I went was six years ago, and it was so crowded we had to stand up the whole time we were there.

"It may interest you to know that right now, there is a supper planned to raise money to buy more seats. They plan to hold the supper in the middle of the B.C., so everyone can watch and talk about this great event. I would like to say it pains me very much, not to be able to go more regularly, but it is not for lack of desire on my part. As we grow older, it seems to be more and more of an effort, particularly in cold weather. If you decide to come down to the campground, perhaps I could go with you the first time you go . . . sit with you . . . and introduce you to all the other folks. This is really a very friendly Christian community."[3]

To avoid becoming like the camper, speaking only Christianese, stay in touch with non-Christians so that you are always mindful of their sticking points to faith. Expose your mind to literature that covers a wide array of topics including science, politics, current events, sports, and culture without losing your strong Christian worldview. Also consider eavesdropping on the conversations of non-Christians (where it is acceptable to do without violating their privacy) so that you can hear their language and maintain your bilingual skills. Too much Christianese will disconnect you from their world. Consequently, when an opportunity presents itself for you to share Christ with them, they will not be able to understand your Christianese, though they want to learn of the salvation your God freely offers.

Unlike Jonah, who cared little about the Ninevites' sticking points to faith, God has called all of us to share His love of people within our sphere of care. In so doing, we are perfecting our purpose within the parameters of His purpose, and we will be on the way to sure success.

DAY 39 Points to Reflect Upon

Part of Jonah's mission was to remove the Ninevites' sticking points to faith. However, he preached a message that warned them without including a desire to see them repent. Remember these lessons:

1. Warn lost people to avoid becoming blinded by their own lust.

2. Be a godly witness.

3. Avoid getting lost in your subculture.

DAY 40

Finish Well

Good Hollywood scriptwriters know how to keep movie watchers on the edge of their seats with cliffhangers. Cliffhangers include plots that keep you guessing, characters who add suspense, and believable scenes. In my opinion, the most important part is the last few minutes of the film. I want to know how the characters overcame their temptations and hazardous circumstances. Did they finish well? Did the good guy get the pretty girl? Did the woman in distress punish her attackers? Were they able to stop the embezzlers and crooks from stealing the family farm? In other words, finishing well is just as important as starting well.

Most people start off in pursuit of their life's purpose with good intentions and great energy, but somewhere along the line, they slip into a poor disposition and are no longer mindful that perfecting their purpose is a spiritual calling. You must fight against the temptation *not* to finish well. Perfecting your purpose must include more than executing cold, mechanical, and zombielike action plans; you must strive to finish well by having a right perspective, attitude, and emotional disposition about your purpose.

Jonah's 40-day Transforming Interval keeps us in a cliffhanger mood. The prophet started off by sailing to Tarshish rather than going to Nineveh, which was a clear act of disobedience to God's commands (Jon. 1:2–3). Fortunately, through a series of divine interventions, he was able to get back on track with his assignment of delivering a 40-day warning to the wicked Ninevites. Frightened at the prospect of the impending wrath of God, the people repented with citywide prayer and fasting.

Although Jonah got on board in executing the will of God, he struggled with anger against the Ninevites because he saw no meaning in his purpose. He thought, *Why go to Nineveh and warn these wicked people? If they repent, You [God] will certainly forgive them. This would mean that I wasted my time and I wasted my breath telling them they had 40 days till destruction. In essence, my whole purpose of preaching to the Ninevites brought no satisfaction or real meaning.* Let's check the biblical account:

> *Jonah was greatly displeased and became angry. He prayed to the* LORD, *"O* LORD, *is this not what I said when I was still at home? That is why I was so quick to flee to Tarshish. I knew that you are a gracious and compassionate God, slow to anger and abounding in love, a God who relents from sending calamity. Now, O* LORD, *take away my life, for it is better for me to die than to live."*
>
> *But the* LORD *replied, "Have you any right to be angry?"*
>
> (Jon. 4:1–4)

The prophet's perspective captures a faulty approach to his mission. He did not like the fact that the Ninevites had repented. And he certainly did not like the fact that God spared them from destruction. Jonah's anger was so hot that he prayed to die. Talk about depression and dissatisfaction—Jonah fell into both holes, big time. How can you avoid becoming disillusioned about your own mission and purpose? How can you wage a battle against the temptation to see your purpose as meaningless and a waste of time? God gave Jonah three responses to these questions that you can implement: (1) you are not God; (2) you are to keep the people in proper focus; and (3) you are to keep the mission in proper focus.

1. You Are Not God!

In the mental ward, all patients ate together in the main cafeteria on Tuesday. A single line that wound around the perimeter of the large room was formed. Suddenly, one patient jumped from the rear, ran to the front of the line, looked over his shoulder at everyone, and loudly announced: "God said I was first." Everyone paused. In a few moments someone standing about four or five persons behind him yelled: "I never said you were first; get in the back of the line!"

Whether mentally challenged or not, we struggle with the idea that we're in charge—in charge of our lives, in charge of our goals, in charge of our money. We want to be in charge of everything. Jonah was angry at God because he thought that his take on the whole Nineveh issue was the correct perspective.

After Jonah warned the Ninevites, he found a place to sit immediately outside the city so that he would see what would happen next (Jon. 4:5). God allowed a vine to grow above the prophet's head to further ease his discomfort from the scorching sun. To make a point to Jonah, God allowed a worm to chew the vine, causing it to wither and die. Jonah became angry because his shade was destroyed. Here is God's lesson:

> God said to Jonah, "Do you have a right to be angry about the vine?"
>
> "I do," he said. "I am angry enough to die."
>
> But the LORD said, "You have been concerned about this vine, though you did not tend it or make it grow. It sprang up overnight and died overnight. But Nineveh has more than a hundred and twenty thousand people who cannot tell their right hand from their left, and many cattle as well. Should I not be concerned about that great city?"
>
> (Jon. 4:9–11)

In not so many words, God told Jonah: "There is only one God, and I'm He." Jonah, get over it! You're not God! The Lord was instructing the confused prophet that his mission would go well if he didn't lose sight of the truth that he was not God. This often is a sticking point for people journeying toward their purpose. Invariably, something goes in an entirely different direction than planned, and they get bent out of shape. Jonah thought the best approach to dealing with the Ninevites was to wipe them off the face of the earth. God's perspective conflicted with his view, so he used his anger to try to manipulate God.

God would not be bullied or manipulated. Jonah was one of *His* subjects, not the other way around. How about you? Are you struggling with the notion that if things don't work out the way *you* think they should, you're going to become angry with God? Fight against that temptation. Your job is to execute the assignment given to you. It is God's job to deal with the outcome, whatever it may be. Find your purpose and pleasure in *obeying* God, not in trying to *be* God. This viewpoint helps ward off the temptation to surrender to a fruitless attitude concerning your purpose.

2. You Are to Keep the People in Proper Focus

Working with people is an art form. There is very little science to it. If you don't properly view people, you can lose sight of the reason why you're trying so hard to help them. Remember that a major part of your purpose is serving God by serving people He placed around you. Jonah was forgetting that. He struggled to shake off his anger and resentment toward the Ninevites. He was hoping that God would destroy them, but God was hoping to save them. Fortunately, God's decision was final, though He attempted to refocus the prophet's perspective toward the Ninevites by saying, "Nineveh has more than a hundred and twenty thousand people who cannot tell their right hand from their left, and many cattle as well" (Jon. 4:11). Anyone can tire of serving people. They are so fickle, so temperamental, so hard to please; yet we are called to love them.

Love anything, and your heart will certainly be wrung out and possibly broken. If you want to make sure of keeping it intact, you must give your heart to no one. Simply wrap it carefully round with hobbies and little luxuries; avoid all entanglements; lock it safe in the casket of your selfishness. But in that casket—safe, dark, motionless, airless—it will change. It will become unbreakable, impenetrable. The only place outside heaven where you can be perfectly safe from all the dangers of love is—hell.[1]

To be trusted with the spiritual lives of people is an awesome responsibility. As a pastor, I take my job quite seriously, knowing that the people in my congregation belong *first* to Christ; I am only their undershepherd. Even if you are not a pastor, any level of involvement in the spiritual lives of God's prized possession—people—is a great task. The way you approach the task, however, is of the utmost concern to the Lord. The method that Jesus would employ is to recognize the person's primary goal and use the most caring approach to pull him out of whatever pit he may have fallen into.

3. You Are to Keep the Mission in Proper Focus

Several months after I became a Christian, I was sitting in a church service one Sunday evening thinking: *Is this all that there is?* Unbeknownst to me, I was caught in spiritual warfare. If I did not get past the question, my spiritual development would be halted. I was contemplating the life that I was now to live as a Christian. *Certainly, there must be more to life than going to church, going to school [or going to work], and going home,* I thought. I had become mentally and emotionally stuck on the idea that it was not the life I wanted as a twenty-year-old college student. The answer to my dilemma was found in the song being sung by the choir. It was one of the great hymns of the church, "Blessed Assurance."

> *Blessed assurance, Jesus is mine!*
> *Oh, what a foretaste of glory divine!*
> *Heir of salvation, purchase of God,*
> *Born of His Spirit, washed in His blood.*

> *Perfect submission, perfect delight,*
> *Visions of rapture now burst on my sight:*
> *Angels descending bring from above*
> *Echoes of mercy, whispers of love.*

> *Perfect submission, all is at rest,*
> *I in my Savior am happy and blest:*
> *Watching and waiting, looking above,*
> *Filled with His goodness, lost in His love.*

Chorus
This is my story, this is my song,
Praising my Savior all the day long;
This is my story, this is my song,
Praising my Savior all the day long.[2]

The chorus provided my answer. Fanny Crosby, the song's author, penned these words in response to Mrs. Phoebe Palmer Knapp's question, "What does it [this tune] say to you, Fanny?" Fanny's answer was, "Blessed assurance, Jesus is mine." In a few minutes she handed the completed lyrics to Mrs. Knapp, and the rest is history.[3] These powerful words helped me to accept my life's mission of serving Jesus Christ and not faltering along the way by becoming a casualty to meaninglessness. I wanted to finish well. Certainly, I could do something about my boredom. That night I embraced the overarching goal of serving Christ in perfect submission and perfect delight. I belonged to God; He chose me as an object of His affection. This is what Augustine meant when he said, "O God, Thou hast made us for Thyself, and our souls are restless, searching, 'til they find rest in Thee."

Jonah had become confused. God needed to remind him about *why* he was sent to Nineveh. Jonah's journey was all about God's mission, not about his happiness. God's word brought a clear perspective: "Should I [God] not be concerned about that great city?" (Jon. 4:11). The question must have stung the prophet because it revealed that to finish his course well, he must remember the reason why he was doing what he was doing. Likewise, you are on a mission from God, and the mission is the most important thing! Remember why you are doing what you are doing!

The bee has been aptly described as busy. To produce 1 pound of honey, the bee must visit 56,000 clover heads. Since each head has 60 flower tubes, a total of 3,360,000 visits are necessary to give us a pound of honey for the breakfast table. Meanwhile, the worker bee has flown the equivalent of 3 times around the world. To produce 1 tablespoon of honey for our toast, the little bee makes 4,200 trips to flowers. He makes about 10 trips a day to the fields, each trip lasting 20 minutes on average and 400 flowers. A worker bee will fly as far as 8 miles if he cannot find a nectar flow that is nearer. Therefore, when you feel that perfecting your purpose is a difficult task, think of the bee.[4]

And remember the encouraging words from the apostle Paul that direct us to walk with God in order to know true success:

> *So, what do you think? With God on our side like this, how can we lose? If God didn't hesitate to put everything on the line for us, embracing our condition and exposing himself to the worst by sending his own Son, is there anything else he wouldn't gladly and freely do for us? And who would dare tangle with God by messing with one of God's chosen? Who would dare even to point a finger? The One who died for us—who was raised to life for us!—is in the presence of God at this very moment sticking up for us. Do you think anyone is going to be able to drive a wedge between us and Christ's love for us? There is no way! Not trouble, not hard times, not hatred, not hunger, not homelessness, not bullying threats, not backstabbing, not even the worst sins listed in Scripture:*
>
> *"They kill us in cold blood because they hate you.*
> *We're sitting ducks; they pick us off one by one."*
>
> *None of this fazes us because Jesus loves us. I'm absolutely convinced that nothing—nothing living or dead, angelic or demonic, today or tomorrow, high or low, thinkable or unthinkable—absolutely nothing can get between us and God's love because of the way that Jesus our Master has embraced us.*
>
> (Rom. 8:31–39, The Message)

Armed with these promises and God's commitment to watch over your life, stay the course! Finish the work to which Christ has assigned you! Perfect your purpose to the glory of God!

DAY 40 Points to Reflect Upon

Jonah had to learn that to perfect his purpose, he had to avoid falling into the trap of meaninglessness. He had to view his mission as important at the beginning of his journey and at the end. To finish well, you are urged to

1. realize that you're not God.

2. keep the people you are called to serve in proper focus.

3. keep your mission in clear focus.

NOTES

Introduction: The Search for a More Meaningful Life
1. John Pollock, *The Billy Graham Story* (Grand Rapids, Mich.: Zondervan, 2003), 25.

Day 1: Understand the Power of 40 Days
1. Charles Paul Conn, *Making It Happen* (Grand Rapids, Mich.: Fleming H. Revell Company, 1981), 95.

Day 2: Establish Conviction: The Fuel of Purpose
1. Sam Wellman, *Mother Teresa—Missionary of Charity* (Uhrichsville, Ohio: Barbour Publishing, 1997), 76.

Day 5: Explore Where You Would Like to Go
1. Paul Lee Tan, *Encyclopedia of 7,700 Illustrations,* Logos Bible Software (Garland, Tex.: Bible Communications, Inc., 1996).
2. Anna Muóio, "All the Right Moves," Issue 24 (New York, N.Y.: Fast Company, May 1999), 192.

Day 6: Have a Mountaintop Experience
1. James M. Washington, *Martin Luther King, Jr.: I Have a Dream* (New York, N.Y.: HarperCollins, 1986), 105.
2. Source unknown.
3. Sermon Notes, Illustration on Adversity (Accessed July 2004), http://www.sermonnotes.com/members/deluxe/illus/p.htm.

Day 7: Keep Your Ideas Quiet for Now
1. Victor Kiam, *Going for It!: How to Succeed as an Entrepreneur* (New York, N.Y.: HarperCollins, 1986).
2. James S. Hewett, ed., *Illustrations Unlimited* (Wheaton, Ill.: Tyndale House Publishers, 1988), 134.

Day 8: Sample the Fruit
1. Hewett, ed., *Illustrations Unlimited,* 495.

Day 9: Determine Who Is in Charge

1. Hewett, ed., *Illustrations Unlimited*, 312.

2. *Bits & Pieces* (Fairfield, N.J.: The Economics Press, May 28, 1992), 5–6.

3. Frank Damazio, *Intercession* (Portland, Oreg.: BT Publishing, 1998), 18–19.

4. John Eldredge, *Wild at Heart* (Nashville, Tenn.: Thomas Nelson Publishers, 2001).

Day 11: Allow God's Love to Rescue You

1. James E. Bordwine, *A Guide to the Westminster Confession of Faith* (Jefferson, Md.: The Trinity Foundation, 1991).

2. Kenneth W. Osbeck, *101 Hymn Stories* (Grand Rapids, Mich.: Kregel Publications, 1982), 28.

3. Ronald Nash, *Worldviews in Conflict* (Grand Rapids, Mich.: Zondervan, 1992), 26.

4. Bordwine, *A Guide to the Westminster Confession of Faith*.

Day 12: Come Out of the Rain!

1. Francis A. Schaeffer, *How Should We Then Live* (Wheaton, Ill.: Crossway Books, 1976), 24.

Day 13: Make the Transition

1. E. Bratcher, R. Kemper, and D. Scott, *Mastering Transitions* (Sisters, Oreg.: Multnomah Publishers, 1991), 55.

2. Max Lucado, *The Cross* (Sisters, Oreg.: Multnomah Publishers, 1998), 12.

Day 15: Overcome Worldly Appetites

1. J. Patterson and P. Kim, *The Day America Told the Truth* (New York, N.Y.: Plume, 1992).

Day 16: Determine How God Wants to Be Worshiped

1. J. E. Burkhart, *Worship* (Philadelphia, Pa.: The Westminster Press, 1982), 16.

2. Robert E. Webber, *Worship Is a Verb* (Peabody, Mass.: Hendrickson Publishers, Inc., 1992), 26.

Day 17: Live By a Moral Code

1. Madonna Gets Religion and Remakes Herself Yet Again, http://lounge.teamshania.com/showread.php?t-4548 & highlight=madonna +religion (Accessed July 2004).

2. R. C. Sproul, *Loved By God* (Nashville, Tenn.: Word Publishers, 2001), 65.

3. W. C. Kaiser Jr., B. K. Waltke, and R. H. Alexander, *The Expositor's Bible Commentary*, vol. 2 (Grand Rapids, Mich.: Zondervan, 1990), 420.

4. Chuck Colson, *The Body* (Nashville, Tenn.: Word Publishers, 1992), 124.

5. Sermon Notes, Illustration on Happiness (Accessed October 2003), http://sermonnotes.com/members/deluxe/illus/p.htm.

Day 18: Understand How to Treat God

1. C. F. Keil and F. Delitzsch, *Commentary on the Old Testament: The Pentateuch, Exodus 12–40, Leviticus* (Peabody, Mass.: Hendrickson Publishers, 1989), 114.

Day 19: Understand How to Treat Yourself and Your Family

1. C. F. Keil and F. Delitzsch, *Commentary on the Old Testament: The Pentateuch, Exodus 12–40, Leviticus*, 120–21.

2. Hewett, ed., *Illustrations Unlimited*, 197.

3. George Rekers, ed., *Family Building: Six Qualities of a Strong Family* (Ventura, Ca.: Regal Books, 1985), 36, 38, 43.

Day 20: Understand How to Treat Others

1. C. S. Lewis, *Mere Christianity* (New York: Macmillan, 1943).

2. Hewett, ed., *Illustrations Unlimited*, 195.

Day 21: Survive the Loss of a Significant Relationship

1. Hewett, ed., *Illustrations Unlimited*, 185.

2. Success.org., John McCain, *Fight for a Cause.* (Accessed November 2004), http://www.success.org/AP/others/552.shtml.

Day 22: Overcome Painful Memories

1. H. C. Leupold, *Exposition of Genesis*, vol. 2 (Grand Rapids, Mich.: Baker Book House, 1942), 1217.

2. *Narcotics Anonymous* (Van Nuys, Ca.: World Service Office, 1988), 26.

Day 23: Practice the Habit of Letting Go

1. Hewett, ed., *Illustrations Unlimited*, 221–22.

2. John Stott, *The Contemporary Christian: An Urgent Plea for Double Listening* (Downers Grove, Ill.: InterVarsity Press, 1992).

3. Corrie ten Boom, *Tramp for the Lord* (New York, N.Y.: Jove/Revell Company, 1978), 53.

4. Lewis Smedes, *The Art of Forgiving* (New York, N.Y.: Ballantine Books, 1996).

Day 24: Learn to Live Again

1. *Dale A. Hays Leadership*, vol. 10, no. 3 (summer 1989), p. 35, April 7, 1965, 11:00 A.M.
2. Aleksandr Solzhenitsyn, *The Gulag Archipelago* (New York, N.Y.: Harper-Collins, 1975), 615.
3. M. G. Easton, *Easton's Bible Dictionary* (Oak Harbor, Wash.: Logos Research Systems, Inc., 1996).

Day 26: Accept God's Correction

1. Frank E. Gaebelein, ed., *The Expositor's Bible Commentary, 1 & 2 Kings*, vol. 4 (Grand Rapids, Mich.: Regency Reference Library, 1988), 150–51.
2. *Merriam-Webster's Collegiate Dictionary*, 11th ed. (Springfield, Mass.: Merriam-Webster Inc., 2003).
3. Daniel Goleman, *Working with Emotional Intelligence* (New York, N.Y.: Bantam Books, 1998), 26.
4. Abraham J. Heschel, *The Prophets*, vol. 2 (New York, N.Y.: Harper Torchbooks, 1962), x.

Day 27: Impact the Next Generation

1. Thomas Toch, Ted Gest, and Monika Guttman, "Violence in Schools," U.S. News & World Report, vol. 115, no. 18 (November 8, 1993), p. 30, citing data from Congressional Quarterly Researcher.
2. Josh McDowell and Bob Hostetler, *Right from Wrong* (Dallas, Tex.: Word Publishing, 1994), 6.
3. Ron Hutchcraft, *Five Needs Your Child Must Have Met at Home* (Grand Rapids, Mich.: Zondervan, 1995).
4. Ministry Matters, *Ministry Today*, (Palm Coast, Fl.: March/April 1998), 13.

Day 28: Leave a Spiritual Legacy

1. Benjamin Carson, *Gifted Hands* (Grand Rapids, Mich.: Zondervan, 1990).

Day 29: Gain Strength from Past Experiences

1. Wendyl K. Leslie, The Courage to Care (Accessed July 2004), http://www.selfgrowth.com/articles/Leslie4.html.
2. Arthur F. Lenehan, *The Best of Bits & Pieces* (Fairfield, N.J.: The Economics Press, 1994), 39.

Day 30: Make a Faith Confession

1. Hewett, ed., *Illustrations Unlimited*, 391.
2. David D. Ireland, *Why Drown When You Can Walk on Water?* (Grand Rapids, Mich.: Baker Book House, 2004).

3. Elie Wiesel, Nobel Prize Acceptance Speech, 1986. (Accessed July 2004), http://www.pbs.org/eliewiesel/teaching/activity3.html.

Day 31: Develop Your Own Style of Fighting

1. Bruce Lee Story, mysite.freeserve.com/pohb/jeetkunedo.html. (Accessed July 2004).
2. Hewett, ed., *Illustrations Unlimited*, 496.

Day 32: Recognize that God Is Almighty

1. C. F. Keil and F. Delitzsch, *Commentary on the Old Testament: The Book of 1st Samuel*, vol. 2 (Peabody, Mass.: Hendrickson Publishers, 1989), 183.

Day 33: Pass the Test

1. A. W. Tozer, *The Pursuit of God* (Camp Hill, Pa.: Christian Publications, 1982), 83.
2. J. B. Phillips, *The New Testament in Modern English* (New York: Touchstone Books, 1947, 1957).

Day 34: Welcome Supernatural Experiences

1. Jack Deere, *Surprised By the Power of the Spirit* (Grand Rapids, Mich.: Zondervan, 1993).
2. Rick Warren, *The Purpose-Driven Life* (Grand Rapids, Mich.: Zondervan, 2002), 58.

Day 35: Seek the Kingdom of God

1. Source unknown.
2. John Calvin, *Institutes of the Christian Religion*, III.3.19, Beveridge trans.
3. Tan, *Encyclopedia of 7,700 Illustrations,* Logos Bible Software.

Day 36: Enjoy Intimacy with God

1. Spiros Zodhiates, *The Complete Word Study Dictionary—New Testament* (Chattanooga, Tenn.: AMG Publishers, 1992), 947.
2. John Foxe, *Foxe's Christian Martyrs of the World* (Ulrichsville, Ohio: Barbour and Company, 1989), 69.

Day 37: Dig for Gold

1. Viv Grigg, *Companion to the Poor* (Sutherland, Australia: Albatross Books, 1984), 13.

Day 38: Care for Others with a Sense of Urgency

1. J. D. Douglas, Philip W. Comfort, and Donald Mitchell, eds., *Who's Who in Christian History* (Wheaton, Ill.: Tyndale House Publishers, 1992).

2. Billy Graham, *Storm Warning* (Dallas, Tex.: Word Publishing, 1992), 35–36.

Day 39: Remove Sticking Points

1. Charles G. Finney, *Revivals of Religion* (Grand Rapids, Mich.: Fleming H. Revell Company, 1993).

2. Illustrations on Lust (Accessed Nov. 2004), http://www.bible.org/illus.asp?topic-id=924, Consumed by Your Own Lust *(Chris T. Zwingelberg)*.

3. Hewett, ed., *Illustrations Unlimited*.

Day 40: Finish Well

1. Sermon Notes, Illustration on Love (Accessed July 2004), http://www.sermonnotes.com.members/deluxe/illus/p.htm.

2. Joyful Noise Music Company, *Logos Hymnal* (Fort Worth, Tex.: Joyful Noise Music Company), 1994.

3. Http://schfrs.crosswinds.net/hymns/assurance.htm (Accessed July 2004).

4. Tan, *Encyclopedia of 7,700 Illustrations*, Logos Bible Software.